Managing Disasters through Public–Private Partnerships

TITLES IN THE SERIES

Managing Disasters through Public–Private Partnerships

Ami J. Abou-bakr

GEORGETOWN UNIVERSITY PRESS
WASHINGTON, DC

Library of Congress Cataloging-in-Publication Data

Abou-bakr, Ami J.
    Managing disasters through public-private partnerships / Ami J. Abou-bakr.
        p. cm. — (Public management and change series)
    Includes bibliographical references and index.
    ISBN 978-1-58901-950-8 (pbk. : alk. paper)
    1. Disaster relief—United States. 2. Emergency management—United States.
3. Public-private sector cooperation—United States. I. Title.
    HV555.U6A53 2013
    363.34'80973—dc23
                                    2012012671

♾ This book is printed on acid-free paper meeting the requirements of the American National Standard for Permanence in Paper for Printed Library Materials.

20 19 18 17 16 15 14 13   9 8 7 6 5 4 3 2
First printing

To J. R. G. and R. C. A.

CONTENTS

TABLES

PREFACE

In 2010 and 2011 the world watched as an Icelandic volcano brought European air travel to a standstill, was horrified at the devastation caused by the earthquake in Haiti, and was appalled by the Tohoku earthquake, tsunami, and nuclear disaster in Japan. Disasters, be they caused by nature or man, occur and invariably affect the United States. The question is not, how can we stop disasters? For the most part, we cannot. The question is, how can we ensure that we are adequately prepared and sufficiently resilient to cope when disaster strikes our home, our neighborhood, or our country? The issues addressed in this book are applicable and directly relevant to a broad range of practitioners in government, the private sector, media, and academia (particularly academics in the fields of public policy and public administration). This book also proposes new ways of approaching disaster management given the global, interconnected world in which we live.

The events of 9/11 and Hurricane Katrina demonstrated that the US government alone is not equipped to respond to disasters. Most of the physical and virtual networks we rely upon are owned and operated by private corporations. For example, after Katrina it was Walmart, not the government or law enforcement, who was the first responder, providing 2,498 trailers of emergency merchandise and $8.5 million to the relief effort. These crises focused national attention on the importance of cooperation between the government and the private sector and made it no longer a question of whether the private sector had a role to play in national security and disaster management, but a question of what that role should be, and how effective public–private partnerships (PPP) for these purposes could be established.

Where once government, military, and law enforcement took full responsibility for disaster mitigation and resiliency, 9/11 and Hurricane Katrina made two things apparent. First, private ownership of an estimated 85 percent of US critical infrastructure makes industry a significant stakeholder in critical infrastructure protection for the foreseeable future. Second, during disasters, the private sector demonstrated its constructive use and understanding of global networks, systems, and patterns as a means to enhance the speed of recovery efforts. With these realizations emerged a further awareness that as partners with government, the private sector may be able both to respond to physical events after they occur and to use this knowledge of networks and trade patterns to assist the US government in mitigating the impacts of future events.

A decade after 9/11, despite a widespread acknowledgment by both sectors that public–private collaborations for these purposes would be beneficial, significant barriers to cooperation persist that have limited their effectiveness on a federal level. This book attempts to assess disaster-oriented PPPs through December 2011 and aims to understand why these collaborations have proven so difficult and to determine whether they can be built to last.

Managing Disasters through Public–Private Partnerships ultimately argues that change is possible but is only likely to occur in the event of a disaster of greater magnitude than any the United States has yet experienced. In the meantime, policymakers and analysts should explore, debate, and assess the potential challenges of cross-sector cooperation so that when disaster does strike, new contributions can make a positive and immediate impact on policymaking.

This research would not have been possible without the generosity of those who shared their time and experiences with me. I tried to capture and reflect these conversations with the greatest possible accuracy, and any errors in the interpretation of what any of these individuals shared with me are, of course, my full responsibility. I would like to particularly thank Archie Dunham, Bob Liscouski, Nitin Natarajan, Lynne Kidder, Steve Carmel, Bryan Koon, Erin Mullen, Jim Young, Bob Grimaila, Rick Holmes, Clay Detlefsen, Capt. George McCarthy, and Frances Fragos Townsend. The insights, anecdotes, and willingness of these interviewees to speak frankly and openly about their experiences allowed this book to take shape. I would like to offer special thanks to Darryl Williams for his tremendous help, and in particular to Gen. Charles C. Krulak for his unwavering support of this project and continued assistance. I would also like to acknowledge Randy Lerner, who first realized the potential for the Federal Reserve System to serve as a model for formalized cooperation between the public–private sectors after 9/11.

This book is based on a PhD thesis originally supervised by Ken Young and Wyn Bowen at King's College London. It was an honor and a privilege to have an opportunity to work with both of them. I offer my sincerest thanks and appreciation to P.E.O. International for their help in funding a significant portion of this research, and in particular to P.E.O. Chapter BE in Twin Falls, Idaho. I would also like to thank Beryl Radin, series editor, and Don Jacobs and the staff of Georgetown University Press.

My list of thanks would be incomplete without recognizing my family, especially my husband, Stephen, and my mother. Stephen was not only patient and supportive but also read every word of this book (more than once) and provided innumerable comments and insights throughout its development.

ABBREVIATIONS

BENS   Business Executives for National Security
BP   British Petroleum
CIA   Central Intelligence Agency
CIKR   critical infrastructure and key resources
CND   Council of National Defense
C-TPAT   Customs Trade Partnership against Terrorism
DHS   Department of Homeland Security
DoD   Department of Defense
EO   Executive Order
EPA   Environmental Protection Agency
FBI   Federal Bureau of Investigation
FDA   Food and Drug Administration
FDIC   Federal Deposit Insurance Corporation
Fed   Federal Reserve Bank
FedEx   Federal Express
FEMA   Federal Emergency Management Agency
FOMC   Federal Open Market Committee
GAO   Government Accountability Office (General Accounting Office prior to 2004)
GCC   government-coordinating council
GMB   General Munitions Board
HHS   Department of Health and Human Services
HSIN   Homeland Security Information Network
HSPD   Homeland Security Presidential Directive
I&A   DHS Office of Intelligence and Analysis
ISAC   information-sharing analysis center
NARA   National Archives and Records Administration
NCB   Naval Consulting Board
NDRF   National Disaster Recovery Framework
NIMS   National Incident Management System
NIPP   National Infrastructure Protection Plan

NRF	National Response Framework
NRP	National Response Plan
NYCH	New York Clearing House
NYSE	New York Stock Exchange
PCCIP	President's Commission on Critical Infrastructure Protection
PDD	Presidential Decision Directive
PPD	Presidential Policy Directive
PPP	public–private partnership
SCC	sector-coordinating council
TSA	Transportation Security Administration
UP	Union Pacific Railroad
WIB	War Industries Board
WTC	World Trade Center
Y2K	Year 2000

Introduction

In *Managing Disasters through Public–Private Partnerships*, I examine the viability of public–private partnerships (PPP) as tools of disaster mitigation, preparedness, response, and resilience in the United States.[1] I explore how and why "disaster-oriented PPPs" developed in the United States, understand the infrastructures that have been developed to facilitate cross-sector cooperation for these purposes, and determine if these partnerships are viable in the long term. As globalization inexorably interconnects the social, economic, and political elements of society through physical and virtual networks, the need for the United States to evolve and cope with the reality of this new world order becomes increasingly evident. Disaster-oriented PPPs could become one aspect of this evolution.

The US approach to disaster management is no longer organized in the same way it was a decade ago, when government, military, and law enforcement took full responsibility for disaster mitigation, preparedness, response, and resilience. The attacks of September 11, 2001, and catastrophic natural disasters such as Hurricane Katrina in 2005 made two things apparent. First, they highlighted the fact that the private sector owns and operates a significant amount of US critical infrastructure (estimated at 85 percent).[2] If the nation hoped to have a comprehensive and efficient disaster-management strategy going forward, these events made it clear that industry is a significant stakeholder in the protection of critical infrastructure.[3] Second, in the aftermath of both 9/11 and Katrina, the private sector illustrated its sophisticated understanding of and access to global networks, systems, and patterns, and it showed how this knowledge could be brought to bear on disaster response to enhance the speed of recovery efforts. There emerged a further realization that, as partners with government, the private sector may be able to use its knowledge of global networks and trade patterns not only to respond to physical events but also to assist the US government in mitigating the impact of future events. The crises focused national attention on the importance of public–private cooperation and made it no longer a question of whether the private sector had a role to play in national security

1

and disaster management but a question of what that role should be and how effective PPPs for these purposes could be facilitated.

The attacks on the World Trade Center were unique because they constituted an attack *on* private-sector resources, *using* private-sector resources, and with devastating effect. The aftermath of the attacks had crippling economic impacts on the businesses of south Manhattan, nearly brought the New York Stock Exchange to its knees, and, in the long term, had a significant effect on a number of industries, notably the airline industry. In short, 9/11 brought the issue of public–private cooperation to the forefront by demonstrating that in the case of a terrorist attack, there is a high likelihood that (1) the private sector would be a target; (2) first responders to attacks would be from the private sector, not government or military; and (3) an attack would have dire economic consequences that impact private industry in the first instance but would then spread to the US and international economy as a whole. Each of these factors established that cooperation was in the best interests of both sectors.

The concepts that underpin this book were generated in the aftermath of the terrorist attacks of 9/11, but it has become increasingly apparent that the application of this kind of research extends far beyond terrorism. The electricity outages in the northeast United States in 2003, hurricanes Katrina and Rita in 2005, the Asian tsunami of 2007, multiple disaster events in 2010 (including the earthquakes in Haiti, Chile, and China; the volcanic eruption in Iceland; and the BP Gulf of Mexico oil spill), and the Tohoku earthquake and tsunami in Japan in 2011 all illustrate the value of research into the private sector as a partner to government in times of natural disaster as well.

In August 2005 additional benefits of cross-sector cooperation emerged as a result of Hurricane Katrina. While the local, state, and national governments struggled to coordinate and organize a response, private-sector corporations such as Walmart were largely the first responders on the scene and provided critical supplies to evacuees. Walmart and many of the other private-sector corporations featured in this work found that they were better geared to respond rapidly to the hurricane than the government. While a disaster-oriented PPP cannot generate revenue per se, it appeals to business leaders because it can prevent future losses by first avoiding crisis and then, in the event of a disaster, by helping industry rapidly restore normal business practices. Katrina demonstrated to the nation that (1) the private sector could play a critical role in the response to natural disasters; (2) private-sector corporations could in many cases transport and distribute critical goods and services faster than the government and military; and (3) in the event of a disaster of this scale, industry was ready and willing to assist because rapid recovery is in the shared interests of all—government, the public at large, and industry.

The definition of disaster I have adopted in this book aligns with the definition of "major disaster" provided in the Robert T. Stafford Disaster Relief and Emergency Assistance Act (as amended in 2007), which defines major disasters as

> any natural catastrophe (including any hurricane, tornado, storm, high water, wind driven water, tidal wave, tsunami, earthquake, volcanic eruption, landslide, mudslide, snowstorm, or drought), or, regardless of cause, any fire, flood, or explosion, in any part of the United States, which in the determination of the President causes damage of sufficient severity and magnitude to warrant major disaster assistance under this Act to supplement the efforts and available resources of States, local governments, and disaster relief organizations in alleviating the damage, loss, hardship, or suffering caused thereby.[4]

This definition addresses the severity, scale, and US orientation with which this research deals. This book also supports the broader definition of disaster laid out by the United Nations International Strategy for Disaster Reduction: "A serious disruption of the functioning of a community or a society involving widespread human, material, economic or environmental losses and impacts, which exceeds the ability of the affected community or society to cope using its own resources."[5] Therefore, the use of the word "disaster" in this text refers not to the impact or scale of the disaster agent (such as a hurricane or terrorist attack) but to the devastation that can result, with a particular focus on infrastructure, administrative, and policy failures.[6]

I focus on 9/11 and Katrina specifically because these disasters served as "focusing events" in the development and prioritization of public–private cooperation for disaster management purposes.[7] In addition, both events offer well-documented examples of successes and failures in public–private cooperation and are the foundation from which government and private demands for this form of partnership largely emanate. While many other significant disasters have affected the United States in the last decade or more, and many of these have further underlined the need for PPPs, none have been of the scale or importance of 9/11 or Katrina in terms of national, public, or policy responses regarding PPP development. Events such as the 2011 tornado in Joplin, Missouri, the 2010 BP oil spill, or Hurricane Ike in 2008 are not explored in this study simply because they failed to generate sufficient reaction, policy change, or discussion about PPPs to warrant their consideration. This is not to minimize these disasters in any way but simply to argue that in terms of the progression of national policy on disaster-oriented PPPs, these events were simply not of sufficient scale to explore in depth in this research.

In an interview conducted for this book, one interviewee commented that the phrase "resilience" had become a vague "buzz word."[8] Although resilience is widely used in the context of disaster-oriented PPPs and critical infrastructure protection, it is not an easy term to define. As the National Infrastructure Advisory Council of the Department of Homeland Security (DHS) points out, "A myriad of definitions [of resilience] can be found in a wide range of literature, addressing all manner of public and private concerns. Some blur the lines between what is meant by critical infrastructure resiliency, straying into the realm of infrastructure protection or community resilience. Though infrastructure *protection* and infrastructure *resilience* represent complementary elements of a comprehensive risk management strategy, the two concepts are distinct."[9] The council goes on to define resilience as "the ability to absorb, adapt to, and/or rapidly recover from a potentially disruptive event."[10] I use the word "resilience" in this book with this broader definition in mind because it embraces the ability of the public and private sectors to "bounce back" after a disaster. I focus on public–private partnerships, specifically exploring the viability of developing national frameworks to facilitate these PPPs on a long-term basis and make them more effective in the event of a disaster. To maintain this focus, I adopt this broad definition and do not further engage in semantics of what may or may not be "resilience."

The Federal Emergency Management Agency has defined the four phases of emergency management as "preparedness, response, mitigation and recovery."[11] I have chosen slightly different word order and terminology to describe the focus of disaster-oriented PPPs, instead using the phrase "mitigation, preparedness, response, and resilience." I have done this intentionally because the PPP framework explored in this book is intended to function beyond immediate emergency management. The public and private sectors should first proactively "mitigate," that is, work together to avoid future incidents wherever possible. Second, they should "prepare" for the inevitability of the unexpected disaster event. Third, with preparedness comes the ability to effectively respond. Finally—and perhaps most important—PPPs should be designed to accelerate "resilience" to ensure that the nation is infrastructurally and economically able to rapidly recover. I position mitigation as the primary objective. While resilience and recovery may be synonymous in the immediate aftermath of a disaster, resilience is the phrase more commonly used in the context of PPPs. In addition, "resilience" also implies a more immediate and active engagement in absorbing the impact of the events, adapting to new circumstances, and ultimately facilitating that recovery.

GENERAL APPROACH

This study benefits from two distinctive approaches: one for the historical case studies and another for the assessment of contemporary disaster-oriented PPPs. I conducted primary research for the case studies on the Federal Reserve and War Industries Board at the National Archives and Records Administration (NARA).[12] Beyond archival research, secondary sources about both organizations were invaluable. There are no publications that approach the War Industries Board as a public–private alliance, and only a single work explores the Federal Reserve in these terms.[13] Therefore, nearly every time I consulted a secondary source, I explored the existing body of research in an original way to uncover how these institutions functioned as public–private collaborations. In the case of the Federal Reserve, for example, a number of books chart its organizational history in terms of US monetary policy.[14] I consulted and examined these texts with the specific aim of establishing how the Federal Reserve was created and how it managed its relationship between the public and private sectors. These existing resources, applied in a new way, provide an important foundation from which these Wilsonian constructs can be explored as public–private alliances that are comparable to disaster-oriented PPPs.

A second approach explores the more contemporary aspects of this book. This research was informed primarily by qualitative interviews with key leaders and decision makers in the public and private sectors. Because the topic of disaster-oriented PPPs is so new and constitutes an emerging area of academic research, it is important to base the key findings of the book and the origins of those findings upon the experiences and perspectives of public and private practitioners who have personally dealt with the benefits, challenges, and complications of public–private cooperation for these purposes. As a contemporary issue, a number of serving and retired experts from both sectors contributed to this study. Secondary resources on this topic, when available, were used primarily as tools to verify interview results.

I selected interviewees on the basis of their seniority and experience in cooperating with the US public or private sectors on matters of critical infrastructure protection or tactical disaster response and preparedness planning. Interviewees were either serving currently or recently retired private-sector executives and high-level government officials from the United States who are or have been involved in cross-sector cooperation between the US government and the private sector. (See the appendix for the full interviewee list.) Interviewees were selected in the first instance using existing contacts that I developed while working in the private sector from 2001 to 2006. This list quickly expanded in a "snowball effect" as interviewees facilitated further introductions and made referrals. Twenty-five interviews took place between April 1, 2010, and July 14, 2010.

Senior-level leaders were intentionally targeted as interview candidates. This study aims to propose and test a theoretical framework to assess disaster-oriented PPPs in the hope that the framework can be taken and applied by public and private leaders to make cross-sector collaborations more viable. Only decision makers have the ability to enforce this kind of change, and only those in positions of leadership have a comprehensive understanding of the breadth of public–private cooperation currently taking place. Personnel at mid-to-lower levels within both industry and government may have specialist knowledge of the inner workings of some of these relationships, but they rarely have the direct capacity to institute change or have a sufficient sense of the bigger picture. Understanding this bigger picture is important in order to grasp the extent to which cross-sector cooperation occurs on an industry-wide or agency-wide scale as well as where and how the cooperation may be failing. The interview data are supplemented by documentary analysis of relevant US policy documents and secondary source material.[15]

INTRODUCTION OF TWO ORIGINAL FRAMEWORKS AND THE CASE STUDIES

The organizational guidelines for developing formal disaster-oriented PPPs between the private sector and federal government remain unclear. While overarching policy aims such as "the protection of critical infrastructure" or the "enhancement of US national security" dominate, there are no explicit instructions for policymakers or private-sector practitioners to indicate when or how they are meant to collaborate. Important questions remain unanswered. For instance, should the partnerships be responsive—that is, designed primarily to respond to disasters when they occur? Or should they be more strategic, with the partners collaborating proactively both to prevent disasters and to respond if necessary? I look at two public–private collaborations—one existing and another historic—to help answer these questions; I use precedent as a guide to explore the possibilities of both types of partnerships and identify whether disaster-oriented PPPs would be more effective as responsive or strategic alliances. This differentiation impacts nearly every aspect of the partnership, including the longevity, scope, size, and influence of the alliance as well as the best structural framework to facilitate cooperation.

Although disaster-oriented PPPs are a relatively new form of cross-sector cooperation, the US government and private sector have worked together in the past to address other significant national policy dilemmas. I explore two of these collaborations in depth in this book: the Federal Reserve System (hereafter, Federal Reserve or the Fed), established in 1913 and still in operation today, and the War Industries Board (WIB), created in 1917 and dissolved in 1919. Although each partnership was established to achieve a very different objective, each represents a historic, national, policy-oriented, public–private collaboration. The phrase "public–private partnership" came into use long after either of these collaborations was formed, and it would be an anachronism to refer to either as such; however, both are examples of public–private alliances in which the public and private sectors partnered formally on a federal level to attain a shared objective with direct national policy implications.

At their most basic, the case studies aim to explore the structural framework most applicable to disaster-oriented PPPs. They are not intended to be organizational histories, nor will they evaluate the organizations as tools of monetary, fiscal, or economic policy relative to other options or methods. While I acknowledge that there has been a long history of debate about how the Federal Reserve in particular has executed its remit, this research does not engage in this debate and accepts the argument of Bernard Shull that, having operated for nearly a hundred years, "the Federal Reserve has been a success if only because it has survived."[16]

The Fed and WIB are of particular interest to this research for two reasons. First, the Federal Reserve is arguably the longest lasting, functioning, public–private collaboration established for national policy objectives in US history. When looking at disaster-oriented PPPs, it is important to understand how and why the Federal Reserve was created as well as the role that political and private-sector leadership played in the creation and passage of legislation to construct that organization. Second, an evaluation of the WIB, another policy-oriented cross-sector collaboration from the same era but one that has not survived the test of time, is helpful in understanding why one organization achieved longevity and the other did not. While it would be easy to use the "time test" to dub one of these Wilsonian constructs a success and the other a failure, this approach would be too cursory.[17] The case studies identify key parallels and practices that may be relevant and useful in the development of disaster-oriented PPPs. Each case study is assessed to understand the degree to which disaster-oriented PPPs are unique; whether past cross-sector collaborations faced similar priorities and challenges; and, if they did, how these challenges were overcome to forge a successful cross-sector partnership.

What I describe in this book as a "responsive" PPP may be understood as a partnership that is established *in response to* a particular large-scale problem, issue, or incident. These PPPs are designed to address a specific, focused element of a larger-scale national or international dilemma. Responsive PPPs dissolve either at the resolution of the larger incident or at the completion of the directive that the partnership was established to achieve, whichever comes first. They contribute to national policy by using public–private cooperation as a tool to respond to a particular national crisis that significantly impacts both sectors. In responsive PPPs, cooperation is ensured by a shared sense of urgency and a strong sense of mutual gain that drives both sides to work together. Because these partnerships respond to national events, the partnership structure is institutionalized to provide the organization the wherewithal to cope with large-scale complex issues. At the same time, because they are established and sustained in relation to a particular situation, when the crisis is resolved, the organization naturally dissolves. This makes the partnership ad hoc but institutional.

The WIB is an example of a responsive partnership. As with the other national-level policy partnerships explored in this study, the WIB was established as a result of a major crisis—in this case, World War I.[18] The WIB is an example of a responsive PPP because it was created in response to a pressing national need for the US government to mobilize American industry to ensure it had the industrial resources in place to engage in war. The WIB was not established to solve or resolve the war; it was simply one of many tools put in place by government to address national needs that developed in response to the war effort. In addition, because the organization was established as a mechanism to assist in the larger war effort, there was no expectation that the partnership would carry on after the end of the war.

The WIB experienced a great deal of public- and private-sector support generated by a shared sense of urgency in both sectors, a patriotic desire to contribute to the war effort, and the mutual interest of public and private leaders for industrial mobilization to occur.[19] While government needed industry to increase production and fuel the needs of the war, the private sector was equally eager to partner and see the economic benefits that would come as a result of increased production.[20]

In contrast, a strategic partnership is one that is oriented toward the resolution of a broad, national-level objective. Strategic collaborations are distinguished by their long-term orientation and ability to resolve national dilemmas and develop strategies to avoid them in the future. These partnerships have the ability to react and respond to calamitous incidents but, if ultimately successful, develop the capacity to avoid them altogether.

Strategic cross-sector partnerships are designed to inform national policy by using public–private cooperation as a tool to directly influence national or international policy objectives. Strategic alliances are more forward thinking and long term than responsive partnerships. They seek to develop strategies to avoid crisis and mitigate disaster. When or if a crisis occurs, strategic alliances aim to develop a plan to ensure that the nation is prepared and able to respond rapidly with minimal disruption to either sector. While these partnerships are also created as a result of a large-scale national or international crisis, strategic and responsive collaborations differ in that strategic partnerships are designed to ensure that future incidents are prevented, where possible, and they are designed to mitigate, prepare, and respond to crises as they occur over time.

Strategic partnerships can lack the pressing sense of urgency from which responsive partnerships benefit because effective mitigation often occurs in times of relative calm. During these periods, strategic PPPs rely on institutionalization and the organizational mechanisms it provides to facilitate ongoing cooperation in lieu of a pressing sense of urgency caused by crisis. Unlike responsive partnerships, strategic PPPs have the potential to continue indefinitely, as long as the partnership is effective and the underlying need for the partnership remains.

The Federal Reserve is an example of a strategic partnership. This is reflected in the first report made by the Federal Reserve Board to Congress. It described the duties of the reserve banks in terms of crisis prevention rather than crisis response in saying "the duties of the Federal Reserve Banks were not to await the development of emergencies, but rather, by anticipation, to move to prevent them."[21] The financial panic of 1907 was the catalyst for the creation of this cross-sector partnership.[22] Unlike the WIB, which was created to solve a focused aspect of the war effort, the Fed was not designed to address a piece of the nation's economic problems but to resolve them altogether to ensure that a panic of that scale never occurred again.[23] As a result of this broader remit, the Federal Reserve was forced to develop strategies to prevent panics and adapt to face future challenges. The Fed further illustrates how a strategic PPP can have far greater longevity than responsive PPPs. While the nature of economics has changed since the financial panic of 1907, the need for a national cross-sector tool to avoid economic disaster has not, and nearly a century after the establishment of the Federal Reserve, the organization remains a functional and viable institution.

When considering which partnership approach may be most effective for contemporary policymakers, it is important to understand how the strategic and responsive partnership approaches work and when they have been most effectively employed. The delineation between a strategic and responsive partnership indicates the primary orientation and objectives of the alliance. By assessing the case studies in terms of their strategic or responsive orientation and using this differentiation as a starting point to evaluate both the case studies and disaster-oriented PPPs, one can begin to ascertain some of the conditions that may be necessary to develop PPPs and the factors that influence both their longevity and what they are able to achieve. Table I.1 graphically depicts the primary differences between PPPs designed to accomplish responsive and strategic objectives.

Disaster-oriented PPPs and each case study are also assessed in terms of seven critical factors that have been identified in interviews with public and private-sector leaders either as necessary conditions for the success of disaster-oriented

TABLE I.1: Responsive and Strategic Policy-Oriented PPPs

	Responsive Partnerships	*Strategic Partnerships*
Establishment Precipitated by	Major crisis/incident (national or international)	Major crisis/incident (national or international)
Purpose	Crisis response	Crisis mitigation (preparedness and response if necessary)
Organizational Structure	Ad hoc institutional	Permanent institutional
Duration	Dissolves/short term (naturally ends with resolution of crisis, or completion of aims)	Indefinite/long term (if successful, can continue infinitely)
Motivation for Cooperation	High (shared sense of urgency to cooperate and resolve as quickly as possible)	Moderate (reliance on organizational/institutional mechanisms to maintain and facilitate partnership in lieu of urgency)

PPPs or as challenges that must be overcome for them to function effectively. The seven critical factors are the role of crisis, public- and private-sector leadership, organizational structure, information sharing, benefits to each sector, trust, and adaptability or sustainability. Disaster-oriented PPPs, the Federal Reserve, and the WIB will be assessed in terms of these factors to provide a consistent method of evaluating and comparing the two historical case studies with each other and with disaster-oriented PPPs.

In exploring the chapters in terms of the same seven factors, it may be possible to determine if these factors are relevant to all national policy collaborations or if these concerns are unique to disaster-oriented partnerships. In addition, by using the same basis of analysis for all three partnerships and maintaining this consistency throughout the study, applicable parallels between the organizations are maximized. Finally, the seven critical factors further illuminate key aspects of the strategic or responsive orientation of the Federal Reserve and WIB and thus serve as an indicator for disaster-oriented PPPs.

THE ROADMAP

The chapters that follow are devoted to exploring the degree to which it is possible for disaster-oriented PPPs to be viable tools of disaster mitigation, preparedness, response, and resilience in the United States. Chapter 1 explores specific examples of cooperation between government and the telecommunications, finance, and retail industries to demonstrate how those sectors cooperated during the 9/11 and Hurricane Katrina crises, and how this cooperation has enhanced US disaster-response capabilities. The examples given in chapter 1 illustrate that (1) private-sector distribution networks and technological know-how allowed industry to provide goods and services faster than government could during a disaster; (2) disaster-oriented PPPs were valuable after the attacks of 9/11 and Hurricane Katrina; and (3) corporate and government interests aligned during both disasters to make cooperation a shared priority for the public and private sectors. The chapter also summarizes the organizational history of disaster-oriented PPP policymaking in the United States and lays out the existing federal framework for cross-sector cooperation.

Chapter 2 critically assesses disaster-oriented PPPs using the seven critical factors outlined earlier that public- and private-sector practitioners identified as either critical to the success of the partnership, or as significant barriers to cooperation that must be overcome for disaster-oriented PPPs to function effectively. This chapter demonstrates that considerable obstacles exist that limit the effective development of disaster-oriented PPPs on a federal level. These include challenges of sharing information between sectors, a shortage of sustained congressional and presidential leadership, a lack of trust between would-be governmental and private-sector partners, and flaws within the DHS organizational guidelines for cross-sector cooperation. While disaster-oriented PPPs may be viable in principle, the existing framework is not.

The value of disaster-oriented PPPs was highlighted in the two most significant disasters faced by the United States in the last decade, yet the existing framework to facilitate cross-sector cooperation is falling short. Therefore, the remainder of this book addresses two key questions: Are PPPs for this purpose viable? If they are viable, can the existing framework be improved to make these partnerships function more effectively?

The case studies in chapters 3 and 4 help to answer these questions by providing examples of two other public–private alliances designed, like disaster-oriented PPPs, to achieve national policy objectives. Chapter 3 begins by critically assessing the Federal Reserve as a strategic PPP that is one hundred years old. Within this context, the Fed is analyzed specifically in terms of the same seven critical factors that have been identified as crucial to the development and success of disaster-oriented PPPs. By exploring the Fed in this way, it becomes evident that the seven critical factors were just as relevant to the founders of the Federal Reserve as they struggled to build the organization as an effective cross-sector alliance as they are to public and private leaders developing disaster-oriented PPPs today. The chapter also explores how the Fed has remained institutionally viable for so long.

Chapter 4 explores the WIB as an example of a responsive public–private alliance. This case study tracks the history of the organization in order to understand it as a PPP and provides an alternative to the Federal Reserve model. In exploring the WIB in terms of the same seven critical factors used to assess disaster-oriented PPPs and the Fed, it is evident that these factors were equally relevant to this short-lived, responsive partnership. The WIB's response to each of these critical factors, however, differs greatly from the Federal Reserve's response and thus illustrates the degree to which the responsive and strategic partnership structures differ in purpose and function.

In chapter 5 I compare the Fed, WIB, and disaster-oriented PPPs. This reveals that although policymakers have called for strategic disaster-oriented partnerships, an organizational framework has been created that much more strongly resembles a responsive framework. By using the Fed and WIB as a guide, this chapter argues that in order to make disaster-oriented PPPs viable in the long term (as policymakers have said they want), a strategic framework should be adopted. This would require an act of Congress to cement public- and private-sector roles and responsibilities, establish institutional trust, and encourage consistent leadership from Congress and the president. These steps are unlikely to occur, however, given the lack of urgency and political prioritization that disaster-oriented PPPs receive as time passes since the last significant disaster and as leaders focus their attention elsewhere. Therefore, while disaster-oriented PPPs may be theoretically viable, it appears in practice that there is currently little interest in developing a framework able to sustain lasting cooperation.

The concluding chapter argues that while the Fed provides a framework that could be applied by disaster-oriented PPPs, in reality this is unlikely to occur without a catastrophic disaster of a magnitude greater than anything yet experienced in the United States. Until this occurs, it is important that awareness about these issues is generated so that when disaster does strike, a framework is in place and ready to be applied. The conclusion also outlines the future implications of this work.

NOTES

1. The term "public–private partnership" appeared in the 1980s and quickly came to be used to describe any number of forms of cooperation between the public and private sectors. The phrase was first used in the context of critical infrastructure protection in Presidential Decision Directive 63 issued by President William J. Clinton in 1998. For more on various types of PPPs and the challenges that the generality of the term has

created, see Bult-Spiering and Dewulf, *Strategic Issues in Public–Private Partnerships*; Linder, "Coming to Terms with the Public–Private Partnership"; Schaeffer and Loveridge, "Toward an Understanding of Public–Private Cooperation"; and White House, *Presidential Decision Directive 63*, Washington, DC, May 22, 1998.

2. Critical infrastructure is defined in the 2009 National Infrastructure Protection Plan (NIPP) developed by the Department of Homeland Security as "systems and assets, whether physical or virtual, so vital that the incapacity or destruction of such may have a debilitating impact on the security, economy, public health or safety, environment, or any combination of these matters, across any Federal, State regional territorial, or local jurisdiction." DHS, *NIPP* (2009), 109; and 9/11 Commission, *9/11 Report*, 323.

3. After 9/11 nearly every significant national policy document relating to the development of Homeland Security included at least a mention of developing closer links with the private sector. One of the first was the National Strategy for Homeland Security, issued in 2002. This document speaks at length about the importance of private-sector cooperation with government.

4. The Robert T. Stafford Disaster Relief and Emergency Assistance Act, Pub. L. No. 100-707, was signed into law on November 23, 1988, and amended the Disaster Relief Act of 1974, Pub. L. No. 93-288, June 2007. This act constitutes the statutory authority for most federal disaster response activities.

5. UNISDR, *2009 UNISDR Terminology*, 9.

6. There are number of ways scholars and practitioners have sought to define and distinguish disasters from other types of events. While the author acknowledges this debate, this work aims to focus on PPPs, not disaster theory, and as a result does not engage further. For an excellent summary of the theory surrounding the terminology that may be used to differentiate and describe events of various scales, see Birkland, *Lessons of Disaster*; Faulkner, "Towards a Framework for Tourism Disaster Management"; and Quarantelli, "Catastrophes Are Different from Disasters."

7. A focusing event is defined by Thomas Birkland as "an event that is sudden, relatively rare, can be reasonably defined as harmful or revealing the possibility of potentially greater future harms, inflicts harms or suggests potential harms that are or could be concentrated on a definable geographical area or community of interest, and that is known to policy makers and the public virtually simultaneously." Birkland, *After Disaster*, 22.

8. Nitin Natarajan, Chairman of DHS GCC for Healthcare and Coordinating Director of Health and Human Services/ASPR/OPEO, telephone interview with the author from Washington, DC, May 5, 2010.

9. DHS, NIAC, *Critical Infrastructure and Resilience*, 12.

10. Ibid.

11. DHS, *Federal Emergency Management Agency*, 17.

12. Research conducted about the Federal Reserve was conducted at NARA I in Washington, DC, and all research on the War Industries Board was conducted at NARA II in College Park, Maryland.

13. Rowe, *Public–Private Character*.

14. Friedman and Schwartz, *Monetary History*; and Meltzer, *History of the Federal Reserve*; Kemmerer and Kemmerer, *ABC of the Federal Reserve*; Shull, *Fourth Branch*; Moore, *Federal Reserve System*; and deSaint Phalle, *Federal Reserve*.

15. Policy documents include reports of the Congressional Research Service, the Government Accountability Office, and the US Chamber of Commerce in addition to official publications of the Department of Homeland Security. Additional secondary sources include books, chapters in books, and journal articles. All sources consulted for this book are listed in the bibliography.

16. Shull, *Fourth Branch*, 6. Shull goes on to argue that the Fed has also been a success as a result of the dramatic growth of its "size, powers, and influence" over time. While this work does not engage with the debate surrounding the effectiveness of the Federal Reserve as a tool of monetary, fiscal, or economic policy, an insight into the primary arguments of the proponents, opponents, and academic observers of the organization can be found in the following texts: Kemmerer and Kemmerer, *ABC of the Federal Reserve*; Shull, *Fourth Branch*; Meltzer, *History of the Federal Reserve*; Moore, *Federal Reserve System*; deSaint Phalle, *Federal Reserve*; Warburg, in *Federal Reserve System: Its Origin and Growth*; and Willis, *Federal Reserve System*.

17. President Woodrow Wilson was president of the United States from 1913 to 1921. The Federal Reserve Act was passed and the War Industries Board was created during his time in office.

18. Kester, "War Industries Board"; and Hitchcock, "War Industries Board."

19. When the United States broke diplomatic ties with Germany prior to World War I and the United States' entrance into the conflict was imminent, there was a significant surge of patriotism from American industries with offers to assist the government. Cuff, *War Industries Board*, 46–47.

20. Baruch, *Baruch*, 58.

21. Rowe, *Public–Private Character*, 68.

22. Carter Glass writes, "The frightful panic of 1907, decidedly the severest financial disturbance the country ever had, sharply arrested the attention of Congress and forced those charged with legislative authority at least to attempt remedial action of some kind." Glass, *Adventure in Constructive Finance*, 64. See also Bruner and Carr, *Panic of 1907*, 146; and Friedman and Schwartz, *Monetary History*, 163.

23. Warburg, *Federal Reserve System*, 165.

CHAPTER ONE

The Emergence of Disaster-Oriented PPPs

In the last decade the United States has witnessed no fewer than twenty-one significant disasters within its borders. These include natural and man-made disasters that range from devastating terrorist attacks to catastrophic floods, hurricanes, electrical blackouts, and wildfires.[1] Beyond its borders, the United States has been engaged in Afghanistan since October 2001 in the single longest war in American history; American troops were also in Iraq from March 2003 to September 2010.[2]

Significant international events have also weighed heavily on the US public and private sectors. Some of the more significant incidents since the millennium include the attack on the USS *Cole* in Yemen in 2000, the bombings of expatriate compounds in Saudi Arabia and suicide bombings in Morocco in 2003, the Madrid train bombing and the devastating tsunami in the Indian Ocean in 2004, the 7/7 bombings in London in 2005, the catastrophic earthquakes that shook Haiti and Chile in 2010, the Icelandic volcano that halted all transatlantic air travel for several weeks in 2010, and the Tohoku earthquake and tsunami in Japan in 2011. This list does not include the global public health risks posed by the anthrax attacks in Washington in 2001, SARS in 2002–3, the avian flu pandemic in 2005, or the global H1N1 "swine flu" pandemic of 2009–10.

While the regularity of disasters has served to underscore the importance and potential value of cross-sector cooperation, no two events prioritized disaster-oriented public–private partnerships (PPP) in the minds of the American public and private sectors more than the terrorist attacks of 9/11 in 2001 and Hurricane Katrina in 2005. Although man caused one crisis and nature the other, each was pivotal, shocking the public with its scale and scope while exposing areas of national vulnerability, and each disaster created a heightened awareness of the benefits of cross-sector cooperation.

Hurricane Katrina and 9/11 made the formation of disaster-oriented PPPs a more urgent priority for both the public and private sectors. In this chapter I use specific examples of cooperation between government and the telecommunications, finance, and retail industries to demonstrate how the sectors have cooperated during these crises and how this cooperation has been valuable to US disaster response capabilities. The examples illustrate three key points. First, private-sector distribution networks and technological know-how allowed industry to provide goods and services faster than government could during a disaster. Second, the private sector proved itself to be an invaluable partner after the attacks of 9/11 and Hurricane Katrina. Third, in the crisis generated by both disasters, national interests and corporate interests aligned to make cooperation a shared priority for the public and private sectors.

I also explore the organizational development of federal policy relating to disaster-oriented PPPs in the United States. I track disaster-oriented PPP policy from 1995 to the present to understand how these partnerships developed, how the framework evolved over time, and how these PPPs were prioritized after 9/11 and Katrina. By tracking the historical development of the partnership framework here, the groundwork is established for a more critical exploration of the existing guidelines for cross-sector cooperation in chapter 2.

THE PUBLIC AND PRIVATE VALUE OF DISASTER-ORIENTED PPPS

The 9/11 attacks on the World Trade Center (WTC) were an awakening. Not only were the attacks on civilian targets within US borders; they also forced the nation to acknowledge that unless the critical infrastructure owned and operated by the private sector was better protected, America would be vulnerable.[3] Prior to 9/11 the three al-Qaeda attacks carried out against the United States occurred overseas and targeted US military or government installations.[4] With 9/11, al-Qaeda brought its attacks to the United States, targeted civilians, generated fear in the public, and prioritized matters of defense and security within both the public and private sectors. The attacks of 9/11 constituted attacks on private networks, and using private networks to devastating effect. This use of private infrastructure created the awareness that the private sector had a significant role to play in developing the country's resilience following terror attacks. The *9/11 Commission Report* warns the American people: "The lessons of 9/11 for civilians and first responders can be stated simply: in the new age of terror, they—we—are the primary targets. The losses America suffered that day demonstrated both the gravity of the terrorist threat and the commensurate need to prepare ourselves to meet it."[5]

The attacks also forced the public sector to acknowledge openly the nation vulnerability caused by having such a significant amount of American infrastructure in private hands. The *9/11 Commission Report* says "the private sector controls 85 percent of the critical infrastructure in the nation. Indeed, unless a terrorist's target is a military or other secure government facility, the 'first' responders will almost certainly be civilians."[6] The commission's formal acknowledgment of the importance of the private sector in preparedness represented a dramatic shift from earlier approaches to national security, where responsibility for disaster preparedness and response was seen to be the sole responsibility of local law enforcement, the military, and government.[7] The events of 9/11 highlighted the importance of public–private cooperation and made it no longer a question of whether the private sector had a role to play in counterterrorism and national security but one of what that role should be and how effective PPPs could be facilitated.

The devastation caused by Hurricane Katrina demonstrated that natural disasters have just as much potential to cause panic and disruption as terrorist incidents. As with 9/11, Katrina underscored the value of PPPs and established their applicability to man-made as well as natural disasters. "Coming four years after the September 11, 2001 attacks, the hurricanes of 2005 dramatized the frailties of our nation's disaster response system."[8] While the government, and particularly the Federal Emergency Management Agency (FEMA), struggled to respond, private-sector corporations were, in many cases, the first responders, delivering food, water, blankets, and other vital necessities to those stranded. The US Chamber of Commerce reported: "Private-sector assistance during and following the major 2005 hurricanes—Katrina, Rita and Wilma—totaled about $1.2 billion, 25 percent of that in products and services, the remainder in cash contributions. . . . At least 254 companies made cash or in-kind contributions of $1 million or more."[9]

While 9/11 generated a widespread acknowledgment of the private sector as a terrorist target and highlighted the importance of disaster-oriented PPPs in terms of protecting critical infrastructure vis-à-vis terror threats, Katrina illustrated the capacity of the private sector to serve not only as a defender and protector of national systems and assets but also as a capable and willing responder to all types of disaster, be they caused by man or nature.

The roles of the Verizon Corporation, the New York Federal Reserve Bank, and the New York Stock Exchange during 9/11, as well as the role of the Walmart corporation during Hurricane Katrina, illustrate how and why the development of disaster-oriented PPPs has become valuable to the public and private sectors in the last decade. These examples provide a basis for understanding the role several key industries played in disaster response and how the private sector demonstrated its value as a partner.

9/11: A Response from the Telecommunications Sector, Verizon

When the south tower of the WTC collapsed on 9/11, all mobile phone capabilities were lost at Ground Zero.[10] The restoration of mobile phone communication at Ground Zero was urgent—first responders needed mobile phones as backup for their failing radios, mobile phones could be used by survivors trapped in the rubble to call for help, and, once restored, mobile-phone tracking devices could be used by rescuers to locate survivors.[11] The mobile-phone network—the equipment, technology, and the capability to restore communication—rested in the private sector. Verizon owned the wireless tower that collapsed on the south tower of the WTC (called a switching station) and was responsible for most of the area's telecommunications networks. The public sector could not repair the network independently, so it immediately turned to Verizon.

Verizon was quick to respond. In a September 12, 2001, press conference, the vice-chairman of Verizon's telecom group described the area around the WTC as "probably the most telecommunications-intensive area in the world."[12] They owned the switching station on the south tower and nearly five hundred Verizon employees had been in WTC tower 1 during the attack. While most Verizon employees were on lower floors and escaped, at least a dozen employees who were known to be above the impact zone had been instructed to ascend to the roof and lost their lives when the tower collapsed.[13] The corporate headquarters of the organization, the Verizon Building, was located directly across the street from the WTC. The building remained structurally sound but it sustained serious damage. Burning rubble from the WTC was piled for seven stories around the Verizon Building. The most damaged section of the building contained Verizon's most critical equipment, and collapsed steel and concrete had damaged Verizon's underground cable vaults (thereby disrupting landline and Internet communication for Lower Manhattan) and had severed critical electrical feeders, water mains, and sewer piping.[14] Verizon had a vested interest in cooperating with the government: Verizon employees had been victims of the attack and may have been among the survivors who were trying to use mobile phones as a lifeline, the company headquarters had been damaged, and millions of customers throughout Lower Manhattan were without coverage, including emergency response teams, the New York Stock Exchange, the Federal Reserve Bank of New York, and other key resources.

The public and private sectors immediately realized the importance of cooperation. Authorities in New York City cleared the rubble to help Verizon repair vehicles gain access to Lower Manhattan and even helped bypass a great deal of bureaucratic red tape to bring a fuel tanker into the city, very near the WTC site, so that Verizon could fuel a generator necessary for them to do their work.[15]

The New York City police also forcibly removed a number of parked cars that blocked Verizon engineers' access to a critical substation.[16] Once wireless coverage was restored to Ground Zero, Verizon distributed more than five thousand cell phones to emergency workers.[17] In addition, Verizon and other wireless providers began monitoring all cellular signals near the collapsed WTC site to locate survivors who may still have been trapped.[18]

9/11: A Response from the Finance Sector, the New York Stock Exchange, and the Federal Reserve Bank of New York

While the telecommunications industry provides a very tangible and tactical example of how the sectors cooperated to help in the immediate response to 9/11, the role of the financial services industry provides an equally important, albeit less tangible, illustration. The attacks occurred in the epicenter of the banking community. A document produced for Congress summarizes the severity of the attacks to the financial system:

> The attacks on the twin towers threatened the heart of the US financial system. Their destruction devastated the leading dealer in US Treasury securities, the loss of whose staff accounted for almost one quarter of those killed in New York City. The debris from the collapsing towers and the general chaos in the area brought about the closing of the New York Stock Exchange, the major stock exchange in the United States, as well as closing brokerage houses and banks in the Wall Street area. The grounding of all airplanes severely hampered the clearing of checks and the distribution of paper currency, creating great uncertainty for financial institutions.[19]

The New York financial community was acutely mindful of the potential economic impact of 9/11 and feared financial panic. The New York Stock Exchange (NYSE) and the New York Federal Reserve were located just a few blocks from the WTC. When the towers collapsed, telephone and electricity capabilities for the area were lost. Verizon was not the only company with major infrastructure hubs lying within reach of the WTC. Con Edison, New York City's electricity provider, lost two key substations, which resulted in power outages throughout Lower Manhattan, including the NYSE and the Reserve.[20] These outages shut down the "computer systems that execute, process, and record billions of transactions daily and telecommunications networks that link investors, markets, and financial institutions."[21]

The NYSE closed on September 11 and did not reopen until Con Edison and Verizon restored power and communication to the exchange for an opening on Monday, September 17. This was no easy task, and Con Edison completed work that normally would take weeks in a matter of days.[22] Although the NYSE was closed for the first time since the Great Depression, the Federal Reserve continued operations without disruption, and the resilience of the financial services sector limited the economic impact zone to the Greater Manhattan area and prevented a larger scale economic crisis.[23] The Congressional Research Service attributes this success to the "massive repair effort—organized and carried out by private telecommunications and financial firms with little government assistance" that helped ensure "the markets and banking system were not paralyzed."[24]

Despite the tangible damage that prevented the operation of the exchange, there were some intangible benefits to its temporary closure. The closure of the NYSE may have prevented widespread national and international financial panic. As one Wall Street chief financial officer summarized, "Closing the markets provided more time to collect data and allowed for more informed decision-making which served to diminish panic selling by investors, helped maintain orderly markets and, ultimately, maintain global financial stability." The closure of the exchange hedged the nation against the very real threat that nervous investors, unsure of how the markets would react to the attacks, would "hoard assets and get out of the market at all costs."[25] Waiting to reopen the exchange allowed time for the immediate shock of the event to subside and made it possible for the markets to reopen once key operating systems were back in order and investors could be reassured that the US markets were strong and stable.[26]

The government and the private sector realized the importance of reinstating the exchange and worked in close cooperation to get its operational systems functioning. As the *New York Times* explained the day before the NYSE reopened: "Government officials and financial leaders are eager to open the exchange and resume trading for symbolic, and practical, reasons. Millions of people do not know the value of their investments. Investors who want to sell shares, or buy them, cannot. The government is losing taxes every day the markets remain closed, and the exchange itself risks losing business to other markets."[27] It was important to the economy that the exchange should return to "business as usual." It was equally important to send a message to the world that US industry, and the networks that underpinned its operations, were sound. To signify not only the close cooperation between the sectors but also the importance of the financial services industry as a symbol of post-9/11 resilience, New York mayor Rudolph Giuliani and New York City fire and police officers were on hand for the ringing of the opening bell.[28]

That events in New York did not balloon into a national (or international) panic was important to the national economy and to the mitigation of a more lasting crisis. The maintenance of economic stability is central to a sense of public well-being. In the days that the NYSE was closed, the Federal Reserve did everything it could to maintain stability by remaining operational and serving as the lender of last resort. With many of the nation's largest banks paralyzed by the attacks, this role was critical.[29] By remaining open, the Fed demonstrated its ability to withstand a significant crisis. The vice-chairman of the Federal Reserve Board argues, "We attempted to maintain confidence by indicating through our public statement that the Federal Reserve was open and operating and that we were ready to provide liquidity."[30]

The crisis created by 9/11 shocked both the US public and private sectors, and made them more cognizant of their interdependence. In New York City, the financial sector had been the primary target of the attacks, and beyond the devastating loss of life, the residual damage of the collapsing towers had left Lower Manhattan without key necessities such as water and power. The rapid restoration of these services was not only a practical necessity for those who lived in the area but also a symbolic act that demonstrated the resilience of the city and its economy. None of these things was possible without cross-sector cooperation.

Hurricane Katrina: A Response from the Retail Sector, Walmart

Hurricane Katrina made landfall on August 29, 2005, and refocused the lens through which the nation viewed disaster-oriented PPPs. While 9/11 demonstrated why and how PPPs could benefit the nation in the event of a terrorist attack and shone a light on the benefits of PPPs for national security, Hurricane Katrina generated awareness that PPPs play an equally important role in the event of a national disaster.

Katrina presented a very different type of problem. Unlike 9/11, where the attacks stunned the nation, the Gulf Coast has a long history of dealing with hurricanes. When the levee system in New Orleans failed, the resulting devastation was of such a scale that it immediately became a national crisis. In contrast to 9/11, where the death toll was high (2,973) but the impact area fairly compact, Katrina impacted 93,000 square miles across the states of Louisiana, Mississippi, Florida, and Alabama.[31] Approximately 5.8 million Americans experienced the hurricane, nearly 770,000 were displaced, and there were an estimated 1,500 deaths.[32] More than 2.5 million customers were left without power, an estimated 300,000 homes were destroyed, and approximately 80 percent of New Orleans was flooded.[33] The scale of the disaster, and the crisis that resulted, was enormous.

While the hurricane may not have been a surprise, its impact and the sluggish response of the public sector was a shock. The authorities struggled to respond while corporations such as Walmart, Ford, and Office Depot distributed supplies to the areas most affected.[34] The week after the hurricane, the *Washington Post* argued, "While state and federal officials have come under harsh criticism for their handling of the storm's aftermath, Walmart is being held up as a model of logistical efficiency and nimble disaster planning, which have allowed it to quickly deliver staples such as water, fuel and toilet paper to thousands of evacuees."[35] After the crisis, as the failures of the public sector and the successes of the private sector emerged, PPPs were reprioritized on the national agenda.

The failures of the local, state, and national governments during the Katrina crisis have been extensively chronicled. Since 2005 FEMA in particular has worked diligently to move beyond the now-infamous failures of Katrina. Since FEMA's response to Katrina has been critically explored in detail by the government, academia, and the media, and its response no longer accurately reflects the public response planning in effect today, these failures will not be explored in depth here, with the exception of particular incidents that highlight how the event reprioritized public–private cooperation.[36]

In the days immediately following the hurricane, there was a communication breakdown in the public sector at all levels of government, leaving the government overwhelmed.[37] Disaster response agencies (FEMA in particular) were unprepared and slow to respond. In contrast, Walmart was prepared and rapidly reacted to the event. The ability of retailers such as Walmart to respond immediately while FEMA continued to scramble reinforced the sense that the private sector should be more formally integrated in disaster preparedness strategies because they may have an important role to play. Precisely how that role would play out, however, and whether the government would be able to use private-sector capabilities to assist with the response remained to be seen. Susan Rosegrant argues, "Questions remained about whether the public sector could take full advantage of the retailer's strengths and capabilities, and whether it was ready for Walmart and other companies to carve out a new role for private–sector participation in a national emergency."[38]

In discussing Walmart as first responder to Hurricane Katrina, it is important to take into account the scale of the Walmart network. Walmart is the world's largest retailer. In 2004, the year before Katrina, Walmart saw sales of $256.3 billion. The store had one hundred distribution centers across the United States, eight of which were specifically designated as disaster distribution centers (not storage facilities).[39] The Walmart business model is reliant upon goods constantly moving through their distribution network. This is noteworthy because it suggests that the Walmart business model is dependent upon a complex network that must be open and functional for Walmart to be productive and profitable. "For the vast majority of goods, when they arrive from a manufacturer to a Walmart warehouse, it is there for an average of 45 minutes before it is loaded and dispatched to various facilities."[40] Bryan Koon, Walmart's director of emergency management, estimates that approximately eight thousand truck drivers, seven thousand trucks, and approximately fifty-five thousand trailers support the movement of these goods through the US network.[41] Knowing that it is Walmart's business to get their merchandise to the right stores in a timely manner, they have developed contingency plans (and contingency plans for contingency plans) to work around every possible impediment that may clog their network, including weather, traffic delays, man-made or natural disasters, and equipment breakdowns. Because of their expertise, the strength of their distribution chains, wealth, and extensive contingency planning, they are well practiced at moving goods and services on a scale and at a speed that is simply unrealistic for government.

Walmart recognizes that it is often in the interests of their corporation to assist after significant disasters such as Katrina. Disasters are bad for business— they prevent employees from getting to work, close stores, damage property and merchandise, and ultimately lose retailers' money. Koon argues, "Disasters will happen, and they will happen in areas that Walmart has stores. Knowing this, it's Walmart's aim to restore normalcy as quickly as possible—we want the community back on its feet as soon as possible so that we can continue to operate normally."[42] This is not to argue that corporations such as Walmart have no sense of altruism but to point out that business motives ultimately drive the private sector's ability and willingness to respond.

Walmart has 4,000 stores in the United States, and more than 170 Walmart facilities were in the Katrina impact zone of Louisiana, Mississippi, Florida, and Alabama. Of those 170 stores, 126 were forced to close after Katrina, many because of power failures.[43] As the hurricane roared toward the Gulf Coast, Walmart's Office of Emergency Management in Bentonville, Arkansas, prepared. On the day the hurricane made landfall, the retailer was ready: "Stores in the storm zone had closed early after stocking up on special 'hurricane' merchandise; teams were stationed near New Orleans and the Mississippi coast, ready to sweep in to evaluate damage to stores; and at the centralized emergency operations center, representatives of all major functional areas were gathered to launch a coordinated effort to find displaced employees, reopen stores as quickly as possible and help stricken communities."[44] Walmart disaster distribution centers had space for $4.7 million in emergency merchandise with supplies based on geographic location. In the Southeast these supplies included items such as water, batteries, lanterns, lamp oil, and ready-to-eat food.[45] After Katrina, the scale of the devastation was soon apparent. Phone lines and cell towers were down, electricity was out in most places, and debris and law enforcement kept many Walmart teams from accessing or evaluating the stores. To access their stores, Walmart contacted local authorities with whom they had worked during previous hurricanes to conduct damage assessments. It was not long before reports of the devastation in New Orleans, structural damage to stores, rising floodwaters, and looters breaking into many stores began to arrive from the Walmart regional teams.[46] Law enforcement was too occupied with the disaster response to stop the looting. In one store, police looked on while people stole carts full of supplies and cleared out the entire gun section.[47]

Like Verizon in the aftermath of 9/11, Walmart was motivated to get involved for a number of reasons. First, thousands of Walmart associates were in the flood zone, and the corporation wanted to get emergency supplies to its employees (approximately thirty-four thousand Walmart employees were affected by the storm).[48] Second, Walmart needed assistance getting access to some of its stores.[49] It could not gauge its losses or capacity to help until it assessed the damage and merchandise remaining in its stores. Third, the communities affected were all customers of Walmart, and the corporation was holding goods its customers needed. Fourth, from an advertising and public relations perspective, being seen by customers as an active participant in the response was not only good advertising but could also enhance brand loyalty. It would benefit the corporation, its employees, and its customers to do everything it could to assist. As a result of Katrina, Walmart shipped 2,498 trailers of emergency merchandise, gave $3.5 million in merchandise to shelters and command posts, and customers and associates (employees) donated more than $8.5 million to the relief effort.[50]

As Walmart struggled to coordinate their response with the public sector, numerous shortcomings in public–private cooperation forced the corporation to negotiate with the authorities during the crisis to protect its interests. For example, Walmart negotiated with local law enforcement and gave them store goods in exchange for protection from looters. While Walmart officials argue that this was "the cost of providing community support," there were cases of abuse, including isolated incidents where police and National Guardsmen broke into stores out of desperation and took items without permission. One first responder from Walmart argued: "If people needed water and they needed food and they couldn't get it anywhere else, let them have it. . . . When they took the big screen TVs we had to roll our eyes at that one."[51] In an attempt to distribute goods to those who needed them, stop the looting, and assess the greater damage to Walmart stores, some Walmart facilities were offered as command posts for first responders. This benefited both sides because food, clothes, and cots were made available for exhausted responders, and the retailer was able to keep looters out of stores because of the law enforcement presence.[52]

The lack of governmental preparedness and the failure of the public sector to have an organized plan to coordinate and communicate with the private sector during the crisis were apparent after Katrina. Walmart tried to cooperate with the government on numerous occasions during the crisis and met with the

Department of Homeland Security (DHS) in the days after the hurricane to find out how they could better assist with the response. Walmart offered to send a representative to DHS's operations center and offered to help the Department of Defense (DoD) with logistics, but both agencies refused.[53] In speaking to both FEMA and the Private Sector Office (both part of DHS), Walmart was left with the impression that there had been little thought about how to engage the private sector; and, while privately owned services such as utilities and telecommunications were seen by the government as "critical" as a result of the 9/11 experience, the retail sector was not yet deemed to be an equally valuable partner.[54]

This lack of coordination and information sharing between the sectors impacted relief efforts and ultimately made Walmart the unwitting "first responder" after Hurricane Katrina. Walmart had not been given access to the "red zone" in New Orleans. It had supplies ready for distribution to hurricane survivors but had no sense of where the supplies were needed or where the goods should be distributed. In addition, because the need for supplies was so urgent, Walmart wanted support from local law enforcement to unload the trucks and to safely manage the crowds to avoid fights and rioting.[55] Walmart knew they could help but needed direction.

Walmart also knew from news reports that there were more than twenty thousand evacuees at the Superdome with inadequate supplies. Despite the fact that Walmart had thirteen trailers of water that had been waiting for three days just outside of the city of New Orleans, they could not get access to the stadium.[56] DHS did not return calls, and the New Orleans mayor's office instructed the trucks to wait near a closed-off bridge for a police escort into the city: it never arrived. After waiting for hours, the trucks were forced to turn back.[57] Eventually, there were nearly twenty-five trailers of emergency supplies waiting outside the city with nowhere to go. Despite numerous requests to FEMA for help, "the agency was still trying to get organized and couldn't provide direction."[58] Finally, in desperation, a Walmart executive took action and set up a distribution point on a main road into New Orleans. He recalls, "It felt good for about thirty minutes . . . but when the crowd of a few hundred quickly swelled to more than a thousand, and people began fighting over food, the trucks pulled out."[59] Walmart had the goods and the ability to deliver them but needed direction, support, and protection to do it safety and effectively.

The examples of Verizon, the NYSE, the Federal Reserve Bank of New York, and Walmart demonstrate how and why momentum developed around disaster-oriented PPP initiatives after 9/11 and Hurricane Katrina. The private sector has resoundingly demonstrated its value as a partner as well as the important impact it could make in the event of a catastrophic disaster. In some cases, as seen with Verizon and the NYSE, the government relied upon the private sector and could not have adequately responded alone; in other cases, as seen with Walmart, the private sector demonstrated that its access to transportation systems, goods, and services could significantly augment government's speed and capacity to respond. Industry proved it could dramatically enhance disaster response and resilience by applying its specialist skills and knowledge to achieve the common objective shared by both sectors—the restoration of normality.

THE HISTORICAL EVOLUTION OF POLICY AND ORGANIZATIONAL FRAMEWORKS

Federal attempts to develop disaster-oriented PPPs began during the late 1990s under the Clinton administration as part of the US counterterrorism and national security strategy. Following the first bombing of the WTC in 1993 and the bombing of the federal building in Oklahoma City in 1995, a heightened awareness developed about the importance of critical infrastructure protection in the United States. A directive focused on counterterrorism, Presidential Decision Directive 39 (PDD 39), was signed two months after the Oklahoma City bombing, although much of it was classified. PDD 39 is noteworthy in terms of the development of disaster-oriented PPPs because it established a cabinet-level group to determine the vulnerability of government facilities and critical national infrastructure to terrorist attacks.[60] This exercise resulted in the creation of Executive Order 13010 (EO 13010) in 1996, which established a full-time commission called the President's Commission on Critical Infrastructure Protection (PCCIP), which was designed to monitor critical infrastructure protection issues and make policy recommendations. EO 13010 argues, "It is essential that the government and private sector work together to develop a strategy for protecting [critical infrastructure] and assuring their continued operation."[61] The order was a landmark in PPP development at the federal level because it formally acknowledged the importance of the private sector in national security and critical infrastructure protection and the value of cross-sector cooperation.

In 1997 the PCCIP produced a report for the president that further explored the issues prioritized in EO 13010. The PCCIP report, *Critical Foundations*, defined critical infrastructure, differentiated vulnerabilities as either "cyber" or "physical," and discussed at length the challenges of private-sector ownership of critical infrastructures.[62] The report also continued to reiterate the importance of developing relationships with the private sector: "The critical infrastructures are central to our national defense and our economic power, and we must lay the foundations for their future security on a new form of cooperation between government and the private sector."[63] The report proposed a framework for PPPs through an information-sharing analysis center (ISAC).[64]

The PCCIP categorized "critical infrastructure" into eight sectors. Each sector was then assigned to a federal agency (designated as a "lead agency") to oversee critical infrastructure protection and private-sector outreach.[65] For example, the Department of the Treasury was assigned as lead agency for the banking and finance sector. The PCCIP envisaged the ISAC as a "one-stop/one-call" center for information assurance, protection, and defense.[66]

The recommendations in the final report of the PCCIP, including the establishment of an ISAC, were acted upon in Presidential Decision Directive 63 (PDD 63), signed in July 1998.[67] PDD 63 set the ambitious goal of ensuring that the United States could provide critical infrastructure protection by 2003. PDD 63 again underscored the importance of private-sector involvement and for the first time used the phrase "public–private partnership" to describe cross-sector cooperation for these purposes.[68]

While the PCCIP and subsequent PDD 63 envisioned a single ISAC to coordinate all sectors of public and private information and analysis sharing, the concept soon went in an unanticipated direction as the idea of a single organization able to coordinate all the sectors evolved into each sector having its own ISAC. Kathi Ann Brown explains, "Although it took almost two years for the first ISAC to become operational—one in banking and finance—soon ISACs of all types and arrangements began to appear, not all of them officially sanctioned. Their models and missions also took on varied forms. Some focused mainly on cyber; others incorporated physical security, too."[69]

Not only were there a number of ISACs; their scopes were varied and inconsistent. ISACs did not become the PPP framework that was hoped, and there are two dominant theories about why they have not been more effective. The first, argued by Lewis Branscomb and Erwann O. Michel-Kerjan, is that although the ISACs represented an "increasing recognition of the necessity of sharing information within specific critical sectors," ultimately they were unsuccessful because of the reluctance of the private sector to share information.[70] The private sector was concerned about loss of competitive advantage if they partnered with government, and industry was further hindered by confidentiality agreements with customers and concerns about potential antitrust violations that could emerge from cooperating with the public sector.[71] Jamie Gorelick, a member of the PCCIP advisory committee and commissioner of the *9/11 Commission Report*, argues that industry was not eager to participate in the ISACs because "it's an act against nature for a company to sit down with its competitors and share its vulnerabilities and to share information which is going to give its competitors competitive advantages."[72]

The second theory is that the ISACs were structurally flawed because the sectors were not given sufficient guidance to organize effective frameworks capable of cross-communication. Little direction was given in PDD 63 (or subsequently) to ensure a consistent approach to public–private cooperation. Daniel Prieto argues, "While the ISACs were established as a result of PDD 63, neither PDD 63 nor the policy changes after 9/11 clearly delineates how the ISACs should operate or how the relationships between the ISACs and the federal government should work."[73] Although it was the intent of the PCCIP that there would be a single ISAC, this soon devolved; a series of smaller sector-oriented ISACs sprouted, and, with nothing but a very general mission statement as a guide, each lead agency interpreted the structure and purpose of its individual PPP at will. "With each industry group free to set up their ISAC as they wished, the ISACs differ widely in quality, structure, and in how they are funded, managed, and operated."[74] The differences between the ISACs meant there was no shared platform to communicate and share information among the sector groups. They were silo-driven PPPs, unable to function outside a particular industry and not very useful on a national scale for comparing and assessing information across industries.[75] Jamie Gorelick contends that the ISACs have not been an effective platform for a PPP: "What you hear about the capacities of these ISACs or whatever they're called is just baloney. It's just not true. They do not have substantial capacity."[76]

While the ISACs continue to function on various levels today, they are nowhere near the public–private communication epicenters that the PCCIP and PDD 63 envisaged they would become. The ISACs are an important benchmark in disaster-oriented PPP development—in large part because of their failure. They mark the first serious attempt formally to establish an institution to facilitate PPPs for these purposes at the federal level. Because the ISACs did not provide the viable organizational framework for public–private cooperation that was hoped, they offer valuable insight about what does *not* work in disaster-oriented PPP organizational structures of this nature—loose organizational frameworks and sector-focused, silo-driven approaches to PPPs that fail to facilitate communication between industrial sectors.

As the millennium approached, fears began to circulate about the soundness of international digital infrastructures. Specifically, there was a concern that the internal "clocks" of many computing systems might not transition from 1999 to 2000, leading to a catastrophic collapse of key digital networks, potentially including those used by the Pentagon and critical aspects of national (and international) infrastructure including air traffic control, banks, and electricity providers. Initiatives to minimize the disruption caused by the Year 2000 (Y2K) were widespread and international as governments and the private sector worked together to ensure that all data networks seamlessly made the transition. Y2K further underlined the importance of public–private collaboration and cooperation to cope with national emergencies, particularly those involving US information networks.

As a result of the Y2K experience, a number of policy initiatives came into effect that were designed to encourage public–private cooperation. The Y2K preparedness initiative was primarily led by the White House and was enabled by focused and sustained support from both the president and Congress. Although Y2K discussions began in Washington as early as 1995, it was not until 1998 that preparations began in earnest with the signing of Executive Order 13073, which created the President's Council on Year 2000 Conversion. This push by the executive branch was backed and reinforced by Congress in October 1998 with the passage of the Year 2000 Information and Readiness Disclosure Act. The act was designed to ease restrictions on private-sector firms to encourage information sharing between companies to promote Y2K testing innovations.[77]

There were a number of lessons learned from Y2K that applied more broadly to disaster-oriented PPPs. First, Y2K constituted an unprecedented level of outreach between the public and private sectors to mitigate the risk that Y2K could significantly disrupt services.[78] This proved that collaboration to prevent a shared risk was not only possible but could also be extremely successful. Second, the cooperation that occurred in preparation for Y2K created an extensive network of effective, working partnerships. Third, the importance of information sharing between the sectors was a key contributing factor to the success of the Y2K initiative and was identified as "vital to coordinating efforts and ensuring an appropriate response."[79] Finally, the leadership, prioritization, and sustained focus of the federal government (backed by both congressional and executive leadership) had a significant influence on the ability of the Y2K initiative to achieve such positive results. The General Accounting Office (GAO) argued that the same leadership and focus shown during Y2K should be applied to other areas of national concern, including critical infrastructure protection.[80] The report states: "The priority both the legislative and executive branches gave to the Y2K challenge and the persistence they both demonstrated were crucial to its successful outcome. . . . Applying this leadership to other ongoing major management issues—such as computer security and critical infrastructure protection—will also be essential to adequately confronting these and other challenges.[81] Y2K, arguably the first national test of organized cross-sector collaboration since the Oklahoma City bombings, demonstrated that PPPs for these purposes could be very successful. Despite this recognition, little was done in the aftermath of the Y2K experience to meaningfully apply the lessons learned.

After 9/11, the American security environment changed drastically and with great speed. Federal prioritization and interest in PPPs lagged after PDD 63 (despite cooperation that occurred during Y2K) and did not spike again until 9/11 put them back on the national agenda. In the three years between PDD 63 and 9/11, only a few ISACs had been established, but by 2005—with a renewed sense of urgency, a new Department of Homeland Security, and no better organizational framework to support disaster-oriented PPPs—at least fifteen ISACs were in operation.[82]

Only forty-five days after the attacks of 9/11, Congress passed the controversial USA Patriot Act.[83] In a "sketch" of the USA Patriot Act written for Congress, the Congressional Research Service summarizes the act: "The Act gives federal officials greater authority to track and intercept communications, both for law enforcement and foreign intelligence gathering purposes. It vests the Secretary of the Treasury with regulatory powers to combat corruption of US financial institutions for foreign money laundering purposes. It seeks to further close our borders to foreign terrorists and to detain and remove those within our borders. It creates new crimes, new penalties, and new procedural efficiencies for use against domestic and international terrorists."[84] The Patriot Act significantly loosened the parameters under which law enforcement agencies could engage in activities such as wiretapping and e-mail hacking and resulted in a great deal of concern about a return to McCarthyism and loss of individual privacy.[85]

The Patriot Act was part of a flurry of crisis-response activity by the federal government that took place in October 2001. President George W. Bush used his executive power to set the foundations for a new governmental department for homeland security. He issued EO 13228 to establish an Office of Homeland Security in the White House and the Homeland Security Council, and he issued the first Homeland Security Presidential Directive (HSPD-1), which established the president's Homeland Security Advisory Council. In addition, on October 11, 2001, exactly one month after the attacks, a bill was proposed in the Senate to establish a National Department of Homeland Security.[86] The bill passed through both houses of Congress and the Homeland Security Act was signed into law on November 25, 2002.[87]

This crisis activity in the month following the attacks of 9/11 underscored the role of the private sector in disaster management and preparedness planning. Cooperation with the private sector was understood and assumed to be vital to the creation of a successful homeland security strategy. The establishment of DHS and repeated references to private-sector involvement represented not only the formation of a new comprehensive national plan for coping with America's changing security environment but also the establishment of an environment in which PPPs seemed to be a necessity.[88]

The creation of DHS was the largest governmental reorganization since 1947, when President Truman created the Department of Defense.[89] The founders of DHS had the monumental task of merging twenty-two separate governmental agencies, which involved integrating approximately 180,000 employees and combining an estimated two thousand congressional appropriations accounts.[90]

The bureaucratic scale of the endeavor to create DHS and the organizational challenges involved in trying to make so many disparate entities work together as a collective whole stands out as one of the most significant challenges faced by DHS in its early years.

By 2005, when Hurricane Katrina provided the first real test of the agency, a number of structural mechanisms had been put in place to enhance preparedness and response capabilities, which included PPPs. The National Strategy for Homeland Security issued by the president in July 2002 called for a single national system (the soon-to-be established DHS) to coordinate federal response to disasters.[91] The Homeland Security Act of 2002 formally established DHS, and when the agency set to work on March 1, 2003, it was tasked with developing a national incident management system (established in HSPD-3) and significantly involved the private sector.[92] In February 2003 the president issued the National Strategy for the Physical Protection of Critical Infrastructure and Key Assets, which defined the terms and established thirteen critical infrastructure sectors, and he issued the National Strategy to Secure Cyberspace, which recognized cyberspace as a critical element of overall critical infrastructure protection.[93] That same month the president issued HSPD-5, instructing the secretary of DHS to create the National Incident Management System (NIMS) and the National Response Plan (NRP).[94] NIMS and NRP were designed to work together; NRP provided the overarching structural framework for national response and the NIMS spelled out how that framework should be consistently applied by the government at the federal, state, and local levels and with the private sector and nongovernmental organizations. In December 2003 the president issued two further directives to DHS in the form of HSPD-7 and HSPD-8. HSPD-7 tasked the agency with the establishment of a national policy for critical infrastructure protection and ordered the development of a National Infrastructure Protection Plan (NIPP) by December 2004.[95] The NIPP was to outline how DHS planned to tackle critical infrastructure protection, including how they would work and share information with the private sector. HSPD-8 was intended as a "companion to HSPD-5" and called for the development of a national preparedness goal that was "all hazards" and focused on preparedness, protection, response, and recovery to ensure readiness in the event of a terrorist attack, major disaster, or other emergencies.[96]

The fundamental flaw with the work completed in these early years of DHS was the general lack of specificity about how all of the lofty policy goals, strategies, and directives were to be practically implemented. A December 2005 report by the Democratic staff of the US House Committee on Homeland Security outlines in depth many critiques of DHS.[97] One leading failure cited in the report was that the interim proposal presented in January 2005 was "not a comprehensive plan" but a mere framework that left DHS "without a clear strategy for protecting critical infrastructure in the event of an attack."[98] Stephen Flynn and Daniel Prieto argue that as late as November 2005 DHS continued to "discuss the *process* by which priorities and protective actions [would] be developed."[99] By this time, priorities should have been long decided and under way. Hurricane Katrina illustrated the gravity of this critique. *The Federal Response to Katrina* concluded: "There is no question that the Nation's current incident management plans and procedures fell short," and, the president argued, "the system, at every level of government, was not well-coordinated, and was overwhelmed in the first few days."[100]

Little specific direction was provided about how disaster-oriented PPPs should be structured. The House report argued that DHS "has not worked to effectively involve the owners of critical infrastructure in efforts to prevent terrorism . . . [and] has not clearly defined what it believes are reasonable actions for the private sector to take to reduce vulnerabilities in its critical infrastructure."[101] DHS is further criticized for failing to "address private business fears about their homeland security relevant information being disclosed to competitors."[102]

The organizational disorder within DHS itself also dampened the ability of the agency to achieve its broader objectives in the early years. Between 2003 and 2005 DHS underwent multiple internal reorganizations while turf battles raged among the twenty-two recently merged agencies. These bureaucratic obstacles made consistency in planning and action difficult at best. Brian Lopez argues, "The shifting responsibilities for various aspects of critical infrastructure protection have led to a fractured approach, often changing from year to year, based more on budget allocation than on an overall national strategy."[103] The regular internal reshuffling made the development of disaster-oriented PPPs challenging as bureaucratic disorganization often involved rapid personnel turnover. This also made cohesive private-sector outreach difficult and limited the development of trusted relationships between the public and private contacts.

Beyond the challenges faced by repeated internal reorganization, DHS found itself in direct competition for jurisdiction and authority with more established governmental institutions such as the Federal Bureau of Investigations, Department of Defense, and the Central Intelligence Agency, each of which had a large number of overlapping interests with various aspects of the newly formed DHS mission, particularly relating to counterterrorism. Prieto argues that there was further overlap with some of the sector-specific federal agencies such as the Department of Transportation and the Environmental Protection Agency. He says that DHS "unsettled the federal landscape by splitting duties for information sharing between industry sectors' traditional regulatory agencies and DHS" and argues that "the fragmentation has contributed to a lack of clarity regarding divisions of responsibility."[104]

In many ways, Hurricane Katrina was a watershed moment for DHS and the development of disaster-oriented PPPs because it provided the first test of the agency, illustrated how weak public–private linkages continued to be, and reminded the nation that the parameters of a "disaster" could encompass more than terrorism avoidance and response.[105] The hurricane demonstrated that the public and private sectors continued to lack specific directions from DHS about how to interrelate and cooperate. Charles Wise argues that the sectors "did not understand the principles and protocols in the NRP and NIMS framework that were supposed to guide their decision-making."[106]

As a result of "the Katrina experience," DHS underwent yet another series of organizational changes. FEMA's power grew to centralize the control and authority of the organization, and the NIPP (released in January 2006) outlined a specific framework for cross-sector cooperation and communication. DHS also made further organizational and operational adjustments as required by the 2007 Implementing Recommendations of the 9/11 Commission Act and also updated in the National Strategy for Homeland Security to ensure that the lessons of Katrina were included in the overall strategy for the agency.[107]

The Post-Katrina Emergency Management Reform Act focused largely on FEMA and sought to empower the agency to more effectively avoid, react, and respond to future disasters. Specifically, the act "brought new missions into FEMA and restored some that had been previously removed, and enhanced the agency's authority by directing the FEMA administrator to undertake a broad range of activities before and after disasters occur."[108] FEMA was instructed to lead "national efforts to prepare for, protect against, respond to, recover from and mitigate against" all forms of disaster, whether caused by man or nature.[109] FEMA was also specifically instructed to partner with the private sector and others to "build a system of emergency management" to effectively and efficiently respond to disaster.[110] Since Katrina, FEMA has sought to strengthen its authority to ensure it has the power to act when disaster strikes. It has also tightened its planning and preparedness (as outlined in an updated National Response Framework) and has thoroughly integrated public–private cooperation into its program in an attempt to ensure the mistakes of Katrina are not repeated.[111]

The NIPP, first issued in 2006 and updated most recently in January 2009, provides the "overarching approach for integrating the Nation's many [critical infrastructure and key resource] (CIKR) protection initiatives into a single national effort."[112] The NIPP marked significant progress in disaster-oriented PPP development because it proposed a framework to facilitate cross-sector communication, cooperation, and organization between and among the industrial sectors. First, as in earlier attempts to facilitate disaster-oriented PPPs, the plan assigns each sector to a sector-specific agency that is responsible for developing plans (called sector-specific plans) for each particular industrial sector.[113] For example, the Environmental Protection Agency is responsible for developing sector-specific plans for the water sector, and the Transportation Security Administration is similarly responsible for postal, shipping, and transportation systems.[114] To create these preparedness and response plans, the sector-specific agencies work in cooperation with the DHS to establish sector-coordinating councils (SCC) made up of private-sector executives and government-coordinating councils (GCC) made up of representatives from the sector-specific agencies. The SCC and GCC from each sector would then work together to produce a sector-specific plan. DHS is intended to serve as a coordinating force to oversee, coordinate, and integrate each sector's work to ensure that the sector-specific plans meet the requirements of a comprehensive national strategy.[115]

In creating the SCCs and GCCs, DHS sought to "create a structure through which representative groups from all levels of government and the private sector [could] collaborate or share existing approaches to CIKR protection and work together to advance capabilities."[116] The SCCs and GCCs meet regularly to discuss relevant sector-related issues.[117] While this framework bears similarities to the ISACs created in the late 1990s, the key difference is that the NIPP also establishes the cross-sector council, which is designed to "promote coordination, communication, and sharing of best practices across CIKR sectors."[118] The other key improvement in the NIPP framework over the ISAC platform is that DHS is meant to act as a coordinating force between the various sectors to ensure that there is a degree of consistency and communication between sectors.

Another key element of the Post-Katrina Emergency Reform Act that influenced PPPs was section 682, which called on DHS to create a national disaster recovery strategy within 270 days of the date that the Post-Katrina Act went into effect (October 2006).[119] In February 2010, a draft of the plan, renamed the National Disaster Recovery Framework (NDRF), was released.[120] Following two letters from senators demanding the plan from the US Senate Committee on Homeland Security and Governmental affairs in February 2010 and May 2011, and five years after it was originally requested, the NDRF was eventually issued in September 2011.[121]

Like previous plans, the NDRF recognizes the private sector as an important stakeholder in disaster recovery. The most noteworthy aspects of the NDRF in terms of public–private partnerships are that the framework focuses on the importance of PPPs at the state, local, and tribal levels, and that it adds nothing new in terms of federal-level partnerships but simply defers to the preexisting partnership structure outlined in the NIPP.[122]

In addition to the NDRF, Presidential Policy Directive 8 (PPD-8) and the National Preparedness Goal were also issued in 2011 in response to the requirements of the Post-Katrina Emergency Act.[123] PPD-8, the first disaster-oriented directive of Barack Obama's presidency, was issued on March 30, 2011, and is designed to supersede HSPD-8.[124] PPD-8 is not considered to be a repudiation of HSPD-8 but a "conceptual and strategic" evolution.[125] While PPD-8 did not constitute a substantive shift in PPP policy, the directive marks two noteworthy developments in terms of the general US approach to disaster preparedness. First, it formally recognizes and prioritizes "mitigation" as a crucial aspect of preparedness, including it as part of the preexisting quartet of "prevention, protection, response, and recovery" as a key mission area.[126] Second, the directive calls for the creation of five National Planning Frameworks to apply and administer the strategy outlined in PPD-8. This is a significant change from HSPD-8, which only called for one framework—the National Response Plan (predecessor of the National Response Framework—the NRF).[127]

The National Preparedness Goal issued in September 2011 provides an explanation of each of the five National Planning Frameworks. The frameworks, seen as "core capabilities mission areas," are the National Prevention Framework, the National Protection Framework, the National Mitigation Framework, in addition to the NRF and NDRF.[128] The new frameworks should have been presented by June 30, 2012, with the NIPP expected to provide a "baseline document" for the National Protection Framework.[129] At the time this book went to press in August 2012, none of the frameworks had yet been presented in final form to meet the June 30, 2012, deadline. However, "predecisional" working drafts of the National Prevention Framework, National Protection Framework, the National Mitigation Framework, and the National Response Framework were published (separately) on May 1, 2012.[130] How PPD-8, the National Preparedness Goal, and its corresponding five National Planning Frameworks might impact PPP policy development remains to be seen, but it appears that the SCCs and GCCs as laid out in the NIPP will continue as the primary mechanism for facilitating cross-sector cooperation, communication, and collaboration at the federal level. No other framework has yet been suggested.

The development of PPPs at DHS has been evolutionary, with the organization adjusting as dictated by organizational necessities and national priorities. As evidenced by this brief history of formal PPP development over the last fifteen years, tremendous progress has been made. Whereas involving the private sector in matters of national security and disaster response was a novelty in 1995, a comprehensive national strategy with corresponding frameworks was in place by 2011 to support and develop public–private cooperation. Hurricane Katrina and 9/11 prioritized disaster-oriented PPPs, and both events generated discussion, policy development, and focus on cross-sector cooperation. Although a number of disasters have struck the United States since 2005, none of them have had a similar (or greater) impact in terms of generating PPP-related discussion and motivating policy change. The Post-Katrina Emergency Management

Reform Act of 2006 is the most recent substantive policy development in terms of PPPs. It has driven the development of PPD-8, the establishment of the National Preparedness Goal, and the prioritization of five related "mission areas." The act drove updates to the NRF and the creation of the NDRF. US policy focused on matters of disaster preparedness has identified the private sector as an important partner and stakeholder since as early as 1998. The continued concentration and development of these policies—all of which include the private sector in one way or another—demonstrate an ongoing interest in ensuring cooperation between the sectors to prevent, protect, mitigate, respond, and recover from unexpected events.

CONCLUSION

This chapter provides specific examples of public–private cooperation that occurred as a result of 9/11 and Hurricane Katrina to illustrate why and how disaster-oriented PPPs emerged as an important issue in the United States and why cross-sector cooperation is important. The chapter also offers a summary of the organizational history of US disaster-oriented PPP policy through 2011 and lays out the existing federal framework for cooperation. The next chapter critically assesses the viability of this framework to determine whether it is sufficiently able to support disaster-oriented PPPs on a federal level.

NOTES

1. Specifically (in chronological order) these include (1) The terrorist attacks of September 11, 2001; (2) the Northeast electricity blackout of 2003; (3) Hurricane Charley in June 2004; (4) Hurricane Ivan in September 2004; (5) Hurricane Katrina in August 2005; (6) Hurricane Rita in September 2005; (7) Hurricane Wilma in October 2005; (8) the mid-Atlantic and New England floods in October 2005; (9) the mid-Atlantic flood in 2006; (10) the Washington State flood in November 2006; (11) the Midwest floods of August 2007, (12) the California fires in October 2007; (13) the Oregon and Washington floods in December 2007; (14) the Midwest floods in the spring of 2008; (15) Hurricane Ike in September 2008; (16) the California wildfires from July to October 2009; (17) the Southern floods in September 2009; (18) the southern New England floods in March 2010; (19) the oil spill in the Gulf of Mexico from April to July 2010; (20) the Tennessee floods in May 2010; and (21) the string of deadly tornados in the Midwest that included Joplin, Missouri, in May 2011.

2. Nagorski, "Editors Notebook."

3. See Flynn, *America the Vulnerable*.

4. Specifically, the bombings of the US embassies in Kenya and Tanzania in 1998 and the bombing of the USS *Cole* in the Yemeni port of Aden in 2000.

5. 9/11 Commission, *9/11 Report*, 323.

6. Ibid., 398.

7. The 2007 *National Security Strategy* states, "Disaster response has traditionally been handled by state, local and Tribal governments, with the Federal government and private and non-profit sectors playing ad hoc roles, respectively." White House, Office of Homeland Security, *National Strategy for Homeland Security*, 32.

8. BENS, "Getting Down to Business," 6.

9. US Chamber of Commerce, *From Relief to Recovery*, 23.

10. "The phone system in the WTC continued to work immediately after the planes struck both towers, perhaps with the exception of the floors that were hit and those above them. During the time between 9:03 and 9:59 a.m., however, there was abnormally high calling volumes and the networks, both landline and wireless, could not successfully respond to every request for service which affected those placing 9-1-1 calls. When the South Tower collapsed, the Verizon switching station went down, and all phone service was lost in the 16-acre WTC complex." 9/11 Commission, *Staff Statement No. 14*, 2–3.

11. While most emergency responders had access to radios, there was no consistent use of channels, and there was a general sense that these were not effective communications devices. As a result, access to mobile phone networks was critical. The 9/11 Commission discusses the challenges of radio communication during the evacuation from the towers. They say, "Three factors worked against successful communication among FDNY [Fire Department of New York] personnel. First the radios' effectiveness was drastically reduced in the high-rise environment. Second, tactical channel 1 [used by emergency personnel citywide] was simply overwhelmed by the number of units attempting to communicate on it at 10:00 a.m. Third, some firefighters were on the wrong channel or simply lacked radios altogether." 9/11 Commission, *9/11 Report*, 322.

12. Monroe, "Uncommon Valor."

13. Because of a communication breakdown, emergency dispatchers and fire fighters instructed survivors trapped in the WTC either to stay where they were or to ascend to the roof (which was locked) long after New York City and Port Authority police had given full evacuation orders to descend and escape the building. See 9/11 Commission, *9/11 Report*, 318; and Russell, "Verizon Deals with Loss."

14. Monroe, "Uncommon Valor."

15. Mike Hickey, vice president of governmental affairs and national security at Verizon, interview with the author in Washington, DC, April 9 (in person), and April 22 (by telephone), 2010.

16. Ibid.

17. Russell, "Verizon Deals with Loss."

18. Romero, "Using a Cellphone Signal."

19. CRS, *Economic Effects of 9/11*, 4.

20. Feinstein, "Managing Reliability," 173–74; and Eaton and Johnson, "After the Attacks."

21. CRS, *Economic Effects of 9/11*, 28.

22. Feinstein, "Managing Reliability," 173. For more on the opening of the NYSE, see Eaton and Johnson, "After the Attacks."

23. Norris and Fuerbringer, "A Day of Terror."

24. CRS, *Economic Effects of 9/11*, 28.

25. Robert "Rob" Bolandian, CFO of Brooklyn NY Holdings, interview with the author by e-mail from New York, July 14, 2010.

26. Ibid.

27. Eaton and Johnson, "After the Attacks."

28. Berenson, "After the Attacks."

29. Federal Reserve Board vice-chairman Roger W. Ferguson describes how the Fed stepped in to help banks in the aftermath of the attacks. He argues, "The massive damage to property and communications systems at the hub of financial activity in this country made it more difficult, and in some cases impossible, for many banks to execute payments to one another. The failure of some banks to make payments also disrupted the payments coordination by which banks use incoming payments to fund their own transfers to other banks. Once a number of banks began to be short of incoming payments, some became more reluctant to send out payments themselves. In effect, banks were collectively growing short of liquidity." Ferguson, "Remarks."

30. Ibid.

31. 9/11 Commission, *9/11 Report*, 311; and White House, *Federal Response to Hurricane Katrina*, 8.

32. CRS, *Hurricane Katrina*; Bevan, Avila, Blake, et al., "Annual Summary"; and White House, *Federal Response to Katrina*.

33. White House, *Federal Response to Katrina*, 6, 7, 34.

34. See US Chamber of Commerce, *From Relief to Recovery*. See also *The Economist*, "When Government Fails"; and Barbaro and Gillis, "Wal-Mart at Forefront."

35. Barbaro and Gillis, "Wal-Mart at Forefront."

36. For more on the failures of the US government during Hurricane Katrina, see Shughart, "Katrinanomics," 31–53; Grunwald and Glasser, "Brown's Turf Wars"; Thomas, "How Bush Blew It"; and Steinhauer and Lipton, "FEMA, Slow to the Rescue."

37. See Shughart, "Katrinanomics."

38. Susan Rosegrant's case study is my primary source about Walmart's response to Katrina. During interviews with the head of emergency management of Walmart, Bryan Koon referred to this case study numerous times as representative of Walmart's view of what occurred during Katrina. If asked any specific questions about the Katrina response, he referred me to this study. Because of Walmart's endorsement of Rosegrant's work, I relied on it as the best representation of what occurred. Rosegrant, "Wal-Mart's Response," 1.

39. Ibid., 4.

40. Bryan Koon, director of emergency management, Walmart, telephone interview with the author from Bentonville, Arkansas, April 14 and 23, 2010. (At the end of 2010 Koon was appointed as director of Florida's Division of Emergency Management.)

41. Ibid.

42. Ibid.

43. Koon, interview. See also Horwitz, "Wal-Mart Way in Disaster Preparedness/Response."

44. Rosegrant, "Wal-Mart's Response," 1.

45. Ibid., 4.

46. Ibid., 7.

47. The most common supplies taken by the looters were necessities such as clothes and diapers, although TVs and other merchandise went missing as well. Walmart employees sent to assess the damage of the Tchoupitoulas Supercenter witnessed the looting of the gun section of a store. Once the theft of the guns was reported to headquarters, the emergency operations center at Walmart told managers to pull guns out of any stores to which they could gain access. See Rosegrant, "Wal-Mart's Response," 8.

48. Walmart was highly praised after the storm for its treatment of employees. In addition to creating online message boards in the immediate aftermath of the disaster to help locate employees who were unaccounted for, the retailer guaranteed a job for every Walmart employee who was displaced as a result of the storm. Horwitz, "Wal-Mart Way," 6; Rosegrant, "Wal-Mart's Response," 14; and Barbaro and Gillis, "Wal-Mart at Forefront."

49. Horwitz, "Wal-Mart Way," 6.

50. Walmart also suffered more than $1 million in losses from fourteen stores and estimated losses between $100,000 and $1 million from another sixty-two facilities. Rosegrant, "Wal-Mart's Response," 13, 17.

51. Rosegrant, "Wal-Mart's Response," 11.

52. Ibid., 11.

53. Ibid., 14, 16.

54. Ibid., 13.

55. Ibid., 11–12.

56. Ibid., 12.

57. Ibid.

58. Ibid., 12–13.

59. Ibid., 13.

60. The cabinet group was called the Critical Infrastructure Working Group. Their final report, issued in February 1996, recommended that the president establish a full-time commission to monitor and make policy suggestions about critical infrastructure protection issues. Brown, *Critical Path*, 77–79; and White House. *Presidential Decision Directive 39*, Washington, DC, June 21, 1995.

61. *Executive Order 13010: Critical Infrastructure Protection*, July 15, 1996.

62. Critical infrastructure is defined by the PCCIP as "infrastructures that are so vital that their incapacitation or destruction would have a debilitating impact on defense or economic security." PCCIP, *Critical Foundations*, 3, appendix B-1. For discussion about physical versus cyber threats see ibid., 14–17; for discussion about challenges of private ownership of critical infrastructure protection see ibid., 19–20 and 21–24.

63. Ibid., ix.

64. Ibid., 57–58.

65. The eight CIP sectors were transportation, oil and gas production and storage, water supply, emergency services, government services, banking and finance, electrical power, and information and communications. Ibid., 3–4. For a comprehensive list of lead agency assignments, see also ibid., 55.

66. The PCCIP envisaged that the ISACs would gather "strategic information about infrastructure . . . to better understand the cyber dimension associated with infrastructures" as well as enable "more effective planning and decision-making about investments required within and outside the government." Ibid., 57.

67. White House, *Presidential Decision Directive 63*, Washington, DC, May 22, 1998.

68. Ibid.

69. Brown, *Critical Path*, 155.

70. Branscomb and Michel-Kerjan, "Public–Private Collaboration," 397–98.

71. Ibid., 398.

72. Jamie Gorelick, quoted in Brown, *Critical Path*, 155.

73. Prieto, "Information Sharing with the Private Sector," 406.

74. Ibid.

75. Darryl Williams argues, "If we're dealing with a potential bioterrorism incident at a milk production facility, we need to be able to coordinate a response beyond just the public and private experts in the food and agriculture sectors, we also need to be able to communicate and share information with the transportation industry who move the milk, and the retail industry who sell it." Darryl Williams, architect of STRATCOM Partnership to Defeat Terrorism and CEO of Partnership Solutions International, telephone interview with the author from Omaha, Nebraska, April 1, 2010.

76. Gorelick, quoted in Brown, *Critical Path*, 155.

77. Year 2000 Information and Readiness Disclosure Act, Pub. L. No. 105-271, 112 Stat. 2386 (1998).

78. One example of "unprecedented outreach" was seen in the Health Care Financing Administration, which communicated with approximately 1.2 million Medicare providers in preparation for Y2K. GAO, *Year 2000 Computing Challenge*, 16.

79. Ibid., 4.

80. The General Accounting Office (GAO) was renamed in July 2004 as the Government Accountability Office, but the organization kept the same initials.

81. GAO, *Year 2000 Computing Challenge*, 5.

82. In 2001 ISACs had been established in finance and banking and in telecommunications and information technology. By 2005 ISACs had expanded to include chemicals, food, energy, public transit, water, and real estate, among others. Prieto, "Information Sharing with the Private Sector," 406.

83. The title of the act is an acronym standing for "Uniting and Strengthening America by Providing Appropriate Tools Required to Intercept and Obstruct Terrorism." USA Patriot Act of 2001, Pub. L. No. 107-56, 115 Stat. 272 (2001).

84. CRS, *USA Patriot Act: A Sketch*, 1.

85. Tom Ridge, the first director of the Department of Homeland Security, supports the Patriot Act but acknowledges that it created a great deal of controversy. He

conceded, "The concern over the potential abuse of these new investigative powers undoubtedly echoed the anxiety felt during Joe McCarthy's time. Thoughtful people with an appreciation of history recalled the cultural, legal and political impact of those tumultuous years. Uncorroborated accusations, blacklists, formal government inquiry into the loyalty of citizens or what they were reading—all were manifestations of an abuse of legal authority." Ridge, *Test of Our Times*, 107.

86. DHS, *Brief Documentary History of DHS*, 5.

87. Homeland Security Act of 2002, Pub. L. No. 107-296, 116 Stat. 2135 (2002).

88. In July 2002 the White House released the *National Strategy for Homeland Security*, the result of eight months of work by the Office of Homeland Security. In addition to providing one of the first definitions of "homeland security" after 9/11, the document also spoke extensively about the private sector and the importance of private vigilance and cooperation with the government.

89. GAO, *Department of Homeland Security*, 7.

90. Ibid., 1, 7; and DHS, *Brief Documentary History of DHS*, 3.

91. See White House, *National Strategy for Homeland Security*, 2002.

92. HSPD-3 created the color-coded Homeland Security advisory system to identify "threat conditions" to the public. HSPD-7: Homeland Security Advisory System, March 11, 2002.

93. White House, *National Strategy for Homeland Security*, 2002; and White House, *National Strategy to Secure Cyberspace*.

94. HSPD 5: Management of Domestic Incidents, February 28, 2003, Sec. 15–16.

95. In the actual text of HSPD-7, the president does not call the plan "NIPP"; he calls it the "National Plan for Critical Infrastructure and Key Resources Protection." In the plan created by DHS in February 2005, the name changed to the Interim National Infrastructure Protection Plan. Since then two other NIPPs have been developed (2006 and 2009). Therefore, in the interests of consistency and ease of understanding, it is referred to that way here. See HSPD-7, Sec. 27(a-d); and DHS, *Interim NIPP*, 2.

96. HSPD-8: National Preparedness, December 17, 2003, Sec. 2-7.

97. House of Representatives, Democratic Staff of the US House Committee on Homeland Security, *Leaving the Nation at Risk: 33 Unfulfilled Promises from the Department of Homeland Security; Investigative Report*. Washington, DC, December 27, 2005.

98. Ibid., 4–5.

99. Flynn and Prieto, "Neglected Defense," 13.

100. White House, *Federal Response to Hurricane Katrina*, 19; and Bush, "We Will Do What It Takes."

101. House Democratic Staff, *Leaving the Nation at Risk*, 27.

102. Ibid.

103. Lopez, "Evolution of Vulnerability Assessment Methods," 65.

104. Prieto, "Information Sharing with the Private Sector," 411.

105. For more on Hurricane Katrina as the first test of DHS, see Wise, "Organizing for Homeland Security," 303–4.

106. Ibid., 303.

107. Implementing Recommendations of the 9/11 Commission Act of 2007. Pub. L. No. 110-53, 121 Stat. 266 (2007).

108. CRS, *FEMA Policy Changes after Katrina*, 1; Post-Katrina Emergency Management Reform Act of 2006, Pub. L. No. 109-295, 120 Stat. 1394 (2006) [hereafter, Post-Katrina Act of 2006].

109. Post-Katrina Act of 2006, Title V, Sec. 503 (b)(2)(A).

110. Ibid., Title V, Sec. 503 (b)(2)(B).

111. The National Response Framework replaced the earlier NRP as the strategic guide for FEMA to accomplish the objectives laid out for it in the NIPP.

112. The critical infrastructure and key resources sectors identified in the NIPP are agriculture and food; defense industrial base; energy; health care and public health; national monuments and icons; banking and finance; water; chemicals; commercial facilities; critical manufacturing; dams; emergency services; nuclear reactors, materials and waste; information technology; communications; postal and shipping; transportation systems; and government facilities. DHS, *NIPP*, preface, 15, 19.

113. Ibid., 8.

114. For a complete list of assignments see ibid., 3.

115. Ibid., 50.

116. Ibid., 4.

117. It is common for the SCCs to meet quarterly, and to have SCC and GCC joint meetings semiannually, although this varies by sector. The GCCs also meet independently at least once a quarter.

118. DHS, *NIPP*, 4.

119. Post-Katrina Act of 2006, Title V, Sec. 282.

120. DHS, *NDRF* (draft).

121. Lieberman, Collins, Landrieu, and Graham, *Letter to the Honorable Janet Napolitano in Response to the NDRF Draft*, 2; and Lieberman and Collins, *Letter to the Honorable Janet Napolitano Calling for Long Overdue Disaster Recovery Plan*.

122. DHS, *NDRF*, 19, 14.

123. Specifically, PDD-8 is designed to address the requirements of subtitle C of the Post-Katrina Reform Act of 2006. See Post-Katrina Act of 2006, Subtitle C; DHS, *NDRF*, 58; Brown, *PPD 8 and the National Preparedness System*.

124. White House, *PPD 8*, 1.

125. CRS, *PPD 8 and the National Preparedness System*, 26.

126. Ibid., 2.

127. Ibid., 10.

128. CRS, *PPD 8 and the National Preparedness System*, 2; and DHS, *National Preparedness Goal*, 2–3.

129. CRS, *PPD 8 and the National Preparedness System*, 6–7, 16.

130. Once finalized, the proposed NRF would supersede the 2008 NRF. The National Mitigation Framework remains under development. DHS, *National Protection Framework*; DHS, *National Prevention Framework*; DHS, *National Mitigation Framework*; DHS, *National Response Framework*; and DHS, *Written Testimony*.

CHAPTER TWO

Assessing Disaster-Oriented PPPs

> Private sector preparedness is not a luxury; it is the cost of doing
> business in the post-9/11 world. It is ignored at a potential cost in
> lives, money and national security.
>
> *The 9/11 Commission Report*, 398.

Although there is general agreement among industry, government, and the public in the United States that public–private cooperation is in their shared interests, significant barriers to cooperation remain. Despite the clear progression of policy designed to facilitate cooperation, there has been a significant gap between policymaking and implementation whereby "consensus around the goal of public–private partnerships has not yet translated into clarity as to how such policies should be implemented and improved over time."[1] In this chapter I highlight this gap and examine disaster-oriented public–private partnerships (PPP) more closely to identify the key economic, political, and cultural factors that impact the implementation of policy and the achievement of effective cross-sector cooperation on a national level. My ultimate aim is to determine whether the existing federal framework for disaster-oriented PPPs is—or could be—viable.

To accomplish these objectives, I explore disaster-oriented PPPs in terms of the seven critical factors identified by interviewees as either necessary conditions for the success of disaster-oriented PPPs or as challenges that must be overcome for these partnerships to function effectively. The seven factors are crisis, leadership, organizational structure, information sharing, shared benefits, trust, and adaptability or sustainability.

CRISIS AS A CATALYST FOR CHANGE

Chapter 1 establishes why disaster-oriented PPPs became important in the last decade and provides examples from the telecommunications, finance, and retail industries to illustrate how the private sector worked closely with the government during the 9/11 and Katrina crises. The magnitude of these disasters underlined a number of shortfalls in American disaster management strategies, namely that industry was not sufficiently involved. While there was a modest awareness about the importance of incorporating the private sector into critical infrastructure protection prior to 2001, the crises generated by these two incidents made both sectors prioritize disaster-oriented PPPs as never before.

The crisis created by 9/11 was a significant benchmark in the evolution of disaster-oriented PPPs. While there had been discussions about the theoretical importance of the private sector in terms of American infrastructure in the late 1990s, the attacks on the WTC transformed theoretical discussion into tangible reality. This shift is reflected in the *9/11 Commission Report*: "The private sector controls 85% of the critical infrastructure in the nation. Indeed, unless a terrorist's target is a military or other secure government facility, the "first" first responders will almost certainly be civilians. Homeland security and national preparedness therefore begins with the private sector."[2] With the attacks came the realization that both sectors had to be prepared and manage public expectations of preparedness and security. "The public's expectations . . . cannot be fully realized without government action in concert with the relevant industries. The public will demand that both public and private institutions make themselves accountable for higher levels of service and security. This demand will grow stronger as vulnerability of critical services to both natural and deliberate disasters increases."[3] The US government also began to see the private sector as more than a mere protector of real estate (critical infrastructure) after 9/11. It started to recognize that the global access and knowledge of physical and virtual networks that are embedded in the private sector could make industry an invaluable partner as the government worked to prevent future terrorist incidents. Private companies are ideally suited to notice suspicious patterns or behaviors on their networks. In addition, industry shares an important commonality with modern terrorists: they both operate and rely on interconnected international networks that interact with numerous other industries and nations in the course of doing business. In the case of 9/11, the attacks in New York constituted an attack *on* private sector networks *using* private sector networks.[4] Because industry either owns or uses these same systems, they have a much more sound understanding than government does of both the vulnerabilities within the networks and how terrorists may use them. Goods and services provided by the private sector "are normally delivered by an increasingly complex web of interdependent infrastructure services . . . with highly variable (and generally diminishing) degrees of public regulation or direction."[5]

The private sector's ownership and knowledge of global networks also makes them more able to identify suspicious activity. Steve Carmel, a senior executive at the world's largest maritime shipping company, Maersk, argues, "The biggest help [that industry] can provide to government is our ability to know and understand what 'normal' looks like within our industry and throughout the system we operate on. If we see big drops, surges or absences of certain things that we observe on a regular basis, we can identify these changes easily."[6] The attacks on 9/11 brought a renewed appreciation for the knowledge and access of industry and a hope that further cooperation could avoid future attacks.

While 9/11 illustrated the important role PPPs could play in a crisis caused by terrorism, Katrina dramatically illustrated that these same partnerships could also be of immense value during natural disasters. After 9/11 the priority on PPPs revolved almost entirely around partnering to prevent, prepare, and respond to potential terrorist attacks. The degree to which this kind of collaboration could also benefit preparedness and responsiveness to a natural disaster was not adequately considered, if at all. As one FEMA representative complained in the aftermath of Katrina, "If the billions of dollars that have been spent on chemical, nuclear and biological response ... had come over here, [FEMA] would have done better. But after 9/11, the public priority was terrorism."[7] During Katrina, first responders in both sectors quickly realized that in the event of a catastrophe, be it caused by an act of God or man, cross-sector cooperation was critical. In the chaos of the Katrina disaster, communication was panicked, haphazard, and unorganized. Without an organized framework to facilitate cooperation, information sharing between the sectors was poor, inconsistent, and confused.[8] The private sector struggled to get information from authorities on where and how it could help. The Katrina crisis demonstrated that the private sector had the capacity to react quickly and would do so independent of government, if necessary. This reflected poorly on the public sector, making it appear that the government lacked organization and leadership in the immediate aftermath of Katrina while the private sector appeared to have both.

The Katrina crisis illustrated that the scope of PPPs could extend beyond counterterrorism and the protection of critical infrastructure, and that the partnerships could be useful in a calamitous disaster by using corporate networks to transport and distribute essential goods and services faster than the government or military. What is more, Katrina highlighted shortcomings in disaster-response strategies. Four years after the nation was stunned by 9/11, Katrina showed that government preparedness continued to be inadequate, and this included PPP initiatives. The crisis that the hurricane caused reprioritized PPPs in the minds of the public, for the public sector and for industry. As a result of the crises caused by 9/11 and Hurricane Katrina, it became evident that in the event of a catastrophic disaster, be it a terrorist incident or a major natural disaster, the involvement of the private sector is not, as the 9/11 Commission put it, a "luxury" but is "the cost of doing business."[9]

PUBLIC- AND PRIVATE-SECTOR LEADERSHIP

For disaster-oriented PPPs, crisis is a powerful force that drives urgency, prioritization, and—ultimately—action. The impact when crisis abates is equally powerful, leaving in its wake a series of "action items" that no longer benefit from a crisis-driven sense of urgency or prioritization. Public- and private-sector leaders had a very strong reaction to the national crises generated as a result of 9/11 and Hurricane Katrina.

Political Leadership

In the development of disaster-oriented PPPs, political leadership has been most strong during times of national crises and stress but has abated as new emergencies arise and move disaster-oriented PPPs from the top of the list of "urgent" national priorities. This ebb and flow of interest has created a gap between lofty policy goals on the one hand and implementation of those objectives on the other. "The history of the US government's engagement with the threat of catastrophic terrorism between 1993 and 2006 illustrates both the foresight in identifying critical issues and the difficulty of sustaining focus and creating enduring programs, strategies and institutions to face those challenges."[10] Difficulties implementing policy goals may be caused by a lack of sustained leadership within the government not only by DHS as the policy-implementing agency but also by the president and Congress as the generators of that policy.

Presidential action has been an important aspect of disaster-oriented PPP initiatives in the United States. Research about critical infrastructure protection and the potential value of PPPs began in the Clinton administration with PDD 39 in 1995 and EO 13010 in 1996 in response to the first bombing of the WTC and the bombing in Oklahoma City, which led to the creation of the President's Commission on Critical Infrastructure Protection (PCCIP) in 1997.[11] The PCCIP was responsible for the establishment of the nation's first attempt at formalizing public–private cooperation through the information sharing analysis centers (ISAC). When George W. Bush began his first term in office in 2001, disaster-oriented PPPs continued to be a presidentially driven initiative. After 9/11, driven by the sense of prioritization and urgency resulting from the crisis, Bush issued a series of presidential directives of his own that pushed along the organizational development of disaster-oriented PPPs. The White House issued the *National Strategy for Homeland Security* in 2002, which repeatedly underlined the importance of forging partnerships with the private sector.[12] The 2002 National Security Strategy states, "The Administration's approach to homeland security is based on the principles of shared responsibility and partnership with the Congress, state and local governments, the private sector and the American people." It further argues, "A close partnership between the government and the private sector is essential to ensuring that existing vulnerabilities to terrorism in our critical infrastructures are identified and eliminated as quickly as possible." Once Congress passed the Homeland Security Act in 2002, which established the Department of Homeland Security as a new cabinet-level government agency, Bush quickly instituted several other presidential directives (Homeland Security Presidential Directives, or HSPD) to provide specific direction to the fledging agencies. While neither the Homeland Security Act nor the HSPDs were specifically generated to establish a disaster-oriented PPP, each made it clear that the private sector should be involved as part of the homeland security strategy and that a method to formalize cooperation should be established.[13] The specific organizational framework for the PPP, lines of command, and roles and responsibilities of each sector were left to DHS to develop.

In 2005, when Hurricane Katrina illustrated the shortfalls of DHS's progress, the urgency of the crisis again prompted immediate congressional and executive branch action. As the GAO noted in 2006, "The experience of Hurricane Katrina showed the need to improve leadership at all levels of government in order to better respond to catastrophic disaster."[14] The White House issued an extensive report on Katrina in which it identified "more robust private sector partnerships" as one of its recommendations.[15] Not long after, Congress empowered FEMA and directed it to work with the private sector as well as first responders, state and local governments, and nonprofit organizations to "build a national system of emergency management that can effectively and efficiently utilize the full measures of the Nation's resources to respond to natural disasters, acts of terrorism, and other manmade disasters, including catastrophic incidents."[16]

As with 9/11, once Congress and the executive branch established their lofty policy goals for public–private cooperation in direct response to the disaster, it was up to DHS to interpret, apply, and implement those aims. Since Katrina, DHS has continued to lead disaster-oriented PPP initiatives based on the vague instructions provided in excerpts from a variety of sources, including legislation, executive orders, and presidential directives. The National Infrastructure Protection Plan (NIPP) lays out the structural framework for federal disaster-oriented PPPs. Since Barack Obama took office in 2009, there have been no significant disasters approaching the scale of 9/11 or Katrina, and no additional policy has been made by the president or Congress that would change the organizational structure of DHS or impact the existing PPP organizational framework.

While the shortcomings of the PPP organizational structure established by DHS are clear, placing sole responsibility on DHS for the inadequacy of federal PPP initiatives is too easy a solution. The DHS is a political agency led by a presidential appointee. The agency has no real ability to generate policy but is responsible for implementing it. DHS was created during the Bush administration by an act of Congress.[17] The ability of the organization to function effectively and fulfill its remit depends upon the continued support and backing of the president and legislature. What has happened, however, is that the agency was created, given broad policy objectives, and essentially abandoned as the Bush and Obama administrations have focused their attentions on pressing international issues, such as the war in Afghanistan and the global economic crisis. Lewis Branscomb argues that the Bush administration (2001–8) focused too much on the external wars in Iraq and Afghanistan. He contends that by prioritizing military action overseas, the Bush administration sacrificed domestic security and may have sent the wrong message to the private sector, leading them to believe that "just as in the case of a 'real' war, the federal government would, in the event, assume responsibility for domestic security as well."[18] Rather than provide leadership and prioritize PPPs with the private sector to enhance critical infrastructure protection, share information that could deter terrorists, and defend internal security, PPPs have been deprioritized to such an extent that one interviewee anonymously referred to them as the "stepchild" of the DHS.[19]

Townsend attributes the deprioritization of public officials to the "tyranny of the inbox" where leaders are so overwhelmed by the number of "important" issues on their agenda (or in their e-mail inbox) that they prioritize the issues that are most pressing and simply cannot get to everything.[20] Since taking office in 2009 President Obama has concentrated on exit strategies for the wars in Iraq and Afghanistan, the passage of the health care reform, and has been occupied with a global financial crisis. None of these issues relate to disaster-oriented PPPs, and even the BP oil spill in the Gulf of Mexico in the spring and summer of 2010 was not of sufficient proportion to prompt a reprioritization of disaster-oriented PPPs on the national agenda.

While the president and Congress have focused elsewhere, DHS (and, subsequently, disaster-oriented PPPs) has been left vying for funding and authority, flailing amid other more established governmental agencies eager to maintain control. The result has been presidential and congressionally driven policy, created in the aftermath of crisis, that calls for infrastructure protection through the creation of PPPs, with no designated structure or central authority to ensure that this policy is actualized. The lack of leadership from the executive branch and Congress about what specific purpose the PPPs should serve has created confusion about the roles and responsibilities of government and between the sectors. Lopez argues, "The locus of responsibility has not only moved through government, but it has also shifted back and forth between the government and the infrastructure providers."[21] DHS has been left with the directives but has not been granted the tools, direction, or backing to adequately implement them.

The impact that partisanship can have on the behavior of political leaders can be a further impediment to disaster-oriented PPPs, as highlighted in two examples. First, administration changes every four to eight years can significantly limit the ability to build effective PPPs. Nearly every agency in Washington (including DHS, the FBI, DoD, FDA, the TSA, the Treasury, and EPA) undergoes significant personnel changes every four to eight years when a new president is elected. All of the president's cabinet, including members from the agencies just listed, are appointed by the president. Thus, when the administration changes, almost all of the leaders of the government agencies also change. These changes create a cascading effect throughout the agencies as appointees invariably select their own leadership staff. Under the existing organizational framework, each sector of private industry is meant to cooperate with its "sector-specific agency" in addition to DHS. For example, the airline industry is aligned with the Transportation Security Administration. When a new president is elected, the administration change is disruptive to PPPs because it means that private leaders must reestablish working relationships with new leaders of multiple agencies every time there is a change in administration. Gig Hender, the former chairman of the financial services sector coordinating council from 2006 to 2008, experienced this firsthand. The finance sector coordinating council worked closely with both the Federal Reserve and the Department of the Treasury. According to Hender, one of the great benefits of working with the Fed, as opposed to the Treasury, was that the Fed's quasi-public nature prevented it from being upturned every four years, and that it was relatively immune to the impact of administration changes. The Treasury, in contrast, was completely upturned with every new administration, forcing private partners to "rebuild a new working relationship with their replacements and rebuild that trust."[22] To be sustainable, practitioners in both sectors argue that PPPs must be depoliticized to make them able to withstand political whims and personnel changes in Congress and the executive branch.[23]

Second, individual political agendas of members of Congress and the administration can also interfere with the policy aims of disaster-oriented PPPs. Union Pacific Railroad (UP) experienced this first hand. UP worked closely with the federal government in the aftermath of 9/11 to change the routes of hazardous materials (hazmats), such as chlorine, in an attempt to avoid locations where an attack on cars carrying these substances could have catastrophic consequences.[24] While UP cooperated willingly with the public sector to develop more secure routes for hazmats at first, CEO Jim Young argues that partisan self-interest quickly emerged. "The government has helped us route hazardous materials in the past, but the issue quickly became political. Politicians began getting involved in trying to route things out of or around their constituents' cities for reasons that had nothing to do with security. This would cause UP to use rails that may not be as good, routes that were not as fast, and ultimately cost us time and money. These requests were made of us for political, not security reasons."[25] Once the spirit of cooperation was used for political rather than security objectives, UP became a much less trusting and willing partner.

Lynne Kidder, former senior executive vice-president of public–private partnerships for the nonprofit organization Business Executives for National Security (BENS), argues that keeping politics out of PPPs is a prerequisite to maintain a "strong sense of private involvement and ownership" in the long term.[26] Several industry owners and operators confessed a preference for partnering with the military because of their seemingly task-driven versus politically driven agendas.[27]

Private-Sector Leadership

Private-sector leaders, like their government counterparts, were prompted into action on disaster-oriented PPP initiatives primarily as a result of the 9/11 and Katrina crises. Where traditional, public-sector mechanisms of disaster response fell short during these events, a variety of industrial sectors stepped in to provide support.[28]

The actions of FedEx after both 9/11 and Katrina provide one example. After the attacks of 9/11, fearing that the FedEx network could be used to assist terrorists in preparing for or carrying out an attack, FedEx developed a computer link that allowed employees to immediately alert DHS of suspicious activity. FedEx also used its right to inspect packages, a waiver signed by all customers, to open dubious packages with federal agents on hand. It has "radiation detectors at overseas facilities to detect dirty bombs" and even shared "portions of its databases, including credit card details" with the government. While some privacy advocates argue that this kind of information sharing violates customer privacy, FedEx CEO Fred Smith contends that information sharing is good business practice because the discovery that terrorists use corporate networks could cause disruptions or bad publicity. He argues, "All we are trying to do is to protect our assets and not have our assets be used for bad purposes." Walmart, America Online (AOL), and Western Union engaged in similar cooperative efforts with the US government after 9/11.[29]

After Katrina, FedEx again assisted with disaster recovery by developing a way to get communication capabilities to first responders in New Orleans. Using a FedEx communication tower and replacement parts from elsewhere in the country, and contacting FEMA (who in turn contacted the military), a FedEx technician was flown by army helicopter to the roof of a building where a key communication tower was located. The engineer fixed the tower, provided reliable radio communications, and distributed walkie-talkies to first responders.[30]

Like Walmart, FedEx was prepared for Katrina. The corporation, accustomed to working in and around disasters, regularly cooperates with the Red Cross to transport provisions and ensure supplies are in the right place before a disaster strikes. "Before Katrina, FedEx staged 60 tons of Red Cross provisions (it has since delivered another 440 tons of relief supplies, mostly at no charge)."[31] The corporation also had thirty thousand bags of ice, thirty thousand gallons of water, and eighty-five home generators positioned outside Baton Rouge and Tallahassee for employees to use after the storm.[32] "At any given moment, somewhere in the world, there is a social upheaval, a dangerous storm, a wildcat strike. FedEx, which earns its money by being dependable, can't afford a wait-and-see attitude; it moves in advance."[33]

FedEx and Walmart are only two examples of corporations that responded rapidly and proactively with aid in the aftermath of Katrina. International mining giant Freeport-McMoRan Copper and Gold lent their corporate aircraft hangar in New Orleans to the US Army, which used it as its base of operations.[34] The Ford Motor Company donated 275 vehicles to law enforcement in the impact zone.[35] Maersk shipping company immediately sent tankers of ice and wood to New Orleans.[36] Anheuser-Busch donated 9.4 million cans of drinking water.[37] UP used its network to position goods and equipment near the disaster area so it could access the affected areas more quickly, and it worked with Amtrak to run special passenger trains to evacuate people from the area.[38] The US Chamber of Commerce estimates that American corporations donated $1.2 billion to hurricane recovery in 2005, with 254 corporations donating $1 million or more.[39]

While each of these examples highlights independent private-sector leadership in the aftermath of significant crises, industry also works proactively to avoid potential attacks or disasters by safeguarding their networks. Oil corporation ConocoPhillips, for example, owns and operates thousands of miles of oil pipelines internationally.[40] Oil is not only valuable, it is also highly flammable; attacks or disasters affecting any aspect of the oil pipeline could have devastating repercussions. In an attempt to mitigate an incident, the oil giant has crisis centers in place globally that monitor all of the control valves. Any time there is a leak, break, or other incident on the pipeline, the line is instantaneously cut off, thereby stopping the pressure in the line, which in turn slows or stops the flow of oil through the pipeline. This minimizes any loss of oil and ensures that, in the event of a fire of some sort, oil does not continue to fuel the flames.[41] While ConocoPhillips's network is particularly sensitive, most large corporations have similar "crisis centers" or "emergency operations centers" that monitor corporate networks to ensure the normal flow of business operations. Corporations such as Walmart, FedEx, and UP, for example, monitor weather patterns twenty-four hours a day, seven days a week, to ensure that, regardless of the weather or other unforeseen cause for delay, their global transportation networks suffer minimal disruption.[42]

In each instance of cooperation outlined thus far, corporate and national interests aligned to make cooperation worthwhile for both sectors. American executives are motivated to engage in disaster avoidance and resilience efforts largely because of their corporate interests. This is not to say that altruism and patriotism do not play a role in industry's willingness to engage, but in the event of a significant national disaster, the sectors share the aim of restoring normalcy, even if their motivations may differ. It is in the best interests of all parties to do everything possible to minimize losses and return to business as usual. The benefits and risks faced by industry while engaging in PPPs—including the clash between corporate self-interest, patriotism, and altruism—are discussed later in this chapter but are worth noting here. Private-sector leadership during the disasters of the last decade has been proactive, strong, and, in many cases, life saving; but it has also been driven by corporate self-interest.

In summary, public- and private-sector leadership was strong in the emergency environment immediately following the 9/11 and Katrina crises. In the public sector, leadership surged immediately after each crisis, resulting in the formulation of PPP-related policy. As the sense of urgency waned, however, so did public-sector leadership, prioritization, and support, making the implementation of those policies difficult at best. This lack of sustained, focused public-sector leadership created a significant gap between idealized policymaking, on the one hand, and the realities of implementation by DHS, on the other. Policy implementation was further limited by partisan politics. In the private sector, leadership was also apparent after each disaster as industry executives used their firm's resources to boost national response and recovery capabilities. While this leadership by industry is based on corporate interest just as much as if not more than altruism, industry nonetheless served an important role in the response and recovery to these crises.

THE VIABILITY OF THE ORGANIZATIONAL FRAMEWORK

The struggle by DHS to develop and support an organizational framework for disaster-oriented PPPs is the result of a lack of sustained political focus or leadership on PPP initiatives. While DHS intended to create overarching national guidelines to facilitate cross-sector cooperation with the NIPP, there is currently no single organization that coordinates PPPs for disaster mitigation, preparedness, response, and resilience in the United States. Rather, there are a series of PPPs that reside at the federal, state, and local levels and a further selection of PPPs that have been established by the private sector and by nonprofit organizations. All of these were created because of the awareness and sense of urgency that emerged through the crises of the last decade. Although each PPP initiative was established with the noblest of intentions, the end result was a quagmire of competing PPP organizations established at various levels within government, the private sector, and the nonprofit sector. While some of these PPPs are stronger than others, the result of having no single comprehensive federal framework is a series of fragmented PPPs with no consistent means of cross-sector communication and cooperation, unclear lines of authority, and overlapping jurisdictions.

Perspectives from the Public Sector

The public sector and DHS in particular are keenly aware that the existing framework for disaster-oriented PPPs is imperfect as it stands today.[43] The agency has been left without significant presidential or congressional support and has been riddled with frequent organizational changes as it has attempted to interpret and actualize all that it has been tasked to accomplish. According to a 2009 report by the GAO examining national preparedness, "organizational changes [in DHS] have resulted in turnover of staff and loss of institutional knowledge of previous efforts."[44] DHS leaders are quick to point out that the creation of the agency, with its massive merger of twenty-two organizations into one, occurred only in 2003, and they argue that it simply takes time to work out the kinks with an undertaking of such a large scale.[45] The DHS organizational chart frequently emerges to further underscore the problems of trying to create a coherent PPP framework within the complicated DHS organizational structure. "The size and complexity of the nation's preparedness activities and the number of organizations involved make developing a national preparedness system a difficult task. To lead national preparedness efforts effectively, FEMA is to coordinate with a wide range of federal departments and agencies, such as the Departments of Defense, Health and Human Services, and Justice; 50 states, the District of Columbia, and five territories; city and county governments; a wide range of non-profit organizations; and private entities."[46]

Despite the fact that DHS has faced significant organizational challenges—both generally and regarding PPPs specifically—public-sector leaders are eager to demonstrate that accomplishments have been made and argue that further improvements will occur in time as DHS continues to develop into a more delineated, established agency.[47] Examples of accomplishments include instances of improved levels of participation in a certain sector-coordinating council (SCC), better response and cooperation during a recent flood, and enhancements to PPP organizational frameworks.[48] Public leaders are frustrated that the outside world does not seem to recognize the difficulty of accomplishing the tasks that have been assigned to DHS and the complexity of functioning within the DHS organizational structure, and does not acknowledge when progress has been made despite these impediments.

While the policy objectives of DHS are relatively clear, the implementation of those objectives has been difficult. Bob Liscouski, the DHS assistant secretary for the Office of Critical Infrastructure Protection from 2003 to 2005, contends that while PPPs are very important to the achievement of US national security objectives, challenges in public–private cooperation, congressional intervention, and the general growing pains DHS faced in the early years of the organization have hindered its ability to actualize PPP policy objectives.[49] Fundamental issues surrounding the bureaucratic organization of DHS continue to challenge the agency (in general and with regard to PPPs in particular). DHS leaders remain optimistic, however, and argue that the organization is steadily becoming more effective, it has only been functioning for seven years, and it takes time for a new agency of this scale to find its footing.[50]

While DHS (and FEMA in particular) is keen to demonstrate that it has improved since Hurricane Katrina hit the Gulf Coast, this is no easy task. In order to effectively test the success of PPP efforts to prepare for, respond to, and recover from a disaster, however, there must *be* another catastrophic disaster. While the lack of a crisis or disaster in recent years of comparable scale to Katrina is a good thing, it also means that there is no real way to assess the agency or chart its progress. Despite this, FEMA, in particular, argues strenuously that it is not the same agency today that it was during Katrina. It has formalized many of its private-sector outreach efforts, it has been strengthened institutionally through the NIPP and NRF, and it has worked more closely with states to identify potential disaster-response shortfalls prior to any incidents.

Those who work closely within the GCC/SCC framework for cross-sector cooperation share FEMA's sentiments that the improvement of DHS is steady and significant. For example, Nitin Natarajan, the GCC chair for the health care and public health sector, and his private SCC counterpart, Erin Mullen, argue that their sector has made marked improvement in strengthening cross-sector ties using the existing DHS PPP framework. They point out that the health care and public health sector has dramatically increased use of the Homeland Security Information Network (HSIN), a web-based information-sharing portal. Both Mullen and Natarajan point out that there were twenty people involved in 2008, but by 2010 more than 1,500 used the portal. While Natarajan acknowledges that 1,500 participants is still far short of the kind of participation levels necessary to consider the framework a success, he argues that the dramatic increase in participation and use of HSIN indicates that the existing framework is strengthening.[51]

While floods, hurricanes, and wildfires since 2005 have provided small-scale tests of DHS (and FEMA in particular), there have been no crises on the scale of 9/11 or Katrina to really test the agency. Having undergone substantial and frequent changes, DHS officials have become wary of instituting even more changes to the existing PPP framework until the current strategy has been tested, arguing that further changes will only create more confusion. As Natarajan explains, "Resilience, while defined in the National Security Strategy, is often used as a 'buzz word' to mean a variety of different things. DHS may not have the best framework, but it is a framework. It is not good to create parallel, redundant systems."[52]

Perspectives from the Private Sector

If there is one point that the private sector and the government agree upon, it is this: the existing organizational frameworks for disaster-oriented PPPs are not yet good enough. There is a strong sense among industry leaders that while DHS may have made some progress, PPP efforts continue to be largely uncoordinated, decentralized, and inefficient.

The most common complaint from private-sector executives about the PPP organizational framework is that there is no single governmental point of contact to coordinate federal communication and cooperation with industry.[53] Large corporations that are significant stakeholders in critical infrastructure protection because of their national and international reach as well as their ownership of key physical and virtual networks (e.g. UP, Verizon, Walmart, and ConocoPhillips) have regular contact with numerous government agencies. For example, the director of emergency management at Walmart communicates regularly with FEMA, the Office of Critical Infrastructure Protection, DoD, and the Office of Science and Technology.[54] Clay Detlefsen, the SCC chairman for food and agriculture, speaks to his own industry-specific agencies, which include the FDA, the USDA, the EPA, and various offices within DHS and the FBI.[55] There are approximately fifty programs within DHS alone that involve some kind of private-sector contact, and no single office is responsible for coordinating communication among government offices before they contact the private sector. It is not uncommon for corporations who participate in critical infrastructure protection to speak to four or five different federal offices in addition to contacts in each state.[56] While several of the contacts are often within a single agency (DHS), contact points span the US government at large. This generates confusion about who industry should call in government, and the lack of intragovernmental coordination leads to overlapping efforts. As one executive explains, while "the US government can easily segment the private sector into industries, the private sector has a very difficult time finding the right button to push to get information to the right people."[57] This lack of centralization can create redundancies in both sectors as executives receive several requests for the same information from multiple government contacts. This is not only an irritant to industry but it costs both sectors time and money as they make and respond to numerous requests for the same information.

Fran Fragos Townsend, the assistant to the president for homeland security and counterterrorism from 2004 to 2008 under George W. Bush, recalls seeing this occur on multiple occasions while serving in the White House. She recalls one particular instance:

> The CIA needed information from a corporation. They first sent a subpoena to legally compel the company to provide the information. At the same time, the director of the CIA called the CEO directly and asked for his help in providing the information. The same company was asked for the same information twice from a single agency. The CEO immediately complied, but because the subpoena had already been issued, the corporation was compelled to have its legal team formally respond, thereby unnecessarily costing the company time and money. This example does not even take into account instances where you get overlapping requests from multiple agencies. This is a significant disincentive for the private sector to participate.[58]

Townsend argues that the first step of a PPP framework should be to provide a "deconfliction capability" so that if multiple agencies need something from a corporation, there is a central clearinghouse of some sort to coordinate efforts, maximize the efficiency of private-sector outreach, and avoid overlap.[59] This problem of overlapping requests from government to the private sector extends throughout the agencies and hinders effective cross-sector cooperation, making private leaders such as Jim Young, the CEO of UP, hope for a more centralized approach to cooperation and coordination. "In an ideal world, there would be one contact who is an advocate that helps ensure there is two-way communication between industry and the government."[60]

The confusion and challenges caused by governmental overlap in the broad field of national security are not confined to disaster-oriented PPPs. An investigative piece by the *Washington Post* succinctly explained the bureaucratic complexities that have developed in Washington between 2001 and 2010. "The top-secret world the government created in response to the terrorist attacks of Sept. 11, 2001, has become so large, so unwieldy and so secretive that no one knows how much money it costs, how many people it employs, how many programs exist within it or exactly how many agencies do the same work.... For example, 51 federal organizations and military commands, operating in 15 cities track the flow of money to and from terrorist networks."[61] Beyond the fact that government bureaucracy is overwhelmed as a result of the changes that have taken place since 9/11, some business executives argue that interagency and interoffice turf wars are further inhibitors of a coordinated approach to private outreach.[62] Archie Dunham, president and CEO of Conoco Inc. from 1996 to 2002 and chairman from 1999 to 2004, argues, "DHS lacks good leadership [and] has no coordination or leadership among its departments.... DHS is a series of fiefdoms fighting for jobs and power."[63] Interagency battles for power and authority keep the agencies from communicating with one another. Washington agencies such as DoD, FBI, and CIA want to guard their relationships with the private sector as a means of maintaining their own direct links with the private sector as well as their agency's power and authority.[64]

These internal power struggles prevent the agencies from communicating with each other and mean that they often operate in silos where they are unaware of the partnerships and initiatives that occur in other agencies.[65] The impediments posed by interagency power struggles are further compounded by the sheer number of offices involved in PPP efforts; as mentioned earlier, there are approximately fifty offices involved in private-sector outreach within the DHS alone.[66]

Private leaders argue that they are seen not as part of the preparedness/organizational process but as insular elements to be included after decisions have been made. Gen. Charles Krulak, the 31st Commandant of the US Marine Corps who went on to become the CEO of MBNA Europe and serve on the board of directors of a number of Fortune 500 corporations, argues that a major failure of PPP efforts thus far is that the government is "unwilling to engage [with the private sector] *before* an incident" [italics added]. He argues, "The existing frameworks and structures are ad hoc and need to be formalized to take into account all the elements of national power."[67] Because the government's disaster response and preparedness strategies revolve around the central concept of organizing within the government before reaching out to the private sector, industry has no real input on strategy until after the key decisions have been made. As a result, federal disaster preparedness and response strategies frequently fail to adequately incorporate the potential capabilities of the private sector.[68] This reasoning explains why PPPs were not in order by 2005 and why FEMA's response to Katrina was not better coordinated: one side of the "partnership" is effectively excluded from having any real input on the frameworks and processes that govern the relationship before they are in place.[69]

There is a very real schism in thinking about whether PPPs should be organized and operated at the state and local grassroots level or at the federal level. Advocates of the grassroots approach argue that PPPs will be most effective if organized by and among first responders.[70] State and local governments have taken significant steps to improve their relationships with the private sector and have developed their own mechanisms to facilitate cooperation and coordination independent of DHS in the event of a significant disaster. A BENS report about building PPPs notes, "The initial impact of any disaster is local....

Communities across the nation recognize the inter-dependencies that exist between public and private sectors, among multiple public agencies, non-governmental organization service providers, multiple industry sectors and critical infrastructure.... The nation's preparedness and response policies must be informed by the realities of life in local communities as well as by the federal perspective."[71] Beyond 9/11 and Katrina, the many floods, fires, and hurricanes that devastated parts of the Gulf Coast and Midwest states between 2005 and 2010 demonstrated the legitimate tactical need for state and local governments to have channels through which they can directly coordinate and communicate with the private sector in the event of a local or regional crisis.[72] As first responders who will be working together in the event of a disaster, they must also have ways to ensure effective cross-sector cooperation.

While it is important that preparedness occurs at all levels of government—local, regional, and national—regional PPP initiatives should not supplant the continued development of a national PPP framework. In the event of a catastrophic incident, disaster planning at the state and local levels is inadequate, and interstate capabilities are crucial for two reasons. First, only a national framework can ensure adequate response capabilities in the event of a dual-pronged terror attack on opposite coasts, a large biological or chemical attack, or a pandemic or a catastrophic natural disaster that crosses city, county, or state borders.[73] During Katrina, cross-jurisdictional coordination proved difficult as localities and states struggled to coordinate with one another and with FEMA. As a result, in the official government inquiry published by the White House, *The Federal Response to Katrina*, the committee advocates for a federal framework for disaster response to ensure that in the event of a significant disaster "jurisdiction may rapidly expand into multi-discipline, multi-jurisdictional incidents requiring significant additional resources and operational support."[74]

A second reason for the importance of a federal framework to facilitate disaster-oriented PPPs is because state and local governments do not have the funding in place to adequately support the response to a significant catastrophe. "Only one quarter of state emergency operations plans and 10 percent of municipal plans are sufficient to cope with a natural disaster or terrorist attack."[75] State and local governments, particularly in the current economic climate, rely on federal emergency funding in the event of a significant disaster.[76]

What little funding state and local governments do manage to set aside for preparedness, they allocate to natural disaster preparedness rather than to terrorist threats. While this approach is understandable because it is more likely that local communities will be impacted by natural disasters than any other threat, it also means that if and when a significant nonnatural disaster—such as a pandemic or a biological, chemical, radiological, or other terrorist attack—occurs, local and state responders will be largely unprepared. This becomes more true as time elapses since 9/11, and it becomes "difficult for elected public officials to justify local and state spending on homeland security. . . . The public expects the federal government to cover all defense and homeland security expense."[77] A nationally coordinated cross-sector disaster mitigation management program is what the public expects, and it also appears to be a logistical and economic necessity if the United States faces another catastrophic disaster.

There are widely different perspectives as to whether disaster-oriented PPPs should be organized at the federal level or at the state and local level. Kidder of BENS and Bryan Koon of Walmart favor an approach incorporating both local and national PPP frameworks where local PPPs do not replace federal efforts but support them.[78] In contrast, Krulak and Dunham advocate a more federally oriented approach.[79] While views of the public and private leaders vary, none advocated that disaster-oriented PPPs should reside only at the local or regional level, and all envisaged some degree of federal coordination and communication.

In summary, the public and private perceptions of the organizational framework for disaster-oriented PPPs have evolved over the last decade. Federal efforts to coordinate with the private sector gradually improved. In addition, Katrina underscored the importance of coordination at the state and local levels to ensure that the private sector is more fully utilized in the event of a disaster. While this has constituted very real progress, many business executives maintain that federal PPP initiatives have significant room for improvement.

While the public sector largely advocates "staying the course" to allow the existing framework time to develop and function effectively, the private sector is evidently frustrated with the current structure and perceives the need to change. Despite progress since 2005, the framework is seen to be flawed largely because of governmental shortcomings, including internal disorganization, interagency turf wars, and overlapping PPP efforts.

INFORMATION SHARING

> If I am standing at the back of an elephant, all I see is a big [rear end]. If I am able to talk to someone who is standing in front of the elephant, and someone else who is standing beside it, then an entirely different picture emerges.
>
> George McCarthy, interview

Of the seven critical factors explored in this chapter, information sharing is arguably the most important. For PPPs to work, the public and private sectors must communicate effectively. With a disaster-oriented PPP, this communication becomes complicated as both the government and the private sector have legitimate and significant barriers that limit their ability—and willingness—to share information with each other. There are three distinct layers of information sharing between the public and private sectors that facilitate the effectiveness of disaster-oriented PPPs, each with its own unique challenges. These layers include information sharing that occurs within the public sector itself, between the public and the private sectors, and between private-sector participants. Since the challenges of intragovernmental information sharing have been dealt with in earlier discussions about organizational structure and political leadership, this section concentrates on information-sharing barriers between the public and private sectors and among private participants.

Government Classification Standards

The US government uses a classification system to ensure that information deemed sensitive to national security is seen and shared only among individuals who have been "cleared" by the US government. Classification standards have become a significant barrier to cross-sector cooperation and can prevent public-sector partners from sharing relevant information with the private sector. For example, in the spring of 2010, the Maersk shipping corporation prepared to conduct security drills off the coast of Virginia. The company regularly conducts drills to prepare and practice for unexpected events that could impact the fleet, including storms, potential terrorist attacks, or hijackings by pirates (such as those operating out of Somalia). In preparation for one such drill, Maersk executives asked the coast guard to participate; a significant incident at sea near the US coast would likely involve them, and a joint exercise would help strengthen their working relationship and allow both sectors to be better prepared. The coast guard responded that they would not participate because they had run a similar drill a couple of weeks earlier. Maersk had not been asked to participate. Maersk then asked the coast guard to share any valuable lessons, insights, or tips they had learned as a result of their exercise that could be used to strengthen their own drill. The coast guard responded with an emphatic "no" because, they explained, "that information is classified."[80]

This example is indicative of two common impediments to cross-sector information sharing. First, classification standards limit both sectors by restricting what public participants in PPPs are allowed to share with their private counterparts. The second impediment that the Maersk scenario highlights is a standard private-sector complaint that "information sharing" in disaster-oriented PPPs largely involves a one-way flow of information. Information travels from the private sector to the government, but not vice versa.

As disaster-oriented PPPs became a priority, it became important to share information that had historically resided entirely in the public domain. Problems quickly emerged as the public sector realized that governmental classification standards could restrict information sharing with industry. At the same time, it is also possible for public-sector officials who see disaster-oriented PPPs as a waste of time to use classification standards as a means to avoid sharing information with industry.[81]

The issues of classification pose a significant barrier because in order for the private sector to be a valuable and active partner, they must have access to information that will allow them to defend against and avoid potential threats. At the same time, information sharing on this level is a risk to government. If the public sector shares classified material with private-sector civilians who do not have security clearances, there is the potential for a PPP to leak national intelligence. Prieto argues that information sharing between the sectors is further complicated by "the problem of getting large numbers of security clearances for private sector personnel, by fear of improper disclosure of classified information, and by the fact that federal authorities may not possess actionable or specific intelligence."[82] The Reducing Over-Classification Act in 2010 sought to overcome some of the challenges posed by classification standards. The act seeks to facilitate information sharing by creating both classified and unclassified reports that can be more easily disseminated to partners.[83]

Senior public-sector interviewees argued that the private sector is operating under a false assumption that they would be able to access actionable intelligence relevant to their business if they had security clearance.[84] Townsend claims, "Access to classified documents is not very revealing. There is no 'golden nugget' of information that the private sector is missing. The private sector overestimates the quality of the intelligence they would receive from access to classified materials."[85]

A July 2010 special report in the *Washington Post* suggests that challenges of information sharing are problematic throughout the US government. With at least 263 organizations established or reorganized as a result of 9/11, there are now so many US government agencies siphoning such a large quantity of information that public intelligence gathering has become a complicated quagmire in which locating useful pieces of actionable intelligence is difficult at best. The inability of the US government to keep up with the informational deluge is illustrated by the case of the "underwear bomber," a Nigerian national radicalized in Yemen who attempted to ignite a bomb in his underwear on a Christmas Day flight en route from Amsterdam to Detroit in 2009. The US government received information about the bomber from sources in both Yemen and Nigeria (including from the bomber's father), but the information was buried somewhere within the National Counterterrorism Center—an overwhelmed intelligence sorting unit that receives an estimated five thousand pieces of terrorism-related information each day.[86]

Considering the number of agencies involved in the collection and sifting of information, the sheer volume of reports, and the fact that the system has already failed, it is likely that Townsend is correct. Even if the private sector could see everything, there is a strong chance that the information would be either useless or overwhelming and, as a result, unactionable. As one senior army official argued, "I'm not aware of any agency with the authority, responsibility or a process in place to coordinate all these interagency and commercial activities. . . . The complexity of this system defies description."[87]

Nonetheless, it is possible to share useful information between the sectors so long as industry is specific about what information it wants. While working as the assistant undersecretary for infrastructure protection, Liscouski was responsible for coordinating many of the early PPP efforts in DHS. He contends that one of the hidden challenges of information sharing is that the private sector says it wants information, in theory, but in practice has a difficult time articulating its needs to the government. Liscouski holds that he tried to respond to the frequent private-sector complaints that his office was not providing useful information and asked executives of the ISACs to provide him a "wish list" of what they hoped to see from the government. "Even with classification standards, I knew I could give them at least 80 percent of what they asked for without any trouble, and of the 20 percent that was left, I knew that with a little working, I could get them most of the information. . . . All I needed to know was what exactly they wanted."[88] Liscouski never received a list from a single ISAC executive, which led him to believe at the time that the private sector did not really know what information it wanted to receive from the government and, as some private sector executives expressed to him privately, "if they had the information, they would be duty bound to act on it."[89]

Natarajan holds a similar view that there has not been enough communication about what information the private sector would like to receive from the government. When he became a director in the Office of Preparedness and Emergency Management in April 2009 and head of the health care and public health sector GCC, he identified two flaws in information sharing. "First, the government was providing too much irrelevant information to private partners, and, second, the private sector was not being specific about what it needed . . . or no one was taking the time to find out what it was that they really needed."[90]

For the private sector, classification standards have been a frustrating impediment to cross-sector cooperation. To overcome classification barriers, key executives from various industrial sectors have obtained security clearances in recent years to allow them to engage more productively in PPPs. The executives quickly discovered that even with clearances, challenges remain. Hender recalls that after clearances were secured for top sector leaders, complaints began to surface that no information was coming through.[91] In addition, executives found that after they obtained their security clearances, their hands were tied because they could not share any relevant classified information with their corporations. "If there is only one person in a corporation with top secret security clearance, there is no one else in the company that person can tell because no one else has the clearance to hear it. The government . . . is so security conscious that their hands are tied behind their backs and they cannot tell the private sector the information they really need."[92]

In addition, there have been cases where private-sector executives working in cooperation with the US government have faced a real conflict of interest as a result of having security clearances. Townsend provides an example:

> During the Bush administration surveillance programs, leading telecommunications companies were given the green light to provide information to the government. They were also told they could not share with anyone the fact that the program was happening. This became problematic when the telecom companies got sued and the board of directors began asking the executives questions and wanting to know why they had not been informed. The executives were in a difficult position and the only explanation they could legally give their boards was to say that they were bound by classification standards not to reveal anything.[93]

To overcome the information deluge within government and to give the private sector the information it needs, some government leaders have actively sought to bridge the gap. After hearing complaints from private leaders with security clearances who still failed to receive information from the government, Hender took a more proactive approach. "We set up quarterly meetings where key sector leaders were briefed about key issues by the heads of all the intelligence agencies. The majority thought these meetings were worthwhile."[94]

Natarajan, as head of the GCC for the health care and public health sector, established a similar approach.[95] To improve the quality of information rather than the quantity, Natarajan avoided giving private partners "fifty pages of irrelevant information to wade through" but instead gave them summaries with the information most relevant to them.[96] According to Natarajan, "We distill and categorize the information we receive so that it is most relevant to various aspects of our sector."[97] Sector-relevant, nonclassified policy reports that are not readily available to the public (such as reports by the Congressional Research Service) are also provided to ensure that private-sector partners are aware of what is taking place in Washington. Natarajan argues that information sharing has significantly improved because "once we started sharing useful information with the private sector, they became more willing to share information with us."[98] Natarajan's work to improve information sharing is noteworthy and represents one of the few pockets where information-sharing challenges are being successfully overcome through the actions of proactive leaders, but this is not a consistent theme across all sectors.

One-Way Flow of Information and Information Inundation

Inequity in information sharing is a further impediment to disaster-oriented PPPs.[99] Flynn and Prieto found that information sharing is "too often a one-way street [where] companies provide specific information when appropriate but receive little information of value in return from the government."[100] McCarthy has seen this inequity in the shipping industry, noting that the government wants regular information on ships but often fails to reciprocate.[101] When a Danish cartoon depicting the Prophet Mohammed went to press, the Maersk shipping corporation experienced this firsthand. The US government received intelligence that threats had been made against the Maersk fleet because it is a Danish corporation. Rather than contact the shipper directly to warn them of the risk, the government issued a statement to the press. Maersk had no prior knowledge of this threat, and the announcement by the government took the company by surprise and created unwanted alarm in the corporation's customer base.[102] The problem is not confined to the shipping industry. In 2009, as fears of the H1N1 pandemic spread across the United States, the FDA learned that there was a shortage of pediatric Tamiflu, the drug used to counter the virus. The FDA published the drug shortage on their website one month after the manufacturer notified distributors. By the time the medical profession learned that there was a shortage, it was too late for hospitals, medical practices, or pharmacies to monitor their own distribution of the drug or to prepare for the shortage.[103]

One commonality between the sectors is that they both feel that the other is not specific enough in its requests for information. Just as Liscouski argued that industry would not tell him what specific information they wanted from the government, many private-sector leaders argued that the government frequently makes requests for huge swaths of information that are difficult to gather and even more difficult for government analysts to assess or use to obtain accurate information.[104] "The government does not give the private sector specific requirements, they simply say 'we want it all.' . . . If the government would tell the private sector what they are going to use the information for, industry could target what government is searching for and give them exactly what they need."[105] These broad requests frustrate industry leaders, who argue that if they received more specific insight about what the government was looking for, industry could provide much more accurate, useful information, saving all parties time and money.[106] McCarthy argues that if more information were provided to the private sector, they could "focus their time, energy, and effort and not inundate the government with unnecessary information, while the government would get information that is actually relevant and not have to sift through a bunch of stuff they don't understand or know what to do with."[107]

Verizon has experienced a similar problem while cooperating with federal regulators who require moment-in-time reporting on service outages. The information the regulators want from Verizon does not reflect the way the corporation monitors its systems or conducts reporting. As a result, the corporation is forced to generate entirely new reports specifically to meet the government's requirements. Because of the dynamic nature of the Verizon communication network, outages are occurring and being rectified constantly. Therefore, a moment-in-time report will never accurately demonstrate overall outages or trends on the network. Hickey explains, "By the time Verizon gathers and captures the information on outages, at any one point in time, the report will be outdated by the time the report is printed, and even more outdated by the time it is reviewed by regulators. The problems of service restorations are not black and white and cannot be captured by the kinds of reports the FDC wants. This kind of over-reporting can be a waste of time."[108] While Verizon knows this and has tried to explain to regulators that there is a more accurate way to view the information, the government continues to require the corporation to generate a report that the company knows is not a real indicator of its business.

Antitrust Laws

Antitrust laws are an additional barrier to information sharing. These laws, designed to avoid private-sector collusion to create monopolies or unfairly drive up prices to consumers, come into play with PPPs because antitrust laws can significantly limit the discussions that can legally take place between executives within the same industry. One example where antitrust regulations limit US preparedness is the inability of the private sector to report on inventories of doxycycline, the preferred antibiotic for treating anthrax.[109] To ensure preparedness for a potential anthrax attack, the first questions that emergency health care providers and pharmaceutical companies ask themselves are, where is the doxycycline, who has it, and how much do they have? Despite the compelling security reasons that make the answers to these questions vitally important, antitrust laws prohibit corporations from sharing that information with one another and they prevent third parties, such as Rx Response (an information-sharing forum for all aspects of the health care industry that would need to cooperate in the event of a public health emergency) from collecting that information on their behalf.[110]

Competing companies cannot share information that could reduce competition, be used to agree on pricing, or [be used] to determine what customers to serve. Sharing the amount of inventory [doxycycline] that corporations have and where it is physically located could impact pricing. It is, therefore, illegal for them to compile the information. If Rx Response were to gather the information and it were to be stolen or leaked, it could impact prices and distribution. There doesn't have to be an actual market impact to break antitrust laws, there just has to be the potential for antitrust laws to be broken.[111]

While this example raises serious concerns about the balance between preparedness and antitrust protection for consumers, government officials have argued that cross-sector information sharing has not created serious antitrust issues.[112] Nevertheless, there is little doubt that these laws could have serious repercussions for private-sector firms, and "it is hard to know to what extent that concern lingers in the minds of corporate lawyers so long as antitrust exemptions are not formally provided."[113] To ease antitrust concerns, Branscomb suggests that providing antitrust protections for private-sector firms that participate in disaster-oriented PPPs is one of a number of ways the government could ease the burdens faced by corporations.[114]

Privacy and Maintenance of Competitive Advantage

Private-sector corporations also remain acutely aware of maintaining their competitive edge. By engaging in PPPs and sharing information with the government about their business networks, processes, and technological capabilities, industry runs the risk that information will be shared with competitors, either inadvertently or purposefully. "Companies continue to worry about possible liability issues or being placed at a competitive disadvantage should information they disclose to government authorities not be properly protected."[115] The protection of trade secrets is essential to private interests, and sharing this information places the corporation at some risk. These risks will be explored in more detail later in the chapter.

The private sector is also concerned that sharing information with government could alienate or have an adverse impact on customers. American telephone giants AT&T, MCI, and Sprint touched off a national furor after 9/11 when customers learned that the companies had granted federal authorities "access to their systems and provided call-routing information to help physically locate callers" without a warrant.[116] While privacy-rights advocates called the cooperation an "unconstitutional invasion of privacy," the companies risked further liability and brand damage by "providing commercial data for intelligence purposes to federal authorities when a company's customers have certain expectations or even legal claims to privacy protection."[117] Prieto argues that this kind of information sharing resides in a "legal gray zone" and constitutes a reputational and legal risk to corporations.[118] As a result of this risk, many corporations are hesitant to share information with government and do not provide customer information without a subpoena, warrant, or court order.[119] It is also important to remember that, although sharing customer data comes with significant risk, there are other forms of information that can be shared between the sectors that involve minimal risk, such as general observations about overall customer or industry behavioral patterns that make no reference to a particular client.

The impediments of cross-sector information sharing—classification standards, one-way information flow, information inundation, antitrust concerns, privacy issues, and the maintenance of competitive advantage—are symptoms of a larger problem that stems from the inability of the US government to adequately organize disaster-oriented PPPs. The existing framework fails to create a central authority capable of streamlining cross-sector communication and cooperation. The result is an ad hoc approach to information sharing that exacerbates and further embeds the barriers to effective communication between the sectors.

THE RISKS AND BENEFITS OF COOPERATION

To assess the extent to which the public and private sectors may be willing to engage in disaster-oriented PPPs, this section explores both the benefits each sector may gain as a result of cooperation as well as the risks that partnering may pose. Because disaster-oriented PPPs are still in the developmental stages, exploring both the risks and the benefits of cooperation is important to determine the degree to which both sectors will ultimately be willing to participate. It is important to remember that the partnerships will only be viable in so far as the benefits of cooperation outweigh the risks both sectors face in participating. While the benefits of a partnership to avoid and respond to disaster may be clear, significant legal, economic, cultural, and information-sharing barriers may inhibit disaster-oriented PPPs in the long term by making the risks too great for the benefits to be deemed as worthwhile.

Public Sector

Disaster-oriented PPPs serve a direct and explicit national policy objective, and cooperation is in the national interest. Working with the private sector is beneficial to government because it minimizes the probability and potential impact of disasters, aims to improve response and resilience capabilities, and reduces the likelihood of panic. In addition, because so much of America's critical infrastructure is owned by the private sector and because the government frequently quantifies the value of PPPs in terms of critical infrastructure protection and information sharing, cooperation serves public-sector interests.

Beyond safeguarding physical and virtual networks, disaster-oriented PPPs also provide a way for the government to learn and benefit from industry expertise. This includes imparting technological know-how, sharing organizational best practices, or passing industry insights about how the networks that support critical infrastructures function.[120] Additionally, the private sector may be able to provide the government with valuable insight as a result of the access, knowledge, and contacts the private sector possess.[121]

The advantages of disaster-oriented PPPs are not obvious to all public officials. Some remain unconvinced that the private sector is a necessary partner, and this skepticism has inhibited PPP development.[122] One example involved the Katrina emergency, when Walmart found it difficult to convince the DHS and DoD that they could add value to the response.[123] Although Walmart is now a favored government partner, executives in other industries continue to face similar challenges as they attempt to establish cooperative practices with the government.[124]

Steve Carmel of Maersk argues that many public officials believe that PPPs serve no substantial public benefit. He says:

> Government is going through the motions at the moment in their attempts to create public–private partnerships. They have the meetings, they gather the people together, but they don't really "get it" or see how the private sector can make an impact. They don't take private sector capabilities seriously and don't take our offerings of help seriously. I don't think the government really believes industry has anything to offer. . . . They say, "we have our own technology, ships, and satellites, we don't need your [private sector] information and knowledge." This is a huge mistake.[125]

For example, since 2001 UP has had a tracking mechanism in place that enables authorized operators to know exactly what kind of freight is being transported and where the freight is at any given moment. This mechanism is used specifically to monitor the location of hazardous materials. In 2006 UP discovered that the US government wanted to develop a new system to track all hazardous materials moving along their rail network. UP already had the technology in place and fully operational. According to UP CEO Jim Young, "There is no need for the government to be involved with that level of detail. We manage this freight daily as it travels across the country, and we have the technology already in place to monitor it very closely. Rather than build their own unique system that would cost taxpayers and we would have to inform and comply with, all they need to do is ask us. We'll tell them."[126] Beyond the benefits that disaster-oriented PPPs can bring to the US government, they also present a number of risks. First, by engaging with industry as an equal partner, the government risks diffusing power and authority by including the private sector in matters that have traditionally been the sole prerogative of the state. It has been argued that, given today's global and interconnected environment, industry and the technology it possesses is threatening to the public sector because it undermines the necessity of the state.[127] While the validity of this argument is open to debate, it nonetheless reflects a legitimate and central preoccupation in Washington: the maintenance and control of power and authority. Several public and private leaders interviewed cited the governmental preoccupation with holding on to power as a constraint on the development of PPPs.[128] The challenges caused by interagency turf wars certainly provide further evidence of regular struggles for power and authority in the context of PPPs.

Information sharing poses a second potential risk that PPPs may bring to the government. For PPPs to function properly and legitimately to enhance disaster preparedness and response, the government may need to discuss or share classified national intelligence. As mentioned previously, this poses a risk to the government because of the potential for intelligence leaks if information is not adequately protected.

A third risk faced by government is that, by engaging in disaster-oriented PPPs, government may be perceived as practicing favoritism by closely partnering with certain corporations and not others. Williams argues, "The government has said that it does not want to give competitive advantage to any private partners, so unless everyone can benefit from intelligence, no one gets it."[129]

Private Sector

To assess the fundamental benefits and risks that the private sector faces by engaging in PPPs, it is important to start by revisiting the motivating factors that drive the private sector in this area. Businesses are driven by profits, and corporate executives are accountable to their shareholders. While a disaster-oriented PPP, by its nature, cannot generate revenue per se, it appeals to business leaders because it has the ability to prevent future losses first by avoiding crises and then, in the event of a disaster, by helping industry rapidly restore normal business practices. Koon of Walmart explains, "Given that disasters happen, that those disasters will impact communities, and that Walmart is in those communities, it is Walmart's aim to restore normalcy as quickly as possible. It is in our and our customers' interest for us to get involved."[130] Susan Rosegrant argues that,

ough Walmart—as a profit-driven corporation—acts out of self-interest,
ing a disaster, corporate and national interests are often the same. "Walmart
is not an altruistic organization. Virtually everything it does is for its own good.
While they are not altruistic, their interests often align to the common good
and they are able to work in everyone's interest."[131] Although the motivations of
the public and private sectors may differ, during a significant crisis, it is in the
shared interests of both sectors to respond and to cooperate.

While certain industries may be devastated by the effects of a disaster and may
sustain significant losses, these events can be extremely profitable for others. In
the aftermath of Katrina, CNN reported that investors were rapidly purchasing
stock in the industries that might benefit from the rebuilding process.[132] As one
industry analyst commented, "Big national retailers and home improvement
outlets will see the benefits first."[133] Other industries that benefited from past
disasters include the contract oil-drilling sector, the oil and gas exploration sector, and companies involved with construction and building—including tractor
firms such as Caterpillar.[134] In addition, as businesses and people shift away from
a disaster zone, they create business for other cities.[135] Houston, Texas, experienced a tremendous boom after Katrina with small businesses such as low-cost
hotels reaping the economic benefits of the displaced population, while larger-
scale endeavors, such as the city port, assumed delivery of shipments that had
been diverted from their original destination in the hurricane zone.[136]

Disaster-oriented PPPs can also boost a corporation's brand image and enhance customer loyalty. "Americans want sincere and credible corporate involvement after September 11, 2001 and seek restoration of their confidence in
corporate America following the scandals of Enron, World-Com and others.
Providing evidence of good corporate citizenship can help restore confidence
and build trust in the company and in the brand. One way to operationalize
corporate social responsibility is to partner a brand with a cause."[137] Customers
who saw Walt Disney characters in shelters after Hurricane Katrina and who
watched newly donated Ford pickup trucks help their local police locate survivors are likely to feel more loyal to those brands in the future.[138] For Walmart
in particular, Hurricane Katrina was a public relations coup. In 2004, one year
prior to the hurricane, the corporation had discovered that up to 8 percent of
its customers in the United States had stopped shopping at the superstore because of negative press about wages, health care, and the corporation's environmental record.[139] As a result of its quick, capable, and well-publicized response
during Katrina, the corporation was soon presented in the press not as a villain
but as a hero. The president of Jefferson Parish (New Orleans) said on national
television just after the hurricane, "If the American government would have responded like Wal-Mart has responded, we wouldn't be in this crisis," and *Fortune* magazine labeled the corporation as "the only lifeline" during the crisis.[140]

In doing the "right thing" by helping with the response, Walmart's leaders were simultaneously able to minimize the impact of the disaster on corporate earnings by enhancing the speed of the response and opening its stores more rapidly and to significantly boost its public image. It is important to acknowledge that there are distinct incentives beyond altruism and patriotism that can prompt private-sector participation during a disaster. This is not to imply that the motives of one sector are "good" while the others are "bad"; this is to recognize crucial and inherent differences between the sectors that impact their behavior. Therefore, while during a disaster it can be in the shared interests of both sectors to cooperate, the motives that drive that cooperation can be very different.

Without the urgency of a crisis, the benefits of PPPs can be less appealing to industry, and business priorities take over. While patriotism drove a great deal of PPP participation post-9/11, as time has passed with no other significant terrorist attacks in the United States, "patriotism is no longer a motivating factor.... As the nation reverts back to calm and time passes, the private sector refocuses on the bottom line."[141] Clay Detlefsen, the SCC chair for the food and agriculture sector, argues: "The economic problems facing the nation have considerably shrunk the willingness and ability of corporations to lend people to focus on these types of [PPP] initiatives."[142] There have been no attacks on the food system, and although natural disasters were disruptive, they were not crippling.

A significant aspect of the federal vision for disaster-oriented PPPs involves the private sector shouldering the financial burden for security enhancements made to privately owned infrastructures. Often these investments align with the long-term best interests of the corporations and, as a result, are not problematic.[143] As seen with the earlier example of FedEx, the corporation believed it would be better to create additional safeguards rather than risk having its network used to facilitate a terrorist attack. Dunham argues that in his experience the government has never asked for safeguards that were not already in place or in the corporation's best interests to put into place.[144] This is not always the case, however, and when government preparedness initiatives fail to align with private-sector business practices, the costs to industry can be tremendous and strain the PPP.

An instance in which the public sector has requested industry investment in critical infrastructure protection but the investment does not align with business interests can be illustrated by using an example from the maritime shipping industry. A policy requiring 100 percent scanning of cargo containers arriving in US ports was instituted as a result of the 9/11 Commission Act in an attempt to reduce the risk of a dirty bomb arriving in the United States through a shipping container. There are two primary points of contention with the 100 percent scanning initiative. The first, according to Carmel, is that while the government requires that all cargo containers be scanned upon arrival into US ports (a process that lengthens unloading time and results in increased costs to shippers) the coast guard and border control lack the manpower to check all of the scans. The second is that the 100 percent scanning requirement is a knee-jerk reaction to 9/11 that is costly and ineffective.

> The 100 percent scanning requirements destroyed the preexisting Customs Trade Partnership Against Terrorism [C-TPAT]. C-TPAT is targeted at cargo shippers and is an agreement that says that shippers will secure their supply chain from where it originates to the point of destination. Maersk wants to participate because it makes its customers feel more comfortable knowing that the supply chain is secure. The shippers supply customs information about the ships and cargo to demonstrate their compliance with C-TPAT. The agreement provides assurances that in exchange for their participation, the shippers get "Green Lane" access upon arrival in US ports. "Green Lane" gives shippers expedited passage through customs on arrival and makes it faster for them to unload once they arrive in US ports.
>
> 100 percent scanning eliminated Green Lane and reduced the effectiveness of the C-TPAT because the shippers are no longer encouraged to proactively secure their supply chain. 100 percent scanning has made the process more expensive and far less secure. Even if you do succeed in scanning every single container, you still need eyes to review the scans and Customs and Border Control do not have the staffing necessary to view every scan. It's a pointless and expensive exercise.[145]

A second reason that private companies are less likely to be interested in PPPs in times of calm is because of the potential for earnings to suffer if one corporation decides to invest in critical infrastructure protection as a result of engaging in a PPP but its competitors do not. Flynn argues that without industry-wide investment, a single corporation "faces the likelihood of losing market share while simply shifting the infrastructure's vulnerabilities elsewhere. If terrorists strike, the company will still suffer . . . right alongside those who did nothing to prevent it."[146] The investment in critical infrastructure protection or terrorism insurance, without federal regulation requiring such measures of all, is an expensive and very risky proposition that could directly impact shareholder profits.

A third risk to the private sector is that PPPs have the potential to cause reputational damage if customers fear that their information is being provided to the government without their authorization. Since 9/11, the US government has taken numerous steps toward enhancing federal access to the information of private citizens. The USA Patriot Act, enacted forty-five days after the attacks, raised "critical questions regarding the scope of government empowerment in accessing private information in the interest of security."[147] The Patriot Act significantly loosened the parameters under which law enforcement agencies could engage in activities such as wiretapping and e-mail hacking and resulted in a great deal of concern about a return to McCarthyism and loss of individual privacy.[148]

Privacy fears generated by customers in the aftermath of the Patriot Act were troubling to private-sector leaders for two reasons. On one hand, their customers knew the government could compel them, by law, to comply with requests for information about their telephone calls, Internet habits, purchasing patterns, and so on. On the other hand, during this period of increased government demand for personal information and customer concern about privacy infringements, the government began ramping up efforts for cross-sector critical infrastructure protection collaborations.[149]

This created a dilemma for corporations who were compelled by law to share information that could have serious repercussions for their customers. Corporations were mindful of the fact that customers may react badly if they discovered that, in addition to sharing the information they were forced to provide through the Patriot Act, a company was voluntarily cooperating in a PPP. This could result in a violation of trust, a loss of business, or, worse, legal action.[150] As Branscomb and Michel-Kerjan point out, "most firms have confidentiality agreements with their customers not to reveal information about who they are, what their buying behavior is, among other attributes. Releasing that information, even only in part and in limited context could not only compromise a firm's image, but could also send them to court."[151] In the case of many international corporations, it also created an additional level of concern that the business could be perceived as a US government spy, or could lose business internationally if it emerged that they share information with the US government about observations made overseas.[152]

Finally, in addition to the negative repercussions that participating in a PPP could have on customer confidence, industry leaders are protective of their competitive edge. By engaging in PPPs and sharing information with government about their business networks, processes, and technological capabilities, the private sector runs the risk that shared information will, inadvertently or purposefully, be shared with competitors. "Companies continue to worry about possible liability issues or being placed at a competitive disadvantage should information they disclose to government authorities not be properly protected."[153] The protection of trade secrets is important to private interests and sharing this information places the corporation at some risk.

In sum, it is apparent that disaster-oriented PPPs can be risky for both the public and private sectors. In a disaster, however, both sectors benefit from partnering to speed recovery efforts. During a crisis, this shared benefit is substantial enough to outweigh any perceived risks of cooperation. It is only when there is no immediate crisis to cement cooperation that the risks begin to carry more weight. As with many of the aspects of disaster-oriented PPPs, a more centralized and structured approach to facilitating cooperation could assist in overcoming some of the perceived risks. How these efforts can be sustained in times of crises and calm remains to be seen, but sufficient incentives do appear to exist (at least in theory) to warrant continued cooperation.

TRUST

The development and maintenance of trust is the linchpin of any successful relationship, and disaster-oriented PPPs are no different. In Robert Agranoff's study of public management networks (for which disaster-oriented PPPs would qualify) a great deal of emphasis is placed on the importance of trust between partners. He argues, "The foundation of trust within the network is a central factor in establishing and maintaining network cohesion."[154] For a disaster-oriented PPP to have any hope of success, there must be a solid foundation of trust, whether that trust is between the sectors, a company and its customers, the government and the public at large, among government agencies, or between private sector firms. Liscouski also stresses the importance of trust in building disaster-oriented PPPs. "Trust is a critical element that must be built at the individual and institutional levels. Institutions can build standards that help build trust. . . . When considering a framework or structural partnership model, you cannot underestimate the importance of trust between people."[155]

The development of trust between industry and government in national disaster-oriented PPPs has been undermined by a number of factors, two of which directly relate to the challenges of information sharing. The first involves the government making requests or instituting industry-wide regulations without adequately taking industry impacts into account. This was seen in two examples in this chapter where the government made requests from Verizon for outage reports and again in the institution of 100 percent cargo-container scanning at ports. Townsend argues that this barrier "could be overcome if the private sector were, or felt it were, understood by government." To emphasize this point, Townsend provides a further example: the bans of liquids on airlines. "Banning liquids on airlines is something that costs the government nothing and it enhances security. In their view it is an easy adjustment that can be made at no cost. For the private sector, the costs are tremendous and government continues to fail to adequately recognize this."[156] McCarthy argues that the public sector fails to take industry into account because the government is too big, too powerful, and, as a result, does not feel compelled to engage.

This arrogance is compounded by what he argues is a pervasive feeling among many in Washington that "any information they need, they can get within the [Washington] Beltway."[157] While McCarthy's views cannot be supported by the interviews conducted with other public-sector leaders, it does reflect a feeling in the private sector that there is a pocket within the Washington bureaucracy that stubbornly refuses to share information with industry and, as a result, ultimately fails to see the value of PPPs.[158]

These strong-arm tactics where the government makes requests without considering, or apparently caring about, the cost implications to industry do not reflect a spirit of cooperation and result in a loss of trust. Industry leaders recognize that many officials in Washington do not value their assistance and cooperation, which further undermines their confidence in the government. This is only enhanced by factors such as the perceived inequity in information sharing. As BENS argues, "Collaboration cannot be mandated by government, but rather is grounded in trusted, tested relationships and common purpose."[159]

A second factor that impacts the development of cross-sector trust lies in the general lack of institutional trust in the existing DHS framework for cooperation. Because neither sector has institutional trust in the NIPP as a strong national framework, both government and industry fail to rely solely on this one mechanism to coordinate cross-sector cooperation. As a result of this lack of institutional trust, key private-sector players have developed multiple layers of partnerships throughout the federal government as well as on the state and local levels and with nonprofit organizations to ensure that if the national framework fails, as it did during Katrina, there are other partnership channels available.

At the same time, the public sector's lack of trust in the institutional framework is evidenced by regular turf wars and the insistence of individual agencies that they must maintain and guard their direct relationships with private leaders. In the event of a major incident, they do not want to rely on the framework but on their own direct access to industry. Townsend argues that many public-sector leaders purposefully undermine the PPP framework because they do not trust that it will develop viable relationships with industry. During her time in the White House, Townsend gathered together all of the agency heads to discuss how to develop PPP cooperation. She notes: "They were not interested in cooperating with each other. Not because of turf wars but because they did not want anyone controlling their relationships with the private sector."[160] Thus, a lack of institutional trust undermines both public and private participation and the viability of the existing PPP framework. As Agranoff points out, when partners have "real and economic differences [they] are less likely to engender high levels of trust among all involved parties."[161] He argues further that to establish trust in these circumstances, a strong trusted network is important to build "the collective confidence of the group" to ensure the partnership is strong.[162] As it stands, there is little institutional trust in the partnership framework, with both sectors preferring to rely on known and established contacts.

ADAPTABILITY OR SUSTAINABILITY

Because disaster-oriented PPPs remain in the formative stages, it is still unclear whether the existing framework is adaptable or sustainable for the long term. Quite simply, these PPPs are "too new to rate." At the moment, PPP initiatives are dispersed throughout the federal, state, and local levels of society, and although there is a federal structure for these PPPs, it is not yet fully functional as an overarching national framework. Until this occurs, the DHS PPP structure will likely continue its path of ad hoc evolutionary development that adjusts according to specific bureaucratic and political needs. Whether this evolution is representative of a long-term structural adaptability is impossible to tell at this stage.

There is a general sense in both sectors that disaster-oriented PPPs are important and that the existing federal structure needs improvement, which indicates a shared belief in the potential development of a viable overarching national framework. However, without a significant event that reprioritizes and depoliticizes disaster-oriented PPPs, it is unlikely that any further significant change will occur. Even then, without a shift in support by public leaders and a more delineated infrastructure to specifically support the PPP, it is likely that attempts to facilitate cross-sector collaboration will continue on their current disjointed trajectory.

A significant question remains about what the public and private sectors want from disaster-oriented partnerships. As it stands, the government and private sector seem to agree that a strategic partnership that is sustainable for the long term is necessary, but they have only set up a structure that facilitates responsive cooperation. Until the organizational framework evolves to the stage where the strategic or responsive "mission" of the PPP is clear, or until some significant development to the framework is made, it will be impossible to determine whether the organization can or should adapt and be sustainable.

BEYOND PPPs

Although this book focuses on disaster-oriented PPPs, it is important to recognize that not all of the challenges that have emerged in the establishment of these partnerships are unique to public–private cooperation. Other stakeholders (including nonprofit organizations and state, local, and tribal governments) have confronted similar obstacles while seeking to cooperate with the federal government to ensure that they, too, are able to contribute to the comprehensive approach to disaster preparedness demanded by the 9/11 Commission Act and the Post-Katrina Emergency Reform Act. Beyond disaster preparedness, some of the primary issues that emerge in PPPs have a broader relevance to the more general study of public networks, organization, and management.[163]

While the stakeholders listed in the previous paragraph are beyond the scope of this work, a brief exploration of the fusion centers established to facilitate information sharing between federal agencies and state and local governments after 9/11 illustrates how the partnerships established between the federal government and other stakeholders face many of the same core challenges as those between the public and private sectors. This similarity indicates that this study may have a broader relevance. If some of the more substantive issues raised in this chapter were resolved, residual benefits might be realized to improve not only public–private cooperation but also partnerships with other key stakeholders.

Like PPPs, fusion centers were created and prioritized as a result of the terrorist attacks of 9/11 and the findings of *The 9/11 Commission Report* that identified a breakdown in information sharing as a major contributing factor to the attacks. As a result of this finding, fusion centers were established to "promote greater collaboration and information sharing among federal, state and local intelligence and law enforcement entities, states and some major urban areas."[164] Fusion centers were originally designed to focus primarily on criminal and terrorist activity but have been more practically tailored over time to suit various local environments.[165] As a 2010 report by the GAO explains, "the missions of fusion centers vary.... Some fusion centers have adopted an 'all-crimes' approach, incorporating information on terrorism and other high risk threats into their jurisdiction's existing law enforcement framework to ensure that possible precursor crimes such as counterfeiting or narcotics smuggling are screened and analyzed for linkages to terrorist planning or other criminal activity. Other fusion centers have adopted an 'all-hazards' approach.... These fusion centers identify and prioritize types of major disasters and emergencies, such as hurricanes or earthquakes, which could occur in their jurisdiction."[166] There are currently seventy-two designated fusion centers throughout the United States, at least one in each of the fifty states.[167] Most fusion centers have a statewide jurisdiction and are operated by state law enforcement entities such as the state police or the bureau of investigation.[168]

Fusion centers are seen as the primary mechanism for information sharing between federal agencies and state and local governments and have been regularly scrutinized by Congress to determine the adequacy of the fusion centers, the challenges they faced, and the degree to which their partnership with the federal agencies (DHS in particular) functioned effectively.[169] It is evident that many of the same core issues affecting cooperation between the public and private sectors have also emerged in the fusion centers' attempt to partner with federal agencies. These include information-sharing barriers caused by classification standards, information inundation or inability to obtain relevant reports, lack of centralized coordination by the federal government to streamline the centers, and uncertainty about the long-term sustainability of the centers.

Like disaster-oriented PPPs, classification standards have proven to be a significant barrier to information sharing. Despite the fact that both law and executive order make it clear that a security clearance provided by one federal agency should be universally accepted, the GAO found that a lack of reciprocity of security clearances between federal agencies continued to complicate and slow the security clearance process.[170] This is somewhat surprising given that these partnerships are primarily with members of the law enforcement community and not members of the public, as would be the case in with most disaster-oriented PPPs.

Classification barriers have persisted as an impediment to more effective information sharing. A December 2011 report issued by the DHS Office of the Inspector General further reiterates earlier findings by the GAO and argues, "The classification of information impedes effective information sharing."[171] This conclusion further implies that the Reducing Over-Classification Act of 2010 has not significantly improved information sharing between federal agencies and other stakeholders. Like disaster-oriented PPPs, interagency politics and a lack of federal coordination and centralization are the leading barriers to effective information sharing with the federal government, and although classification is an impediment, it may be best understood as a symptom of an illness but not the underlying disease.

Fusion centers have also claimed that much of the information that they do receive is unfiltered, untailored to suit their needs, and cumbersome to access. Centers have faced "challenges accessing and managing multiple information systems" and have reported that officials "found the multiple systems or heavy volume of often redundant information a challenge to manage."[172] This information deluge mirrors the experiences described by private sector executives. As Agranoff argues, to ensure that cooperation is effective in complex networks such as these, "participating organizations need to do more than acquire knowledge; they want to be able to use knowledge."[173] Receiving vast quantities of largely irrelevant information that is difficult to access has made it challenging for both the private sector and fusion centers to most effectively use the information they receive.

What is more, the fusion centers also shared similar frustrations with the private sector about a general lack of feedback from the federal agencies about the usefulness of the information they provided. This caused the G͵ ommend in December 2010 that the DHS Office of Intelligence an͵ (I&A) work to provide better feedback to fusion center partners. The gues: "Periodically informing state and local partners of how I&A ana ͵ ͵͵ ͵ ͵ne feedback they provided and what actions I&A took in response to this feedback and analyses could help strengthen I&A's working relationship with these partners and encourage them to continue to provide I&A feedback, which could ultimately make I&A's products and services more useful."[174]

A further similarity that fusion centers share with disaster-oriented PPPs is the challenge caused as a result of a lack of centralized coordination and outreach. Since 2006 there has a been a tremendous focus on providing fusion centers with a certain level of "baseline capabilities" to ensure that the centers are to some extent streamlined across the country and able to achieve some level of consistency across all centers while leaving room for each center to individualize their focus slightly based on locality. In 2007 the primary challenge lay in the fact there was no central coordination or training for fusion centers.[175] By December 2008 this had evolved somewhat when the baseline capabilities were established and assessed.[176] Despite this progress, in 2010 the I&A, the department responsible for oversight of the fusion centers, was criticized because it had failed to establish an adequate framework to effectively share information with state and local partners.[177] In 2011 challenges persisted as many centers lacked sufficient federal guidance or funding to implement the baseline capabilities and the federal government remained unable to meaningfully assess the overall effectiveness of the centers.[178]

A final similarity that the fusion centers share with disaster-oriented PPPs is an ongoing sense of uncertainty about the long-term sustainability of their cooperation with the federal government. Doubts about the continuation of funding significantly inhibit the improvement and development of the centers.[179] Fusion centers are funded annually through a grant process and must compete with other state, law enforcement, and emergency management agencies for a portion of the Homeland Security grant funding awarded to each state.[180] The insecurity about future funding is likely to continue in the near term as the federal government decreases the Homeland Security budget as part of an overall strategy to reduce the federal deficit.[181] Fusion centers have little sense of security or longevity because they face the continuous prospect that their funding could be canceled in any given year. The inability to plan for the future has already been problematic for some centers because, "without sustained funding, centers could not expand operations to close the gaps between their current operations and the baseline capabilities, negatively impacting their ability to function as part of the national framework."[182] Like disaster-oriented PPPs, although fusion centers have been assigned long-term strategic objectives, they have been provided short-term responsive capabilities that limit their ability to achieve these aims.

In briefly looking beyond PPPs and exploring some of the key issues facing the fusion centers, clear similarities emerge. Should some of the core issues identified in this chapter surrounding public–private cooperation be resolved, there may be residual benefits that could be applied to other forms of federal outreach to improve not only public–private cooperation but also cooperation with other key stakeholders as well.

CONCLUSION

Several important elements discussed in this chapter indicate that although disaster-oriented PPPs may be viable in principle, the framework they currently exist within is not. This is due in part to the fact that the PPP initiatives remain under development, but there are strong indicators that if the federal framework for disaster-oriented PPPs continues on its current trajectory, it will not become an effective long-term tool for disaster response. While some regional disaster-oriented PPPs have been successful, these localized efforts are not of sufficient scale to cope with a significant national disaster. In the event of a catastrophic event, the ability to coordinate a national cross-sector and cross-border response at the federal level remains important.

Organizationally speaking, disaster-oriented PPPs have developed in an ad hoc, piecemeal fashion. The existing framework has broad, overarching aims and lacks a centralized structure capable of providing a set of "rules for engagement" that would ensure a coordinated approach to cooperation, define a leadership structure while establishing lines of authority, and lay out a set of roles and responsibilities for each sector. In the absence of a structured center, the organization is likely to mirror the ISACs (the federal government's first attempt at building PPPs in the late 1990s), where PPPs are sector-specific, are largely silo-oriented, fail to communicate and cooperate effectively between industrial sectors, and are too myopic to serve national interests across multiple industrial sectors in an emergency.

While a number of government policy documents indicate that a strategic PPP is what the public and private sectors want, the existing framework seems to follow a responsive model, indicating a gap between idealized policymaking and the realities of implementation. This is significant because responsive PPPs are only viable during a crisis, and they lack the authority, cross-sector trust, and backing to sustain themselves in times of calm. If government leaders intend for disaster-oriented PPPs to be sustainable in the long-term, a strategic partnership structure would be more appropriate.

In addition to the bureaucratic and organizational disorder that limits the further development of disaster-oriented PPPs, there are a number of intangible disruptive forces that also currently limit the effectiveness of cooperation. These have been explored in depth in this chapter and include factors such as the lack of trust (within the government, between the public and private sectors, and in the existing PPP organizational framework), the impact of partisanship and politics, and the residual effects of the passing of time that make these partnerships less of a priority for public and private sector leaders.

More than a decade after the bombings of 9/11 and several years after Hurricane Katrina, without another large-scale disaster, public and private leaders have begun to shift their focus away from PPPs to more immediate pressing issues such as the global economic crisis. Without legislation that provides a mechanism to sustain cross-sector cooperation in times of calm, interest will lag in both sectors. Given the challenges of cross-sector cooperation, it seems unlikely that either sector will be adequately motivated to prioritize disaster-oriented PPPs without a catastrophic national disaster to refocus their attention and prioritization.

The complexity of developing these partnerships cannot be overestimated. Not only are they organizationally complicated because of the sheer number of actors involved, they can also be politically challenging as local, regional, and national governments balance self-interests with the national need. (An example of this balance between self-interest and national need was seen after 9/11 when members of Congress asked UP to reroute trains carrying hazardous materials around certain constituencies. These requests were made for political rather than for national security reasons.) This issue is even more complex when one takes into account interagency contests for power and authority at the federal level, such as those described by Townsend. On top of all these competing political interests, the private sector—in all its various forms—must perceive some sort of benefit as a result of the partnership. The individual agendas of all the actors can significantly impact the viability of a national PPP framework. Whether it is possible to build an organizational structure able to streamline and manage these competing agendas remains to be seen.

NOTES

1. Auerswald, "Complexity and Interdependence," 162.
2. 9/11 Commission, *9/11 Report*, 398.
3. Auerswald, Branscomb, La Porte, and Michel-Kerjan, "Leadership: Who Will Act?," 494.

4. Terrorist organizations are also known to use a variety of international networks to operate and finance themselves. Interfering with methods of international terrorist financing was a cornerstone of the US response to 9/11. A 2003 report by the GAO described how terrorists used international networks more indirectly to finance themselves. "Terrorists use many alternative financing mechanisms to earn, move, and store assets. . . . They earn assets by selling contraband cigarettes and illicit drugs, by misusing charitable organizations that collect large donations, and by other means. They move funds by concealing their assets through nontransparent mechanisms such as charities, informal banking systems, and commodities such as precious stones and metals. To store assets, terrorists may choose similar commodities that maintain their value and liquidity." GAO, *Terrorist Financing*, 2.

5. Auerswald, Branscomb, La Porte, and Michel-Kerjan, "Leadership: Who Will Act?," 493.

6. Steve Carmel, senior executive vice president of Maersk, telephone interview with the author from Norfolk, Virginia, April 14, 2010.

7. Steinhauer and Lipton, "FEMA, Slow to the Rescue."

8. This was illustrated by the accounts in chapter 1 of when Walmart waited for days, trying to get access into New Orleans, while DoD and DHS refused to respond to Walmart's repeated offers of assistance.

9. 9/11 Commission, *9/11 Report*, 398.

10. Lopez, "Critical Infrastructure Protection," 49.

11. The importance and significance of PDD 39, EO 13010, and the PCCIP were discussed in depth in chapter 1. For further information, see also White House, *Presidential Decision Directive 39*, Washington, DC, June 21, 1995; *Executive Order 13010: Critical Infrastructure Protection*, July 15, 1996; and PCCIP, *Critical Foundations*.

12. White House, National Strategy for Homeland Security (2002), 2, 12.

13. See Homeland Security Act of 2002, Pub. L. No. 107-296, 116 Stat. 2135 (2002); *HSPD-5: Management of Domestic Incidents*, February 28, 2003; *HSPD-7: Homeland Security Advisory System*, March 11, 2002; and *HSPD-8: National Preparedness*, December 17, 2003.

14. GAO, *Catastrophic Disasters*, 6.

15. White House, *Federal Response to Katrina*, 95.

16. Post-Katrina Emergency Management Reform Act of 2006, Pub. L. No. 109-295, 120 Stat. 1394 (2006), Title V, Sec 503(b)(2)(B) [hereafter, Post-Katrina Act of 2006].

17. On October 11, 2001, a bill was proposed in the Senate to establish a National Department of Homeland Security. The bill passed through both houses of Congress, and the Homeland Security Act of 2002 was signed into law on November 25, 2002.

18. Branscomb, "A Nation Forewarned," 20.

19. Anonymous, interview by the author.

20. Frances "Fran" Fragos Townsend, assistant to President George W. Bush for homeland security and counterterrorism and chair of Homeland Security Council (2004–7) and CNN contributor on counterterrorism and homeland security, interview with the author in Washington, DC, April 6, 2010.

21. Lopez, "Evolution of Vulnerability Assessment Methods," 66.

22. George "Gig" Hender, chairman of DHS finance sector SCC 2006-2008 and vice-chairman of Options Clearing Corporation (retired), telephone interview with the author from Chicago, April 13, 2010.

23. Capt. George McCarthy, US Navy Office of Global Maritime Situational Awareness, telephone interview with the author from Washington, DC, April 22, 2010; Jim Young, CEO of Union Pacific Railroad, telephone interview with the author from Omaha, Nebraska, April 12, 2010; Hender, interview.

24. Young, interview.

25. Ibid.

26. Lynne Kidder, senior executive vice president BENS, interview with the author in Washington, DC, April 8, 2010.

27. Interviewees who expressed a preference for partnering with the military include Jim Young, Bryan Koon, and Archie Dunham.

28. The actions of Verizon, the NYSE, the New York Federal Reserve Bank, and Walmart are detailed in chapter 1. Examples from other private corporations are outlined here to demonstrate the depth and variety of sectors involved.

29. Block, "Private Eyes."

30. Kratz, "For FedEx It Was Time to Deliver."

31. Ibid.

32. FedEx executives argued that it was their business to be prepared for the disaster and to help in the response. Just after the hurricane, a senior FedEx executive commented, "We're used to dealing with crisis." In ibid.

33. Ibid.

34. Richard Adkerson, CEO of Freeport-McMoRan Copper and Gold, telephone interview with the author from Phoenix, Arizona, April 22, 2010.

35. US Chamber of Commerce. *From Relief to Recovery*, 26.

36. Carmel, interview.

37. US Chamber of Commerce, *From Relief to Recovery*, 24.

38. Young, interview.

39. US Chamber of Commerce, *From Relief to Recovery*, 23.

40. ConocoPhillips is the third-largest integrated energy company in the United States and the fifth-largest oil refiner in the world.

41. Archie Dunham, CEO and chairman of ConocoPhillips (retired), telephone interview with the author from Houston, Texas, April 22, 2010.

42. Susan Rosegrant, author of Harvard case study, "Wal-Mart's Response to Hurricane Katrina: Striving for a Public-Private Partnership," telephone interview with the author from Dearborn, Michigan, March 26, 2010; Bryan Koon, director of emergency management, Walmart, telephone interview with the author from Bentonville, Arkansas, April 14 and 23, 2010; interviews with Adkerson, Young, Carmel, and Dunham; and Kratz, "For FedEx It Was Time to Deliver."

43. Bob Liscouski, assistant secretary of critical infrastructure protection at DHS (2003–5) and president and COO of Steel City RE, interviews with the author in Washington, DC, April 8 (in person), and April 16 (by telephone), 2010; Nitin Natarajan,

Chairman of DHS GCC for Healthcare and Coordinating Director of Health and Human Services/ASPR/OPEO, telephone interview with the author from Washington, DC, May 5, 2010; Brian Scott, deputy director of the partnership and outreach division, Department of Homeland Security, Office of Infrastructure Protection, interview with the author in Crystal City, Virginia, April 9, 2010; and Townsend, interview.

44. The report gives one specific example of the exercise program within DHS, which has undergone five organizational changes between 2003 and 2009. GAO, *National Preparedness*, 20.

45. DHS interviewees included the first DHS undersecretary of the Office of Critical Infrastructure Protection (now called the Office of National Protection and Programs), the director of the Domestic Nuclear Detection Office, the deputy director of the Private Sector Outreach Division of the Office of Infrastructure Protection, and the senior policy adviser in the Office of Policy.

46. GAO, *National Preparedness*, 1.

47. Interviews with Natarajan and Liscouski.

48. This includes the 2009 update of the NIPP and FEMA's most recent National Response Framework. Interviews with Scott and Natarajan. (Natarajan is included in this grouping as the head of the DHS Government Coordinating Council chair for health care.)

49. Specific challenges perceived by Liscouski include barriers to information-sharing and trust and are detailed later in this chapter. Liscouski, interview; see also McKay, "Former DHS Assistant Secretary."

50. Interviews with Natarajan and Scott.

51. Erin Mullen, chairman of the healthcare sector coordinating council and director of Rx Response, telephone interview with the author from Washington, DC, April 22, 2010; and Natarajan, interview.

52. Natarajan, interview.

53. Gen. Charles C. Krulak, 31st Commandant US Marine Corps (retired) and CEO MBNAEurope Bank (retired), telephone interview with the author from Wilmington, Delaware, April 2, 2010; and interviews with Dunham and Koon.

54. Koon, interview.

55. Clay Detlefsen, chairman of DHS Food and Agriculture SCC and vice president of regulatory affairs and general counsel for International Dairy Foods, telephone interview with the author from Washington, DC, May 6, 2010; Mike Hickey, vice president of governmental affairs and national security at Verizon, interview with the author in Washington, DC, April 9 (in person), and April 22 (by telephone), 2010; and interviews with Koon, Natarajan, and Mullen.

56. Interviews with Kidder, Koon, Detlefsen, Natarajan, Mullen, and Hickey.

57. Krulak, interview.

58. Townsend, interview.

59. Ibid.

60. Young, interview.

61. Priest and Arkin, "Top Secret America."

62. Interviews with Koon, Hender, Mullen, and McCarthy.

63. Dunham also serves on the board of directors for Union Pacific and Phelps Dodge Corporation and works in an advisory capacity at Deutsche Bank. Dunham, interview.

64. Townsend, interview.

65. Interviews with Koon and Hender.

66. Mullen, interview.

67. Krulak, interview. Krulak has spoken and written extensively on the importance of developing a multidisciplinary planning approach that includes nongovernmental entities in national security plans at every level. The "five elements of national power" he identifies include the military, government, academia, the private sector, and media. Krulak began presenting his "Ne Cras" presentation within the US government as early as 1996 while serving as the commandant of the US Marine Corps and presented it publicly at the Council on Foreign Relations on November 17, 1997. Krulak, "Ne Cras."

68. Darryl Williams, architect of STRATCOM Partnership to Defeat Terrorism and CEO of Partnership Solutions International, telephone interview with the author from Omaha, Nebraska, April 1, 2010.

69. Ibid.

70. Project Impact is an example of a grassroots initiative that was established by FEMA to create community- and neighborhood-level PPPs. Project Impact was established in 1997 and dissolved in 2001. DHS, *Project Impact*; and Holdeman and Patton, "Project Impact."

71. BENS, *Public Benefit Coalition*, 4.

72. As mentioned in chapter 1, there were no fewer than twenty-one disasters that struck the United States in the last decade. The majority of these were floods, fires, and hurricanes and include Hurricane Charley in June 2004, Hurricane Ivan in September 2004, Hurricane Katrina in August 2005, Hurricane Wilma in October 2005, the mid-Atlantic and New England floods in October 2005, the mid-Atlantic flood in 2006, the Washington State flood in November 2006, the Midwest floods of August 2007, the California fires in October 2007, the Oregon and Washington floods in December 2007, the Midwest floods in the spring of 2008, Hurricane Ike in September 2008, the California wildfires from July to October 2009, the Southern floods in September 2009, the Southern New England floods in March 2010, and the Tennessee floods in May 2010.

73. Interviews with Krulak and Williams; see also White House, *Federal Response to Hurricane Katrina*.

74. White House, *Federal Response to Hurricane Katrina*, 13.

75. Flynn, *Edge of Disaster*, 5.

76. Hakim and Blackstone, "Role of the Private Sector," 1–2.

77. Ibid., 19.

78. Lynne Kidder argues that the federal frameworks provided through the NIPP, SCCs, the Critical Infrastructure Partnership Advisory Council (CIPAC), and the private sector offices for FEMA and DHS have not been effective at the local level but contends that there is a need for an "independent and honest broker" to ensure that PPP efforts can result in resiliency and disaster mitigation. Koon says that a successful

framework should be able to operate on both the national and local levels, and argues: "At this point, any [federal] model pushed down from above will fail. At the same time, pushing from the bottom will get hundreds of different models and they will fail as well. We need a menu of two or three different options that suit varying business and government models and allow businesses and local governments to choose which will work best for them. This would both help narrow the range of options and provide best practices that others can follow." Interviews with Kidder and Koon. See also BENS, *Public Benefit Coalition*, 4.

79. Williams also advocated a federal approach. Interviews with Krulak, Dunham, and Williams.

80. Jim Young, the CEO of UP, had a similar experience and claims that although UP regularly conducts security drills to test various scenarios along their rail network, the government does not and will not participate. Interviews with Carmel and Young.

81. Several private and public leaders interviewed implied during interviews that the excuse "that is classified" was often used to avoid sharing information with industry. I assume that interviewees did not want to make direct accusations. Because this was inferred and observed and not explicitly stated by interviewees, no direct references are provided here to protect the anonymity of those interviewed.

82. Prieto, "Information Sharing with the Private Sector," 422.

83. Reducing Over-Classification Act, Pub. L. 111-258, 124 Stat. 2648 (2010).

84. Interviews with Krulak, Liscouski, and Townsend.

85. Krulak and Liscouski argued similar points in their interviews. Interviews with Townsend, Krulak, and Liscouski.

86. Priest and Arkin, "Top Secret America."

87. Retired army Lt. Gen. John R. Vines, quoted in ibid.

88. Liscouski, interview.

89. Ibid.

90. Natajaran's role as director in the Office of Preparedness and Emergency Operations is within the Health and Human Services Office of the Assistant Secretary for Preparedness and Response. Natarajan, interview.

91. Hender, interview.

92. Krulak, interview.

93. Townsend, interview.

94. Hender, interview.

95. Natajaran holds meetings four to five times a year in various locations around the country for private-sector executives within his sector to receive briefings from the intelligence agencies on issues relating to public health. Natarajan, interview.

96. Ibid.

97. Natarajan and his team organize the information for the cyber/technology experts, the pharmaceutical companies, hospital administrators, and health care providers so they can quickly and easily locate the most pertinent information. Ibid.

98. Ibid.

99. Kidder, interview.

100. Flynn and Prieto, "Neglected Defense," 15.

101. McCarthy, interview.

102. Carmel, interview.

103. Mullen, interview.

104. Interviews with Carmel, Williams, Young, and Hickey.

105. McCarthy, interview.

106. Williams, interview.

107. McCarthy, interview.

108. Hickey, interview.

109. Mullen, interview; and "Doxycycline Becomes Anthrax Drug of Choice in Washington," *CNN.com/HEALTH*, October 28, 2001, http://archives.cnn.com/2001/HEALTH/conditions/10/27/doxycycline/.

110. Mullen serves as the assistant vice president for Rx Response in addition to acting as the chairperson of the health care SCC. For more on Rx Response, see "Rx Response Preparedness Plan," *RxResponse.org*, www.rxresponse.org/Pages/default.aspx.

111. Mullen, interview.

112. Branscomb and Michel-Kerjan, "Public-Private Collaboration," 398.

113. Ibid.

114. Additional public policy options that Branscomb suggests to government include "(1) extension of current safety regulations to cover security exposures; (2) research and development subsidies and partnerships with government's technical resources; (3) tax or financial benefits to reduce the economic impact of required capital investments; (4) facilitation of secured information sharing between private firms and government agencies and departments that respects privacy issues; (5) public provision of information on private vulnerabilities for which firms may consequently be held financially accountable by courts; (6) provision of publicly funded terrorism (re)insurance and incentives to insurance and reinsurance firms to offer rates scaled to risk reduction, and (7) encouragement of voluntary collective actions through trade associations." Branscomb, "A Nation Forewarned," 24–25.

115. Flynn and Prieto, "Neglected Defense," 15.

116. Prieto, "Information Sharing with the Private Sector," 417.

117. Ibid.

118. Ibid., 424.

119. Ibid.

120. Interviews with Dunham, Krulak, Natarajan, Mullen, Kidder, Young, McCarthy, and Carmel.

121. Interviews with Dunham and Krulak; Branscomb and Michel-Kerjan, "Public-Private Collaboration," 397.

122. Interviews with McCarthy, Williams, and Carmel.

123. For more about DoD and DHS refusals of Walmart's offers of help, see Rosegrant, "Wal-Mart's Response," 12–16.

124. Interviews with Carmel, Dunham, Young, and McCarthy.

125. Carmel, interview. Jim Young, the CEO of UP, similarly argues that the government fails to understand industry, its priorities, how it operates, and how it can be useful to government. Young, interview.

126. Young, interview.
127. Strange, "States, Firms and Diplomacy," 8.
128. Interviews with Carmel, Krulak, McCarthy, and Townsend.
129. Williams, interview.
130. Koon, interview.
131. Rosegrant, interview.
132. Kelley, "Rebuilding Post-Katrina."
133. Ibid.
134. Ibid.
135. Romero, "Houston Finds Business Boon."
136. Ibid.
137. Lafferty and Goldsmith, "Cause–Brand Alliances," 423.
138. For more information about donations provided by the Disney and Ford Corporations, see US Chamber of Commerce, *From Relief to Recovery*.
139. Faber, "New Age of Wal-Mart."
140. Comments made by Aaron F. Broussard on *Meet the Press*, aired on September 4, 2005, quoted in Barbaro and Gillis, "Wal-Mart at Forefront." See also Leonard, "Only Lifeline Was the Wal-Mart."
141. Williams, interview.
142. Detlefsen, interview.
143. Interviews with Young, Hickey, and Dunham.
144. Dunham argues, "The government has made no requirements above and beyond what [Conoco] ought to be doing. . . . Nothing the government has done has been a burden for UP or Conoco." UP CEO Jim Young contends that nothing the government has asked of them has had a material impact on their bottom line. Interviews with Dunham and Young.
145. Carmel, interview.
146. Flynn refers to this as the "tragedy of the commons" principle. Flynn, *America the Vulnerable*, 54–55. See also Flynn, " Neglected Home Front," 28–29.
147. Branscomb and Michel-Kerjan, "Public-Private Collaboration," 399.
148. Tom Ridge, the first director of the Department of Homeland Security, supports the Patriot Act but acknowledges that it created a great deal of controversy. In his memoir he comments, "The concern over the potential abuse of these new investigative powers undoubtedly echoed the anxiety felt during Joe McCarthy's time. Thoughtful people with an appreciation of history recalled the cultural, legal and political impact of those tumultuous years. Uncorroborated accusations, blacklists, formal government inquiry into the loyalty of citizens or what they were reading—all were manifestations of an abuse of legal authority." Ridge, *Test of Our Times*, 107.
149. The Patriot Act renews the calls for better PPPs for critical infrastructure protection and calls for private involvement in a number of critical infrastructure protection-related efforts including the generation of modeling, simulations, and analysis for "responses to incidents or crises involving critical infrastructures including the continuity of government and private sector activities through and after such incidents or crises." It is interesting to note that the private sector is not mentioned in title VIII of

the act, which explores information sharing for critical infrastructure protection. Uniting and Strengthening America by Providing Appropriate Tools Required to Intercept and Obstruct Terrorism Act of 2001 [Patriot Act], Pub. L. No. 107-56, 115 Stat. 272 (2001), Title X, Sec. 1016(d)(2)(b) (iii). For more on the importance of incorporating the private sector in critical infrastructure protection initiatives in the Patriot Act, see also Patriot Act, Title X, Sec 1016: (b)(2), (c)(2.1), and (d)(2)(b).

150. Branscomb and Michel-Kerjan, "Public-Private Collaboration," 398; and Prieto, *Seeds of Disaster*, 424.

151. Branscomb and Michel-Kerjan, "Information Sharing with the Private Sector," 398.

152. This applies in particular to disaster mitigation and preparedness efforts that could entail information sharing for counterterrorism purposes. Interviews with Adkerson and Carmel.

153. Flynn and Prieto, "Neglected Defense," 15.

154. Agranoff, *Managing within Networks*, 119.

155. Liscouski, interview.

156. Townsend, interview.

157. McCarthy, interview.

158. Interviews with Carmel, Krulak, and McCarthy.

159. BENS, *Public Benefit Coalition*, 1–2.

160. Townsend, interview.

161. Agranoff, *Managing within Networks*, 120.

162. Ibid., 121.

163. For example, the work of Robert Agranoff that aims to understand public management networks and Kathleen Hale's work on the links between public policy and nonprofit organizations highlight many parallel themes and underlying challenges identified in this book. Agranoff, *Managing within Networks*; and Hale, *How Information Matters*.

164. Fusion centers are also part of the information-sharing environment established by the Intelligence Reform and Terrorism Prevention Act of 2004, Pub. L. No. 108-458, 118 Stat. 3638 (2004); GAO, *Homeland Security*, 1; and DHS, OIG, *Relationships between Fusion Centers*, 2.

165. GAO, *Homeland Security*, Highlights; and GAO, *Information Sharing: Federal Agencies Are Helping Fusion Centers*, 8.

166. GAO, *Information Sharing: Federal Agencies Are Helping Fusion Centers*, 8.

167. GAO, *Information Sharing: DHS Could Better Define*, 19.

168. Some regional fusion centers that operate in major urban areas are operated by city or county law enforcement or emergency management agencies. GAO, *Information Sharing: Federal Agencies Are Helping Fusion Centers*, 1.

169. GAO, *Homeland Security*; GAO, *Information Sharing: Federal Agencies Are Helping Fusion Centers*; GAO, *Information Sharing: DHS Could Better Define*; and GAO, *Information Sharing: Progress Made and Challenges Remaining*.

170. The two presidential orders and two acts of law that specifically address the issue of classification and aim to ensure that agencies accept security clearances issued

by other agencies are (1) the National Security Directive 63 issued in 1991 by President George Bush; (2) President William Clinton's Executive Order 12968 in 1995; (3) Section 3001 of the Intelligence Reform Act of 2004; and (4) the Reducing Over-Classification Act of 2010. National Security Directive 63: Single Scope Background Investigations, October 21, 1991; Executive Order 12968: Access to Classified Information, August 2, 1995; Intelligence Reform and Terrorism Protection Act; Reducing Over-Classification Act; and GAO, *Homeland Security*, 6–7.

171. DHS, OIG, *Relationships between Fusion Centers*, 1.

172. GAO, *Homeland Security*, 6; see also GAO, *Information Sharing: DHS Could Better Define*, 13.

173. Agranoff, *Managing within Networks*, 227.

174. GAO, *Information Sharing: DHS Could Better Define*, 38.

175. GAO, *Homeland Security*, 7.

176. Baseline capabilities were jointly published in September 2008 by the Department of Justice and DHS. GAO, *Information Sharing: Federal Agencies Are Helping Fusion Centers*, 10.

177. GAO, *Information Sharing: DHS Could Better Define*, 25.

178. DHS, OIG, *Relationships between Fusion Centers*, 18.

179. GAO, *Homeland Security*, 10; GAO, *Information Sharing: Federal Agencies Are Helping Fusion Centers*, 17–18; GAO, *Information Sharing: Progress Made*, 11–12.

180. GAO, *Information Sharing: Progress Made*, 11.

181. In 2011, for example, Homeland Security grant funding was $780 million less than the previous year. GAO, *Information Sharing: Progress Made*, 12.

182. Ibid., 11.

CHAPTER THREE

The Federal Reserve, a Strategic Alliance

The concept of a public–private partnership for disaster management is in its infancy in the United States. While there is a widespread sense that cross-sector cooperation is imperative, there no clear way forward. In this chapter I aim to determine if any lessons from an established, strategic cross-sector partnership (the Federal Reserve System) may be applied to the contemporary dilemma to offer historical precedent and guidance.

This case study evaluates the Federal Reserve System as a strategic public–private alliance that is nearly a century old. Within this context I analyze the Fed specifically in terms of the seven critical factors that have been identified as crucial to the development and success of disaster-oriented PPPs: the role of crisis, leadership, organizational structure, information sharing, shared benefits, trust, and adaptability or sustainability. Using this approach, the chapter is designed to assess if the problems facing disaster-oriented PPPs are unique; if the founders of the Fed had similar priorities or challenges as policymakers do today; how the Fed has remained institutionally viable for so long; and, finally, if any lessons from the past may be applicable to disaster-oriented PPPs.

In this chapter I examine the early years of the Fed to understand what drove the creation and early development of the organization. Because disaster-oriented PPPs are still in the formative stages, parallels between the contemporary situation and the Federal Reserve System most readily emerge through an exploration of the same formative period of the Fed. I do not seek to provide a historical summary of the Fed since its formation in 1913; instead I explore certain critical points during its developmental years to provide an understanding of how the need for cross-sector collaboration came about, how the organization was formulated, and what factors have enabled it to survive for so long. Additionally, the case study hones in on the early years of the Fed because the later developments of the Fed, for the purposes of this research, simply demonstrate the organization's continued ability to adapt.

Because this chapter is primarily concerned with the Fed as a long-standing, federal cross-sector alliance, debates about the viability and success of the Fed as an instrument of monetary policy are not assessed in this study. Rowe argues in his 1965 exploration of the Fed: "When the past half century of Federal Reserve System existence is reviewed, there arises a nagging suspicion that the conflicts over the continuance of private representation in the Federal Reserve System are peripheral and that the major reasons for conflict are recurring disagreements about the appropriateness of various monetary policies."[1] These conflicts are beyond the realm of this study and are not addressed here. The fact that the Fed is a public–private alliance that has been in existence for nearly a century is sufficient justification for considering the organizational framework viable and worth evaluation.

CRISIS AS A CATALYST FOR CHANGE

> The panic first strikes the bank, but within the next succeeding
> moment strikes the depositor of the bank; it strikes the borrower
> from the bank; it strikes the business of the country; it goes
> down and strikes the man who digs in the trench and who toils
> in the mine. A sound financial system is essential to a sound
> business system, and a sound business system is essential to a
> sound industrial system, and all are essential to the happiness
> of the people.
>
> Senator James A. Reed, in defense of the
> Federal Reserve Bill in the US Senate, 1913.[2]

Crisis played a crucial role in the formation of the Fed. Although the financial panic of 1907 was relatively brief, the repercussions of the crisis were far-reaching and resulted in the formal establishment of the Federal Reserve System. The extremity of the situation focused the minds of politicians, businessmen, academics, and citizens alike and created a consensus that urgent change was imperative to ensure that future panics were avoided.[3] As described by historian Robert Wiebe, "The panic of 1907 acted as a catalyst in the [political] ferment. Most obviously, it convinced everyone, including the bankers, that financial reform was imperative. . . . The panic released countless little pockets of pressure, turning concerned but comfortable citizens into active reformers and opening many more calls for change."[4]

The panic of 1907 was not a single, isolated incident but the culmination of decades of disjointed banking regulation and a changing national economy. Robert Bruner and Sean Carr argue that to "understand fully the crash and panic of 1907, one must consider its context."[5] The panic was preceded by three failed attempts to create a centralized banking system in the United States: the Bank of North America (1781–85), the First Bank of the United States (1791–1811), and the Second Bank of the United States (1816–36).[6] Each of these institutions failed to have its original charter renewed by Congress, and by 1836 the United States was without a centrally regulated or controlled banking system.[7] During the remainder of the nineteenth century, the US economy was weak and highly unstable, not only because of the lack of a central bank but also because of the Civil War and the growth of new "wildcat banks" throughout the country. The term "wildcat bank" arose in the late nineteenth century to describe a breed of bank located primarily in the "wild" West of the United States. To redeem notes from these institutions, depositors would often have to travel through dangerous parts of the country where wildcats roamed. The remote nature of these banks made them difficult to control or regulate, they were highly unstable, and they often issued their own unique currencies. This was problematic because by 1900 there were at least twelve different US currencies in circulation. The growth of "wildcat banks" also contributed to distrust in the banking system and generated skepticism among the public about the value of American currency.[8] This distrust, combined with the effects of the Civil War and the lack of an institutionalized central bank, resulted in an American banking system plagued by corruption, instability, and a lack of centralized control.

At the same time, the very nature of business was changing. Technological innovations such as the railroad, telegraph, and steam engine created the capacity to transmit goods, services, and information at speeds and scales never seen before. The use and dissemination of each of these innovations was reliant upon a trustworthy bank-issued currency. Through the latter half of the nineteenth century, the failure to develop a stable banking platform in the US left Americans unsure whether the money they kept on deposit with the bank was safe. This uncertainty led to a number of "runs on the bank."[9] A run on the bank would occur when depositors, fearing a bank collapse, would "run" to their bank in an attempt to withdraw their holdings to avoid losing all of their savings if the bank were to fail. During these runs, depositors stood for hours, sometimes paying others to hold their place in line, to ensure they could withdraw their funds. In *The House of Morgan*, a work about the powerful Morgan banking family, Ron Chernow describes the mayhem surrounding the bank runs in 1907: "As panic increased, depositors thronged banks across the city. People sat overnight in camp chairs, bringing food and waiting for the banks to open in the morning. New York police distributed numbers to people to save their places; in other cases exhausted depositors paid enterprising standees to wait for them."[10] The panic of 1907 is considered the worst of the thirteen bank panics that occurred in the United States between 1814 and 1914, and the backstory of the event illustrates that the country was in flux and that a sense of distrust reduced public confidence in the soundness of the banking system.[11]

The panic was sparked by news that Augustus Heinze, a Montana speculator and president of the Mercantile Bank, had lost everything in the stock exchange on October 16, 1907.[12] This resulted in devastating bank runs on the Mercantile Bank, and although the loss of Heinze's wealth alone was not enough to initiate panic, concern was fueled by investors and speculators who knew that Heinze had close connections with numerous financial institutions throughout the country.[13] The crisis really set into motion when news surfaced on October 21, 1907, that Heinze was associated with the president of the powerful Knickerbocker Trust Company.[14] Customers with cash on deposit with Knickerbocker believed that since Heinze's Mercantile Bank was on the brink of collapse, the link between the men might also signify the impending collapse of the Knickerbocker, so they went immediately to reclaim their money.[15] The demand for cash deposits exceeded the cash reserves, and after only three hours Knickerbocker distributed more than $8 million in cash to customers and closed its doors at noon that day, never to reopen.[16] Customers unable to retrieve their cash in that three-hour window lost everything.

The collapse of this institution, feeding on the lack of confidence already felt by many depositors across the country, led to widespread panic and national runs on banks because customers feared their own life savings could be similarly lost. Depositors flocked to trust companies that had nothing to do with Heinze or Knickerbocker to demand immediate cash withdrawals.[17] In attempts to retrieve their savings, some depositors stood for hours in long lines that circled entire city blocks.[18]

The panic of 1907 initiated a much larger national economic crisis. While lasting only fifteen months, the crisis resulted in a 37 percent decline in the overall value of all listed stocks, a giant increase in bankruptcies, and a rise in unemployment from 2.8 percent to 8 percent in the United States.[19] By the time the crisis was finally in hand, at least twenty-five banks and seventeen trust companies had failed and the US economy was spiraling toward a depression.[20]

While the economic crisis was severe, the impact of the panic could have been far worse had it not been for the efforts of J. Pierpont "J. P." Morgan, the founder of J. P. Morgan Bank. Morgan, at the time the single most influential and powerful American banker, led and united a coalition of the most dominant American financiers of the day in a number of massive bail-out plans that saved numerous financial institutions, including the New York Stock Exchange, from collapse.[21] In each case, Morgan led the charge and became known during this period for holding meetings at his home in New York in which he quite literally locked bankers in a room, if necessary, until an agreement could be reached.[22] Kemmerer and Kemmerer describe his role: "Friends and rivals entrusted Morgan with their surplus funds to halt the panic. He, sitting in solitary splendor in a tapestried room, made the final decision as to which banks, brokerage houses, insurance companies, and other institutions should get a loan and be saved and which should have to go without help. . . . Morgan was a one-man Federal Reserve System and Reconstruction Finance Corporation."[23] His leadership was fundamental.

The crisis brought the public and private sectors together to construct a viable way forward for the nation. The panic made banking reform a clear necessity for the government; at the same time, banking reform was prioritized by the private sector because losses were so great during this period that virtually every industrial sector of society felt the impact.[24] Paul Warburg, a New York investment banker who was a foremost commentator on banking and currency issues, said in an essay written in November 1907, "The appalling panic which we have experienced during the last few weeks will do more, I suppose, to bring home to the public the absolute necessity of a change in our present banking and currency system than all the efforts that have hitherto been made to warn the nation of the imminent danger."[25] The early warnings were not heeded, and it took a national crisis, instigated by the panic, to generate the attention and prioritization necessary to activate the reform movement.

The banking community also regularly interacted with the US government. The president and the secretary of the Treasury met with New York bankers at critical moments of the crisis to cooperate and mitigate further damage.[26] "Even President Theodore Roosevelt, who had recently denounced the 'malefactors of great wealth,' granted Morgan a free hand."[27]

The disruption caused by the crisis prompted a quick governmental response. Carter Glass, the primary author of the Federal Reserve Act, described this sense of urgency by saying, "The frightful panic of 1907, decidedly the severest financial disturbance the country had ever had, sharply arrested the attention of Congress and forced those charged with legislative authority at least to attempt remedial action of some kind."[28] In 1908 the Aldrich–Vreeland Act was passed as an emergency measure designed to address many of the more urgent banking reforms deemed necessary.[29] The act also established the National Monetary Commission and assigned it the task of investigating central banks in Europe and providing an assessment as to which central bank, if any, might be a model for a new American central bank.[30] Glass argues that the Aldrich–Vreeland Act was simply "intended to serve emergency purposes until a permanent scheme of currency reform might be contrived."[31]

The panic of 1907, a violent national economic crisis, sharply focused the attention of the nation on banking and currency issues. Although the need for a new central banking structure had been discussed and debated endlessly since the expiration of the charter of the Second Bank of the United States in 1836, the attention of politicians and business leaders was focused elsewhere. The degree of change required after the panic necessitated legislative action to reform American banking laws, restore public confidence in the system, and reduce the susceptibility of the US economy to panic-driven crises.

In summary, the crisis brought three very important issues to the forefront. First, it made the establishment of a system to avoid future panics an unequivocal priority for the US government. Crisis, driven by panic, had to be avoided. One of the most important changes required to achieve this aim was to make currency more elastic and, therefore, able to adjust to the seasonal fluctuations in money supply.[32] The goals of panic avoidance and ensuring greater elasticity in the currency remained priorities for the US government and were later described as some of the most important features of the reserve.[33]

Second, the crisis made it clear that, to avoid future panics, the government needed a national, institutionalized banking system that included a clearinghouse mechanism that would allow banks to share reserves if demand exceeded the supply of cash deposits on hand.[34] The ability to have an elastic currency managed by a national, institutionalized clearinghouse able to facilitate interbank loans in the event of a shortage of money supply was critical to stabilizing the banking system and, at the same time, strengthening public confidence.[35]

Third, the unfolding of the crisis demonstrated the importance of the private sector in the policymaking process and generated a strong sense that bankers should have a part in drafting legislation to establish a new American banking system. This desire for private-sector involvement developed as a result of the involvement, expertise, and influence exerted by J. P. Morgan and other bankers during the panic. At the same time, the degree of power wielded by the banking community made it equally evident that the influence of the "money trust," as the most powerful bankers were called, must be kept in check and must not exceed the power and authority wielded by the US government.[36] There was a sense that while the private sector should be included in legislative reform, the government must be more fully in control of policymaking tools to ensure that policy decisions reflect the interests of the people and not the profit-focused self-interests of the private sector.[37] The crisis generated by the banking panic of 1907 was a catalyst for change. The breadth of the crisis captured the focus and attention of the public and private sectors alike and made action a priority. The Federal Reserve Act of 1913 was the result.

PUBLIC- AND PRIVATE-SECTOR LEADERSHIP

The quick actions of private-sector leaders—led by the New York banking community—were crucial to the ability of the United States to successfully navigate the panic of 1907. After the immediate panic passed, however, it was public-sector leadership, driven primarily by the president and Congress, that was responsible for pushing legislation and developing the Federal Reserve Act.

Public-Sector Leadership

> It was the leadership of the President that banking and currency reform had its surest chance of eventual triumph. Not for an instant did Mr. Wilson ever turn aside from the task or hesitate to apply every resource of intellectual strength and executive power. . . . Without his knowledge of the problem, deprived of his spirit and direction, nothing of a lasting description could have been achieved. It is because no living person, as I believe, knows and appreciates this as I do, that this chronicle is written.
>
> Rep. Carter Glass, author of the Federal Reserve Act, on the role of President Wilson in the passage of the legislation[38]

After an initial flurry of activity following the crisis (during which the Aldrich–Vreeland Act was passed in 1908), there was little progress made in terms of monetary reform. Although President Theodore Roosevelt recognized the need to make changes, he failed to understand the nuances of the currency issue and had little time to enact any further changes before his tenure expired on March 4, 1909. Broz states that Roosevelt "had not acquired enough interest in the issue to study it intently, let alone lead a resolution." He argues that while Roosevelt urged vaguely for reform, he "did not lead" on banking and currency issues, focusing more of his time and energy on building the Panama Canal, launching the Great White Fleet (the first national naval force to circle the world), and supporting conservation causes such as the establishment of the Grand Canyon as a national park.[39] After the 1908 passage of the Aldrich–Vreeland emergency measure, little was done on the issue through the remainder of his tenure in office.

When another Republican, William Howard Taft, came into office in 1909, very little changed. Banking and currency issues were simply not a priority. President Taft's policy was to wait for the completion of the National Monetary Commission study on European banking systems before considering legislative reforms. During his term, he focused primarily on fending off criticism by the newly formed Progressive Party, supporting an act that perpetuated higher than expected tariffs, and attempting but failing to create a trade agreement with Canada.[40] Taft factored so little in the pursuit of any measures that would enact long-term policy reform on banking and currency issues that his name scarcely appears in accounts of the time he was in office.[41] Taft's biographer states that his addresses and correspondences are "singularly bare of references to currency revision," further indicating a lack of interest and prioritization for these issues.[42] The National Monetary Commission study, which took four years and resulted in twenty-three volumes and nearly fifteen thousand pages of research, was not complete until 1911, and no legislation was considered until the Aldrich Plan was composed in 1911, based on the commission's findings.[43]

Unfortunately for Senator Aldrich, his proposal for reform was ill received.[44] "Opinion was unanimous that financial reform was urgent, but the publication of the Aldrich report revealed a profound divergence over the kind of banking system the country should adopt."[45] In the years following the panic of 1907, having seen a demonstration of the power held by a few wealthy bankers, the public questioned who was really running the country—elected officials or the banking community.[46] Republicans were seen to be sympathetic to the interests of overly powerful bankers, and Aldrich, in particular, with his ties to the banking community and marriage into the powerful Rockefeller dynasty, was seen as particularly supportive of the "money trust."[47] These suspicions cast a long shadow over much of Aldrich's work. President Taft, also a Republican, wished to distance himself from any perceived connection to the money trust and backed away from the Aldrich Plan.[48]

Aldrich's efforts to initiate reforms were further hindered when the Democrats seized control of Congress in 1910. Under Democratic control, a plan for monetary reform submitted by a Republican who had a reputation for colluding with the banking community had little hope. For many, including presidential candidate Woodrow Wilson in 1912, "the adoption of the Aldrich plan could mean only the perpetuation of existing Wall Street control."[49] For this reason, the Aldrich Plan was widely unpopular.[50] Therefore, without congressional or presidential support, Aldrich's efforts had little effect.

Banking reform received a second wind when Democrat Woodrow Wilson took office as president of the United States in March 1913. Having run on the Democratic platform that advocated these reforms, Wilson saw banking and currency matters as a priority, and the issue featured prominently in his campaign.[51] While outlining the planks for the Democratic Platform during the election, Wilson stated:

> We recognize the fact that our present banking system and our present system of currency are entirely inadequate to serve the great commercial and industrial operations of the country, either promptly or when most needed, and that their inadequacy subjects the country not only to constant serious inconvenience but also to a constant risk of disastrous financial disturbance and to recurrent panics. We favor, therefore, changes in the regulation and credit basis of our currency . . . and also changes in our banking laws, which

will govern the action of our banks in this matter in a common system of law and furnish the machinery by which the volume of currency may be adjusted with the greatest possible readiness.[52]

It was likely the prioritization of the issue by the Democratic Party, rather than by Wilson himself, that ensured movement on reform after years of near stagnation. Broz notes that Wilson made significant progress on banking reform "only after broad sections of societal support had been mobilized."[53]

Less than a month after election, on November 14, 1912, in a letter sent to Democratic US representative Carter Glass, Wilson reiterated his focus on currency and banking measures. He wrote, "The question of the revision of the currency is one of such capital importance that I wish to devote the most serious and immediate attention to it."[54]

In addition to a president who prioritized these measures, reform was further enabled by the fact that the Democratic Party controlled both the executive and legislative branches, thus clearing the path for the Democrats to create a reform bill able to navigate through the political channels necessary to ensure passage and make the legislation more palatable to the public.[55] Glass, the chairman of the House of Representatives Committee on Currency and Banking, consulted closely with Wilson on the issue and, with his support, presented a bill to the House of Representatives that eventually passed through both houses of Congress and became the Federal Reserve Act.[56] Glass writes that it "became increasingly necessary to carry the currency bill along for introduction as an 'administration measure,' for only thereby could we hope to succeed where so many others had utterly failed."[57]

It was Glass's role as legislator, backed by Wilson's leadership as president, that facilitated the passage of the act. Wilson applied support and pressure to the congressional effort when necessary, issued statements at the White House on currency measures, spoke regularly to the press, and held private conferences with bankers and opposing members of the Senate to help win support for the measure. Broz describes the role of the president as "limited to resolving remaining points of conflict" and questions the degree to which he "demonstrated independent initiative."[58] The efforts of Wilson during the passage of the act, whether independently driven or the result of the party agenda, were made at crucial moments and ultimately helped facilitate its passage.[59] Glass comments on an occasion when the president helped navigate through a difficult issue, arguing, "the determination of this dispute, threatening to wreck legislation, was but another of many instances in which the patience and purpose and firmness of President Wilson prevailed. . . . It represented months of thoughtful consideration and suggestion by Mr. Wilson on one hand and an inestimable amount of labour by the chairman [Glass] and the adviser of the chairman [Henry Parker

Willis]."[60] President Wilson signed the Federal Reserve Act into law on December 23, 1913, only nine months after he took office.[61] The speed and efficiency with which the Glass–Owen Bill, as it was called, was able to pass through both houses of Congress after five years of relative inaction demonstrates that strong executive leadership and legislative support played a key role in instituting the reforms that created the Federal Reserve, a public–private collaboration.[62]

The fact that the Federal Reserve Act was finally able to pass in 1913, six years after the panic of 1907, was the result of two key factors. First, banking reform was made a priority by the Democratic Party leading up to the presidential elections in 1912. This made the development of legislation a priority for Democratic members of the legislature as well as the newly elected Democratic president. Second, when the Democrats won control of Congress in 1910 and Wilson won the presidency in 1912, the aims of the legislative and executive branches were aligned and created an environment where legislation could successfully navigate through the necessary political channels. Wilson's role in the passage of the Federal Reserve Act was crucial, but passage would not have been possible without a political party controlling both the legislative and executive branches and strongly backing the reforms.

Private-Sector Leadership

While political leadership facilitated the technical creation of the cross-sector framework, the events surrounding the panic of 1907 illustrate that private-sector leaders also played an important role in the development of the Federal Reserve System. While the private sector took a back seat during the legislative process itself, they were hugely influential during the crisis, in the formation of legislation, and after the passage of the act.

The leadership of J. P. Morgan and the ability of the New York banking community to mobilize and act, independent of the US government, to save other financial institutions and the US economy during the panic of 1907 made two things very clear. First, it was a strong demonstration of the power held by private industry. While the private-sector response to the crisis clearly served the interests of the nation in this instance, the panic highlighted the sheer power that the private sector held. This made the government recognize the need to ensure that it could sustain authority and control over the national economy so that the interests of the people (rather than the profit-focused industrial sectors) drove national economic policy. As Kemmerer and Kemmerer argue, "That Morgan acted with considerable wisdom and contributed greatly to stopping the panic does not change the fact that the vast power he held over the welfare of his fellow men was not compatible with the principles of a democratic society."[63]

Second, private-sector action during the panic, at a time when the government was unsure of the appropriate response, demonstrated that the private sector should have a "seat at the table" to ensure that the government could be better prepared and respond more rapidly in the future. Additionally, including the private sector in the discussion was an effective way to harness private-sector resources so that a future response could be directed by the government and, thus, act in the interests of the people.

Private-sector leaders also made a significant contribution to the formulation of legislation. Although the private sector had little involvement in the legislative process itself, they exerted tremendous time, energy, and influence informing the drafting of the act. For example, Paul Warburg, an investment banker from the prestigious firm Kuhn, Loeb and Company, wrote and spoke extensively from 1907 to 1913 about his vision for a US central bank.[64] This included a proposal in 1910 for a "United Reserve Bank of the United States," a plan that advocated public and private representation.[65] While Warburg was not directly involved in the physical drafting of the Federal Reserve Act, he worked diligently to influence the debate about the legislation.[66] In congressional hearings held by the subcommittee of the Committee on Banking and Currency in the House of Representatives between January 8 and February 28, 1913, numerous private-sector business leaders from around the nation testified. In these thirteen hearings designed to inform Congress as they prepared to write the legislation that became the Federal Reserve Act, the private sector shared their views about the shape that banking reforms should take.[67] That these people were asked to testify prior to the development of any legislation underlines the degree to which Congress recognized the importance of the private-sector contribution and involvement with regard to these issues. Private-sector leadership, influence, and guidance was a key part of the process.

After the Federal Reserve Act became law in 1913, private-sector leadership again emerged as a critical factor. The success of the Fed was dependent upon the willingness of private-sector leaders to leave their lucrative positions in banking to join the Federal Reserve System where they could use their extensive industry knowledge (including their knowledge of the private sector's capabilities, contacts, and motivations) to benefit and stabilize the national economy. Fortunately, because the banking community saw the establishment of a US central banking structure as so critical to the successful conduct of business and they wanted to ensure that their (private-sector) voices were heard in the new central bank, private-sector leaders were willing to participate. Additionally, some private-sector executives who viewed themselves as industry experts were driven partially by patriotism to get involved in helping reshape the national economy and the platform on which it ran. In a speech made in 1915, Warburg spoke of a "sense of public duty" held by bankers and his belief that they were "animated by the motive of creating the broadest possible foundation for the development of a strong and united banking system in the United States."[68] While there can be little doubt that the primary motivation for private sector involvement in the Fed was to ensure economic stability in the furtherance of private-sector interests, patriotism also played a small role.

Political and private-sector leadership had a significant impact on the formation of the Fed. While political leadership was critical to the establishment of the framework on which the cross-sector partnership would operate, private-sector leadership underlined the importance of including private industry in national economic policy discussions on a long-term, permanent basis.

FORESIGHT AND FLEXIBILITY OF
THE ORGANIZATIONAL STRUCTURE

By 1912 the political environment changed and, with no other major panics since 1907, the sense of urgency to establish a cross-sector alliance ebbed. While a consensus remained that reform was necessary, there was a great deal of disagreement along party lines and, from the private sector in particular, about the shape those reforms should take.[69] Distance from the crisis further reduced the perceived urgency for cross-sector and cross-partisan cooperation. Party politics and industrial lobbies were heavily involved, and vehement debates took place about how the legislation should be written.[70]

There are three primary ways that the organizational structure of the Fed reveals the institutionalized "public–private character" of the system. First, the Fed is organizationally designed so that private-sector professionals are entwined into the leadership and body of the institution. The text of the act itself recognizes the importance of private involvement on the board. The act states the president should have "due regard for fair representation of the different commercial, industrial, and geographical divisions of the country."[71] This stipulation ensured that a range of private interests, not only banking, would be involved in the organization's decision-making.

Sentiments that the private sector should be involved in the Federal Reserve System did not wane in the years following the panic.[72] Shull succinctly describes the cross-sector alliance created as a result of the Federal Reserve Act and describes the private-sector role: "The system was shaped by contemporary concerns about providing a private organization with what, at the time, were viewed as substantial monetary powers. . . . The result was a joint venture affiliating the government with the banking community, characterized by decentralization and diversity."[73]

The private sector has a very definitive role in the Fed at both the national and regional levels. The Fed is composed of twelve regional reserve banks scattered throughout the country that are supervised by a central reserve in Washington, DC.[74] The central reserve is run by a board of governors and is responsible for monitoring and coordinating the actions of the regional banks.[75] Each position on the board is made by presidential appointment and confirmed by the US Senate.[76] While invariably these appointments can be politically motivated, terms last for fourteen years and are staggered so that one term expires every even-numbered year.[77] This helps to ensure that the appointees of a single president do not dominate the leadership of the central reserve. Section 10 of the Federal Reserve Act stipulates that the board of governors should be professionally, industrially, and geographically diverse, thereby ensuring a range of expertise and opinion.[78] The fact that President Wilson took this stipulation very seriously is reflected in his first appointments to the board of governors.[79]

The clear intent that the Fed should function as a public–private collaboration is further demonstrated by the leadership structure of the reserve banks. A committee of nine directors leads each regional reserve bank. Three of the directors represent bankers; three are from "commerce, agriculture, or some other industrial pursuit"; and the final three are from the public sector, with the general idea being that the directorate is equally composed of borrowers, lenders, and public representatives.[80] This structure ensures that the interests of the private and public sectors are represented but in so doing also creates a forum through which cross-sector communication and cooperation is facilitated.[81] Kemmerer and Kemmerer argue that two of the most noteworthy aspects of the Fed are its "democracy"—in that the votes of each reserve bank, regardless of size, are equal—and its "quasi-public nature."[82]

Second, in order to effectively manage public and private demands and expectations, the Fed is not controlled by the government but is "independent within the government."[83] This means that the Fed is neither a wholly private nor a wholly public entity. The Fed is not a private, profit-making institution. At the same time, the Fed is not controlled by government because Congress does not appropriate its funding, and decisions of the Fed do not have to be approved or ratified by the president, Congress, or anyone else within the government.[84] Despite being neither public nor private, the Fed must work within the guidelines of the Federal Reserve Act (and all subsequent amendments) and is subject to congressional oversight, "which periodically reviews its activities and can alter its responsibilities by statute" to ensure that its work is "within the framework of the overall objectives of economic and financial policy established by the government."[85]

Thus, the quasi-public nature of the Fed enables it to look after the interests of the business community while at the same time ensuring that monetary policies in the public interest are considered and represented. Rowe writes that creating a system such as this, that was an "amalgamation in the public interest of a number of quasi-independent bodies with banking, business, and public representation" all supervised and controlled by governmental appointees, was "as American as baseball."[86]

Third, the text of the original act was intentionally written to be vague, an organizational element of the legislation that has allowed the Fed to grow, adapt, and survive over time. "The Federal Reserve Act left many unanswered questions concerning the operation and management of the System and the specific approach to problems to which either the Federal Reserve Board or the Federal Reserve Banks, or both, should direct their attention."[87] The ambiguity made the legislation both politically expedient in the short term and practical for the long term. Politically speaking, a more general text was easier to pass through Congress because it kept legislative debate more philosophical in nature and away from minutiae (much of which had the potential to be controversial and slow to pass).[88]

While the framers of the legislation obviously recognized the political expediency of keeping the text of the act relatively broad, they were also aware that they, as legislators rather than finance experts, were not the most qualified to specify the operational intricacies of the Federal Reserve System. DeSaint Phalle argues that "the Federal Reserve Act only authorized the establishment of new institutions; it was purposely vague because of a conscious desire to make the system flexible and adaptable and because of the prevailing ignorance among both bankers and members of Congress about just what kind of a banking system the country needed."[89] Therefore, while political expediency was a factor, the vagueness of the act also served a very practical purpose in that it empowered the experts, those who would be working within the system, to play a key role in developing the specificities of how the system would function. The fact that these specificities were not included in the original legislation also made the organization able to grow and develop organically over time.

At the same time, the vagueness left questions about the strategic or responsive orientation of the institution and led the leaders of the first Federal Reserve Board to clarify the function of the organization less than six months after the founding of the Reserve. In the first annual report of the Reserve Board, the intended role of the Fed as a preemptive organization was clarified by saying that the Fed is "not to await emergencies but, by anticipation, to do what it can to prevent them."[90] The board felt it important to make this clarification so that the Fed was seen as more than an "emergency institution" that went into action when a financial panic threatened.[91] In other words, the early leaders of the organization clarified the aims of the institution as strategic (working proactively to avoid crisis) rather than responsive (working in response to individual crises).

The Fed continues to operate as a cross-sector partnership largely because of its organizational design. Rowe wrote in 1965 that "the retention of both private and public aspects in the Federal Reserve System during the past half century probably is the best testimonial to the contribution made by this type of management mix."[92] Nearly another half-century later, this assessment still holds true, supported by a framework that has institutionalized the roles of each sector and cemented their shared place in the decision-making process of the Fed.

DEVELOPING A PLATFORM TO SHARE INFORMATION AND RESERVES

Information sharing between sectors is critical to disaster-oriented PPPs. The ability of the sectors to communicate, cooperate, and share key information is an important resource thought to reduce the likelihood that a catastrophic disaster will occur. If a calamitous event does occur, successful information sharing may mitigate its impact by minimizing recovery time, thereby reducing panic, avoiding widespread crisis, and restoring normality as quickly as possible.

The founders of the Fed were equally concerned with panic and crisis avoidance. One of the fundamental ways they sought to mitigate or avoid future crises was to ensure that a platform was developed that allowed banks to share reserves so that, in the event of a run, banks could pool resources and keep troubled banks solvent while reassuring investors that their deposits were safe. The primary "information" that the organization dealt with was in the form of currency and reserves. The Fed provided an institutional platform on which the sectors could cooperate to share reserves in an effort to avoid panics and generate a sense of security in public. Therefore unlike disaster-oriented PPPs, where "information" is data or intelligence, the "information" the Fed shares is currency.

The perceived importance of a central reserve able to pool resources in times of crisis developed from the actions of clearinghouse associations in the United States. Clearinghouses developed in the nineteenth century and provided a platform that member banks could use, in exchange for a joining fee, to cash checks drawn from deposits held at other banks in their city.[93] After the financial crisis of 1857, the role of the clearinghouse adapted, and it became a lender of last resort for banks in trouble.[94] This meant the clearinghouses pooled the risk that any one bank would not be able to honor its checks and it issued clearinghouse certificates, which were a "kind of currency backed by all members of the clearing house."[95] Thus, clearinghouses provided a framework to link financial institutions and served an important role in preventing the spread of panic.[96]

The first clearinghouse association was established in 1853 in New York City, and by the 1880s most towns had a clearinghouse association.[97] A bank's membership in a clearinghouse was entirely voluntary, and the actions of the clearinghouse were not centrally controlled or regulated. In addition, "there was no uniformity to clearing-house organizations and practices; in some geographic areas, no clearing houses existed at all."[98] Thus, while they provided a valuable and necessary service, there was no standardized practice and membership was not inclusive of all financial institutions.[99]

The role of the clearinghouse during the panic of 1907 illustrates the value of the banking services provided by the clearinghouses and the ability of a clearinghouse to mitigate financial crisis in the event of a panic.[100] Although the clearinghouses were not able to avoid panic altogether, the New York Clearing House (NYCH) played an important role in trying to dampen its effect.[101] Largely because of these efforts, the panic of 1907 highlighted the importance of the reserve function provided by clearinghouse associations and made the creation of a national clearinghouse an essential aspect of new banking reforms.[102]

When runs on the Mercantile Bank occurred, Augustus Heinze appealed to the NYCH, of which Mercantile Bank was a member.[103] The clearinghouse conducted an audit of the bank, found it to be solvent, and issued a public statement to reassure and calm the public that Mercantile was safe.[104] Mercantile continued to survive the runs over the next few days based entirely on the support of the clearinghouse association.[105] Despite the work of the NYCH, panic ensued the following week when the bank runs spread to the Knickerbocker Trust Company, which was not a member of the clearinghouse.[106] The NYCH refused to support the Knickerbocker and, without access to a pool of reserves, the organization was decimated by bank runs.[107]

In the aftermath of the crisis, there was a widespread consensus that the clearinghouse function had very important benefits. It provided a mechanism through which banks could pool reserves to avoid bank collapses in the event of a run. What is more, this function had a very important side effect; the establishment of an institutional mechanism to avoid bank collapse increased public confidence in the banks and thereby reduced the likelihood of bank runs that generated mass panic.

At the same time, the panic demonstrated why the existing clearinghouse system in the United States, which was unregulated and entirely ad hoc, was simply not good enough. Bruner and Carr point out that clearinghouse associations failed to prevent the crisis because "they were voluntary (members could quit in a crisis), communication and information were limited, and incentives were perverse."[108] The United States needed a clearinghouse mechanism able to facilitate reserve sharing on a broad, national basis throughout the country, not on a localized, exclusive basis (whereby some financial institutions and localities did not have access to clearinghouse protections).

In addition, as lenders of last resort in times of emergency, the clearinghouses issued certificates to act as emergency currency.[109] Over time, certificates came to indicate "desperate, last-resort attempt[s] to address a deepening, systemic crisis."[110] The public had witnessed this trend numerous times, and the issuance of clearinghouse certificates eventually failed to have a positive impact and actually perpetuated a lack of confidence in the system. Therefore, in addition to being able to pool reserves, the United States also needed the ability to issue currency when necessary to service the needs of a fluctuating economy. This further underscored the pressing need to reform US banking practices and establish a national reserve.

The primary aims of the Federal Reserve Act, to "provide for the establishment of Federal reserve banks, to furnish an elastic currency, to afford means of rediscounting commercial paper, to establish a more effective supervision of banking in the United States," are all goals facilitated by the organization's adoption of a clearinghouse function.[111] The ability of the Federal Reserve System to facilitate the pooling of reserves among member banks was a cornerstone of the original act, and the clearinghouse function of the system continues to constitute one of the core functions of the regional banks. Clearinghouse functions are peppered throughout the Federal Reserve Act and can specifically be seen in sections 13, 16, and 18 of the legislation. These sections not only authorize regional banks to serve as clearing houses for member bank checks but also specify the balances member institutions are required to keep with the reserve banks.[112] Unlike previous clearinghouse associations, however, the act is inclusive among varying types of financial institution.[113] In this way, the Federal Reserve Act attempted to mitigate problems that arose in 1907 by ensuring that all kinds of financial institutions, including trust companies, could enjoy the protections of the reserve.

The Federal Reserve System, as a platform to facilitate reserve sharing between member banks, is noteworthy for two reasons. First, as a cross-sector alliance, the fact that the sectors could agree on a framework where they trusted the Fed to hold their reserves as part of the general "pool" to benefit the greater good of the banking community illustrates confidence in the system and a joint sense that reserve sharing is important. Second, reserve sharing also increases public confidence in the banking system by providing a mechanism to assure deposits will be safe, even in the event of a bank collapse. This increase in confidence reduces the risk of bank runs. Therefore, the reserve function provides the Fed the necessary tools to avoid financial crisis altogether by managing currency fluctuations, but in the event of a crisis occurring anyway, the organization is equipped to mitigate the impact through reserve sharing.

SHARED BENEFITS TO BOTH SECTORS AS A MOTIVATING FORCE

The fact that the public and private sectors perceived great personal benefit in cross-sector cooperation was a significant motivator for cooperation and is important to recognize when evaluating the Fed and exploring its formative years. At the time the Federal Reserve System was established, loss avoidance (rather than straightforward revenue generation) was a compelling motivation for private-sector participation.

Private-Sector Benefits

The private sector wanted to participate in a cross-sector partnership as a means of obtaining the stability it needed to successfully conduct business. In a letter to *The New York Times* on February 12, 1910, banker William Nash complained: "The most glaring deficiency in our banking system is the inability to act in emergencies as a harmonious whole. . . . What we need in a panic, or crisis, is an immediate and sufficient device to stop ruinous liquidation and enable necessary readjustment to proceed on deliberate lines."[114] The Fed is noteworthy in this regard because the banking system was in such turmoil that loss avoidance and stability were seen as crucial. Bankers were interested in the Fed as a safety mechanism that would avoid panic, enhance public trust, and generally create stability so that banks could flourish without the perpetual risk of economic collapse. The generation of revenue was not the first priority but something that would come after the partnership created the right (stable) economic conditions.

The crisis created during the panic of 1907 was so severe that the bankers became convinced that it was in their shared best interests to work together for the common good of the financial community as a whole. A run on one trust company or bank that resulted in collapse simply made them all more susceptible to a loss of confidence. The bankers pooled resources at critical moments of the panic to keep key institutions solvent during the most vicious turns of the panic.[115]

To view the involvement and interventions of the banking community during the panic of 1907 as some sort of philanthropy or patriotism would be naive. While undoubtedly many bankers were great patriots, they had a vested financial interest in ensuring the panic was resolved as rapidly as possible. They wanted an end to the crisis in the short term and governmental banking reform (although they hotly debated the shape that reform should take) in the long term because they recognized that this would strengthen stability, increase public confidence, reduce the volatility of the stock markets, and, ultimately, allow them to make more money.[116] Revenue generation was (and remains) a top priority for private interests. J. P. Morgan, the man often heralded as the private-sector leader who saved the country from collapse during the panic of 1907, saw the panic as an opportunity to make money. Morgan "saw the panic as a time for both statesmanship and personal gain. . . . He told friends that he had done enough and wanted some quid pro quo."[117] For Morgan, this came when President Roosevelt allowed him to orchestrate the takeover of Tennessee Coal and Iron by US Steel, a Morgan holding.[118]

The Fed, as an institutional, long-term mechanism designed to consider private-sector input while stabilizing the economy to allow the business of America to flourish, was an urgent necessity for private-sector interests. As a result of their vested interest in the reforms, from the panic of 1907 through to the enactment of legislation, the private sector played an active role in the development of the dialogue that led to the creation of the organization.[119] Because economic stability is, and will always be, beneficial to industry, the private sector continues to benefit from the partnership and is motivated to remain an active and engaged partner.

Public-Sector Benefits

The public sector also benefited from the Federal Reserve System. As an act of Congress, signed into law by the president of the United States, the Fed is designed to uphold the public interest. The Federal Reserve System provides a mechanism to assure the public that their deposits will be safe in banks, that the banking system itself is sound, and that, if anything goes wrong unexpectedly, the Fed (through mechanisms such as the Federal Deposit Insurance Corporation [FDIC] and the ability of banks to pool reserves in the event of a shortfall) will ensure that people's money will be safe and any crisis will be managed and promptly resolved. Economic stability, free from panic, is in the public interest. A stable economy with low unemployment and a sound banking system makes the public—and thereby the nation—more prosperous.

In defending the Federal Reserve Act on the Senate floor, Sen. James Reed acknowledged that both the private and public interests would benefit from the Federal Reserve System. He argued, "The truth of the matter is that this bill is intended to strengthen our banking system. The truth is the bill will probably benefit the banks by removing from them the great menace of panics and constriction. By removing this menace from the banks we remove it from the country."[120] Wilson also acknowledged the need to engage with the expertise of other sectors of society for the greater good of the nation. He said, "We cannot shut ourselves in as experts to our own business. We must open our thoughts to the country at large, and serve the general intelligence as well as the general welfare."[121]

As a result, both the private and public sectors benefit from their participation in the partnership. They need one another to be most effective and successful. Warburg described the partnership between the sectors: "You may say that this marriage between government and business is not wedlock based on love at first sight. . . . Inasmuch as they must live together, the only wise course is to pull together and let the common interest act as the strong bond uniting them."[122]

INSTITUTIONALIZING TRUST

> Panics are acute infections of the body economic by the germ
> distrust. Varying causes may bring about a crisis, which always
> precedes a panic, but the degeneration of a crisis into a panic is
> invariably an epidemic of distrust. Every modern financial system
> is built on confidence, on credit. Our whole financial structure has
> become a system of clearings of credit, a system of substituting the
> token of confidence for the payment in actual cash.
>
> Paul Warburg, *Federal Reserve System*, 165

Trust and confidence (or lack thereof) were critical in the development of the Federal Reserve System. The events of 1907 highlighted the tenuous relationship between panic, chaos, and trust. On October 23, 1907, the *Wall Street Journal* reported: "The worst and most dangerous feature in the view of Wall Street was the alarm among the public."[123] The need to mitigate this alarm and generate trust in the public about the stability of the banks was critical to the United States economy and a core factor in the creation of the Federal Reserve System.

Bank runs were the root cause of most of the financial turbulence of the period. The public did not believe in the soundness of the banking system and the Fed was intended to strengthen public confidence.[124] The Fed sought to increase trust by adopting a clearinghouse function that would offer national protection, making currency more elastic (thus ensuring adequate supplies of currency would be available during harvest times), and by institutionalizing depositors' insurance in the FDIC.[125] In addition, confidence in the Fed was further enhanced by the organizational construct of the system itself whereby Reserve Banks were intentionally situated across the country to focus on the interests of specific regions. This allayed fears that the New York bankers, the politicians in Washington, or some other group could wholly dictate policies that might not be in the public interest.

Over time the relationship between the Fed and Congress has further enhanced public confidence in the reserve system. Although the Fed is not controlled by Congress, standing orders require it to report to Congress. These reports have been a very effective tool to inform and reassure the public that the Fed is working to avoid financial downturns and attempting to act in the best interests of the country. In the event of an unforeseen incident that the Fed either cannot or somehow fails to control (as seen with the Great Depression and the aftermath of World War I), the public has seen the organization adapt and survive. The longevity of the institution and its capacity to develop and grow to avoid past mistakes also strengthens public trust because the public has seen (and believes) that the Fed has longevity, it will keep them informed, and, ultimately, it will resolve the problem.

The development of trust between public sector and private participants in the system also played a key role in the development and success of this cross-sector alliance. At the most basic level, the ability of the Fed to function is predicated on member banks trusting that their reserves will be just as safe on deposit with the Fed as they would in their own vaults.[126] The private sector had to have confidence that the Fed would clear checks in a timely manner, fairly represent the interests of banks across the country (taking into account their varying geographic needs and functions), and do what it promised in terms of economic stabilization.

In the early days of the Fed, cross-sector trust was assured through a mutual sense of urgency and further cemented through legislation and the institutionalization of the partnership. By establishing a "seat at the table" for private-sector representatives on the boards of the reserve banks, the private sector was assured that their interests would be represented and their views considered. The Fed was thus able to begin to create institutional trust because there was a framework in place to assure the private sector that it would have representation in the organization on a long-term and permanent basis. Because the Federal Reserve System has been functioning for so long, the issue of cross-sector trust has now been incorporated into the organization to such an extent that it is largely taken for granted and seen as part of the inherent and necessary makeup of the institution. Establishing a foundation of trust in the formative years of the Fed contributed to the sustainability of the public–private aspects of the organization in the long term.

ADAPTABILITY OR SUSTAINABILITY

The flexibility and vagueness of the Federal Reserve Act provided the institution with a built-in capacity to adapt and develop as operators within the system became more knowledgeable and experienced, and as demanded by the changing economic needs of the nation.[127] Two early instances in which the Fed adapted as a result of intense "economic distress" and expanded its powers demonstrate how the intentional vagueness of the act enabled the Fed to remain current and transform into an organization that some now argue is the most powerful institution in the United States.[128]

The first example illustrating the adaptation of the Fed occurred after World War I (1919–22). While the vagueness of the Federal Reserve Act afforded the system the opportunity to develop and grow, the lack of specificity also led to confusion in the early days of the system.[129] Following the enactment of the Federal Reserve Act, Wilson took a decidedly "back seat" approach to the Fed and communicated with it only through the Department of the Treasury. As Wilson explained to Glass, he "purposely refrained from contact with the Federal Reserve Board because he wanted the board to feel perfectly free to pursue its course within the law without a particle of constraint or restraint from the executive."[130] The unintended result of this "freedom" was that the Treasury gained greater control of the Fed. Treasury influence over the Fed manifested itself during World War I and in its aftermath.[131]

During the war, the United States economy flourished and the Fed focused its efforts on supporting the deficit financing of the Treasury Department.[132] A postwar recession ensued from the autumn of 1918 until February 1919 and was immediately followed by a postwar boom period of rapid expansion in 1919.[133] Although Fed officials felt that they were fueling the inflation by continuing policies they had adopted during the war, the Fed was prevented by the Treasury Department from taking action.[134] By the time the Fed took steps to curb the inflation, it was already too late and the economy was, once again, heading toward recession.[135]

The slow reaction time of the Fed and the feeling—particularly among hard-hit members of the agricultural sector—that it did "too little too late" to control inflation and avoid recession led to a strong attack on the Federal Reserve System.[136] The result of the outcry was a congressional committee whose hearings constituted the first official investigation of the Fed. A negative review by Congress could easily have resulted in the demise of the organization fewer than ten years after its inception.[137]

Clearly, the hearings did not result in the dissolution of the Fed. On the contrary, the outcome of the hearings actually strengthened the organization because it had proven itself during the war to be a "highly valued institution, whether its policies had been in error or not," despite its postwar mistakes.[138] Congress actively encouraged the Federal Reserve System to break away from the authority of the Treasury. The organization of the institution was left unchanged and, as Shull points out, "these outcomes made clear that here was no congressional inclination to alter the System in any way and suggest, at the least, a modest expansion of System independence."[139] Thus, the Fed, through trial and error, began to learn from its mistakes and adapt to better serve national needs.

A second example that demonstrates the adaptability of the organization occurred in the aftermath of the Great Depression (1929–35), when what are arguably the most significant changes ever were made to the organization. These modifications were instituted in the banking acts of 1933 and 1935, the first major revisions to the Federal Reserve Act since 1913.[140] As with the adaptations that occurred following World War I, the changes in this period were the result of an economic crisis that highlighted shortfalls in the system and mistakes on the part of the Fed operators, and that placed the organization under heavy criticism and scrutiny. Once again, however, the Fed survived the storm and emerged with greater powers and more specific delineations of control.

The banking acts of 1933 and 1935 were the result of a series of events that culminated in a catastrophic US stock market crash in 1929.[141] The Fed failed to respond rapidly enough to ensure that banks had adequate reserves on hand, runs on the banks ensued, and the United States "entered the most serious economic depression in its history" accompanied by high levels of unemployment.[142] Nearly five thousand banks failed from 1930 to 1932, and states began issuing extended "bank holidays" to try to mitigate the damage.[143] Kemmerer and Kemmerer argue that the Fed was not able to mobilize reserves in time to mitigate the panic because "there was one situation that the founders of the reserve System had not provided for, and that the Reserve Banks were powerless to remedy. This was a general loss of confidence in the banks of the United States."[144]

There was little doubt that banking reform was, once again, an urgent necessity. The Fed, if it was to continue to survive, had to have the necessary authority to act and respond in situations such as those leading up to the Great Depression. The Banking Act of 1933 made several changes to the system that were designed to give it the centralization of authority to do just that. Arguably the most important aspect of the 1933 legislation was the establishment of the FDIC, which was designed to enhance public confidence in the system by insuring deposits held at member banks.[145] Additionally, the act stipulated that banks had to be either commercial banks or investment banks, but not both. It also legalized the Federal Open Market Committee (FOMC). This was significant because it limited the ability of reserve banks to pursue independent policies without the oversight and permission of the Reserve Board.[146] A dominant aim of the legislation, drafted largely by Sen. Carter Glass, was to increase the autonomy of the Federal Reserve System by limiting the control of the Treasury Department and the New York Reserve Bank.[147]

The power of the New York Federal Reserve over the rest of the reserve banks and the central reserve was demonstrated during World War I when the head of the New York Reserve, Benjamin Strong, worked directly with US Treasury Secretary William Gibbs McAdoo to double money supply and virtually finance the war effort. Murray Rothbard describes Strong and the New York Fed as "the dominant force in American finance" after World War I.[148] Shull comments that Strong's power came gradually and says that there was a shift in power in the early years of the Fed "from the Board to the Reserve Banks and, among the Reserve Banks, to the Federal Reserve Bank of New York. Then, within the Federal Reserve Bank of New York, the power shifted to Strong, seen as a member of J. P. Morgan's inner circle."[149] Benjamin Strong, a protégé of J. P. Morgan, was the governor of the New York Federal Reserve Bank for most of the 1920s. Kemmerer and Kemmerer describe his power over Washington, saying, "He had more influence than the chairman of the Federal Reserve Board."[150]

The Banking Act of 1935 further centralized the control of the board away from the reserve banks by increasing the power of the board over bank presidents and ensuring that the board was led by the governor in Washington, not the presidents of the reserve banks.[151] The 1935 act further clarified that Congress wanted an even greater distance between the Fed and the Treasury Department by eliminating the secretary of the treasury and comptroller of the currency from the board of governors (both had served as ex officio members of the board as per the original 1913 Act).[152] The act also made the FDIC permanent, liberalized the authority of the board to alter reserve requirements as it saw fit, and specified the rules and functions of the FOMC.[153]

Since the institution of the FDIC, bank failures and the danger of bank runs have been significantly reduced.[154] In the event of a collapse, the FDIC absorbs part of the losses, encourages mergers of failing banks into stronger banks, and transfers depositors' insured funds from one insured bank to another. Additionally, legislation clarified the roles of the reserve banks and the Reserve Board, thereby eliminating the power struggles that had been taking place in the early years of the Fed as the New York Reserve, in particular, sought to wrest control of the organization.

Organizational adaptability was demonstrated in the banking acts of 1933 and 1935 because when the organization fell short there was sufficient space, as a result of the intentional vagueness of the original legislation, for Congress to provide the Fed with the tools necessary to move forward and avoid similar situations in the future. It would have been difficult, if not impossible, for the founders of the Fed to imagine in 1913, with panic avoidance and currency elasticity as their primary focus, that the organization would be engaged with a turf war with the Treasury Department, that power struggles between the central board and the regional reserve banks would make institutionalized centralization of power a priority, or that open market operations would be managed by the Fed. The Fed adapted as dictated by the needs of the economy and of the organization as it grew and developed. "Independent observers have identified behavioral adjustments of the Federal Reserve made in the early 1920s, the 1930s and the 1980s that were critical to its survival."[155] Adaptability made, and continues to make, the Fed current, applicable, and able to adjust if or when institutional shortcomings are exposed because of changes in the economy or by unforeseen circumstances. As Shull argues, "Adaptation has been the way in which the Federal Reserve has navigated through troubled waters."[156]

The Fed has been able to achieve organizational and institutional sustainability. This is most simply demonstrated in the fact that the system is rapidly approaching its centennial anniversary. The key factors that have contributed to the organization's ability to survive lie in the organizational framework of the institution, its ability to adapt, the development and maintenance of institutional trust between the sectors as well as with the public, and the fact that it continues to be in the best interest of both parties to participate in the alliance. Each of these factors ultimately underlines the strategic makeup of the Federal Reserve System. Sustainability—the ability of the organization to last for the long term—is crucial in a strategic organization that must be forward-looking and proactive.

TABLE 3.1: Summary of the Seven Critical Factors in the Federal Reserve System

Critical Factors	Key Elements of Public–Private Cooperation in the Development and Establishment of the Federal Reserve
Crisis	The panic of 1907 was the motivator for the establishment of the Federal Reserve Act. Although the banking system had been in ruin for decades and runs on the bank occurred throughout the late 1800s, it took a large-scale, devastating, economic panic to sufficiently prioritize the need for reform in the public and private sectors.
Leadership	Once the sectors agreed at the most basic level that cooperation was imperative, the interest, involvement, and support of the president of the United States, backed by Congress and his political party, was pivotal in the formulation and successful passage of legislation. It took political leadership, on a practical level, to successfully guide

continued

TABLE 3.1: Summary of the Seven Critical Factors in the Federal Reserve System (continued)

Critical Factors	Key Elements of Public–Private Cooperation in the Development and Establishment of the Federal Reserve
Leadership (continued)	legislation through the necessary legislative channels. At the same time, private-sector leadership enabled the United States to survive the crisis and helped legislators shape the system.
Organizational Structure	The organizational structure of the Fed, as a quasi-public institution, crystallized the role of the private sector in the organization. This served to ensure the ongoing role of both sectors in the Fed. In addition, the fact that the legislation was intentionally vague allowed the organization to develop, grow, and remain current as the global economic environment and the nation's needs changed.
Information (Reserve) Sharing	One key aim of the Fed was to establish a clearinghouse to share reserves and to prevent bank runs. The Fed adopted and adapted the localized clearinghouse system and applied it on a national scale. The Fed made reserve sharing geographically and industrially inclusive as well as sufficiently broad in scope by creating a centralized national platform for sharing reserves.
Shared Benefits	An intangible factor that has influenced the Federal Reserve from the development of the organization to the present is the fact that both the public and private sectors benefit by participating in the partnership. During times of crisis and times of economic prosperity, the sectors have continued to partner largely because the overall aim of the organization (economic stability) remains a priority to both sectors.
Trust	Public trust and cross-sector trust are important elements of the Fed. Public trust maintains financial stability, avoids panics that result in crisis, and allows the financial sector to succeed. Cross-sector trust ensures cooperation between sectors continues. Both forms of trust were facilitated through the Fed because it established an institutional framework that specified and legally cemented a role for each sector.
Adaptability/ Sustainability	The Fed is neither a perfectly designed nor a perfectly developed organizational framework. From inception in 1913, the Fed has been challenged, pressured, and criticized. It has, however, survived because of its ability to adapt and learn from past mistakes. Adaptability permitted the organization to centralize its authority when necessary, and to end power struggles and turf wars that threatened to undermine the institution. Its ongoing operation signifies that it has been deemed a valuable tool to facilitate cross-sector cooperation for the benefit of the US economy.

CONCLUSION

The Fed was created in 1913 as a cross-sector partnership designed to reform banking in the United States. While the Fed was created to accomplish a very different goal from the type of partnership that is the focus of this research, exploring the organization in terms that are relevant to disaster-oriented PPPs informs our understanding of some of the core attributes that have influenced large, national policy–oriented, strategic partnerships of the past. Crisis, leadership, organizational structure, information sharing, shared benefits, trust, and adaptability or sustainability were also important issues during the founding of the Federal Reserve. By exploring the Fed in terms of these seven critical factors, it becomes clear that the Fed may provide historical precedent that is useful when applied to struggles faced by disaster-oriented PPPs.

The Federal Reserve Act did not provide an instantaneous "quick fix" to America's financial problems. While runs on the bank abated, the nation suffered severe economic stress after World War I and as a result of the Great Depression. This form of institutionalized partnership, therefore, should not be seen as an instant short-term solution but as a long-term mechanism able to adapt, strengthen, and grow over time to meet national needs. The Fed today is a much stronger, more powerful, institution than the Fed of 1913.

The Fed is a strategically oriented organization that intends not only to respond to economic crises but also to act preemptively to avoid crisis altogether. While this has been the organization's intent, the Fed has often struggled to do more than simply react. In an ideal world, the Fed would do both, and perhaps as it continues to adapt it will eventually succeed.

Crises, power struggles, political pressures, and divergent opinions about the shape that currency reform should take plagued policymakers in the early twentieth century. These are very similar to the challenges faced by policymakers today. Before determining what lessons the Fed, as a strategic alliance, can provide to current policymakers, the next chapter looks at the War Industries Board to understand how a responsive historical partnership functions against the seven "critical factors" assessed in this chapter. A comparison of the two case studies can determine what practices or lessons, if any, may be applicable to today's disaster-oriented PPPs.

NOTES

1. Rowe, *Public–Private Character*, 178.
2. Quoted in Glass, *Adventure in Constructive Finance*, 220.

3. Numerous unpublished letters from the private sector to Congress in 1907–8 urge immediate action to prevent another widespread crisis. See H.R. Comm. on Approp.—Comm. on Banking and Currency, HR60A-H3.10.H4.1.

4. Wiebe, *Search for Order*, 201.

5. Bruner and Carr, *Panic of 1907*, 2–3. The authors argue that this context includes the impacts of the San Francisco earthquake in 1906, the presidency of a "Republican moralist," societal change driven by immigration and technology, and changes in banking whereby mergers and acquisitions were creating new ways of approaching business. The authors further point to a more interventionist and intrusive government and a poor public opinion of business leaders that was "fueled by a muckraking press." See also deSaint Phalle, *Federal Reserve*, 46–47.

6. For more on these early banks, see Rothbard, *History of Money and Banking*, 62–90; Rowe, *Public–Private Character*, 8–25; and Kemmerer and Kemmerer, *ABC of the Federal Reserve*, 3–10.

7. Moore, *Federal Reserve*, 3–4.

8. See ibid., 4; and Rothbard, *History of Money and Banking*, 78–79, 122–32.

9. Moore, *Federal Reserve*, 4; and Bruner and Carr, *Panic of 1907*, 2–3.

10. Chernow, *House of Morgan*, 124.

11. Bruner and Carr, *Panic of 1907*, 2.

12. Heinze was also on the board of directors of at least eight other banks and two trust companies. The New York Clearing House forced his resignation from all of these after the runs on the Mercantile Bank. Heinze's close business associate, Charles W. Morse, was also forced to resign (because of his close relationship with Heinze) from seven financial institutions. Bruner and Carr, *Panic of 1907*, 62–63; and Shull, *Fourth Branch*, 30.

13. Runs on the Mercantile Bank occurred on October 16, 1907. Heinze was forced to resign from Mercantile on October 17, 1907. See Shull, *Fourth Branch*, 30; and Bruner and Carr, *Panic of 1907*, 64.

14. In 1907 Knickerbocker Trust Company was the third-largest trust company in New York City with nearly eighteen thousand depositors and more than $65 million on deposit. See Bruner and Carr, *Panic of 1907*, 65, 68.

15. The run on the Knickerbocker Trust Company began on October 17, 1907, and increased in severity on October 21 after links were established between Heinze and the president of Knickerbocker Trust Company, Charles Barney. Less than one month later, Barney, forced to resign on October 21, committed suicide in his New York City home. The "trust company" differed slightly from a bank and was a new form of "financial intermediary" that was growing in popularity during the period. While trust companies functioned very similarly to banks, they were less regulated and were able to hold a wider variety of assets than banks. Importantly, trust companies did not enjoy protection from the clearinghouse system that was dominated by large banks, which disliked this form of institution although the larger trust companies created their own small clearinghouses for themselves. See ibid., ix–xi, 66–67.

16. Ibid., 80–81.

17. "It appeared that the runs on the trust companies were not limited to the Knickerbocker. In particular the president of the Trust Company of America told [J. P. Morgan and his associates] he was 'desperately anxious' because the withdrawals from his company on Tuesday had been exceptionally heavy." Ibid., 85–86. An excellent timeline of the panic of 1907 from mid-October to November 6, 1907, can be found in Shull, *Fourth Branch*, 30–32.

18. Bruner and Carr, *Panic of 1907*, 78–79.

19. Ibid., 141–42, 151.

20. Ibid., 151.

21. Because of the power wielded by J. P. Morgan at the time of the panic, heads of institutions on the brink of collapse sought him out for help. In meeting with these individuals, Morgan would then collect a coalition of trust company presidents (if a trust company was in question) or bank presidents to develop a way to pool resources and lend funds to institutions to ensure they would not collapse as a result of a bank run or panic. The Trust Company of America was saved by a trust company–based coalition of businessmen led by Morgan on October 23, 25, and November 2, 1907. The New York Stock Exchange was saved by a coalition of bankers led by Morgan on October 24, 1907. The City of New York was rescued by Morgan himself through a purchase by J. P. Morgan & Co. of $30 million in the city's revenue bonds on October 28, 1907. The brokerage firm Moore and Schley was also bailed out thanks to the New York bankers. Finally, a deal orchestrated by Morgan (and approved by President Roosevelt on November 4, 1907) whereby Tennessee Coal & Iron (TC&I) was acquired by US Steel saved numerous brokerages, banks, and trust companies from financial ruin. Thibaut deSaint Phalle credits Morgan alone for resolving the panic. He writes, "The trigger [of a change in thinking on banking matters] was the panic of 1907 where, strange as it may seem, the financial wellbeing of the country was saved by the confidence and dexterity of one man: J.P. Morgan"; deSaint Phalle, *Federal Reserve*, 46. For more information about these events, see Bruner and Carr, *Panic of 1907*, 92, 99–103, 111–12, 115–19, 131–33.

22. On November 2, 1907, J. P. Morgan invited all the presidents of the trust companies to his home for a third bailout of the Trust Company of America. To ensure that no one left before a resolution was reached, Morgan locked the door to the room, reportedly keeping the key in his pocket until they agreed upon a $25 million plan to save the company. Bruner and Carr, *Panic of 1907*, 124.

23. Kemmerer and Kemmerer, *ABC of the Federal Reserve*, 32.

24. Bruner and Carr, *Panic of 1907*, 151.

25. Warburg, *Federal Reserve System*, 29.

26. After the run on the Knickerbocker Trust, Morgan summoned Secretary of the Treasury George B. Cortelyou for a summit on October 22, 1907. Morgan also arranged an emergency meeting with President Roosevelt and his delegates to ensure the administration would not attempt to interfere with the deal they had brokered to ensure that US Steel would be bought by TC&I, an acquisition that would save numerous financial institutions from collapse. For more on the acquisition, see Bruner and Carr, *Panic of 1907*, 84–86, 131–33.

27. Kemmerer and Kemmerer, *ABC of the Federal Reserve*, 32.

28. Glass, *Adventure in Constructive Finance*, 64.

29. Most importantly, this included allowing currency associations to issue emergency currency backed by commercial paper to allow an element of elasticity in currency flow. For more on emergency currency, see deSaint Phalle, *Federal Reserve*, 48. New York executive and veteran banker William Nash publicly expressed his skepticism about the emergency bill in the *New York Times* on February 10, 1912, saying, "I look with dread at the day when our existing academic emergency currency laws [Aldrich–Vreeland Act of 1908] are applied to for relief. People will have to be educated to believe in them, and there is not time for education in a panic." Quoted in Laughlin, *Federal Reserve Act*, 9.

30. J. Lawrence Broz writes that the National Monetary Commission was an "investigative body with the express mandate to study both domestic and foreign financial structures. . . . Since none of the eighteen politicians on the commission had practical banking experience in such matters, private actors were relied upon to organize the investigations and to recommend institutional changes." The commission published twenty-three volumes of analysis on the financial systems of foreign governments, constituting the most formalized study ever conducted on international monetary systems on January 11, 1911. Senator Nelson Aldrich, the coauthor of the 1908 Aldrich–Vreeland emergency measure and the head of the commission, drafted the Aldrich Plan based on the commission's findings. After the introduction of the Aldrich Plan in 1911, it was soon clear that much further work was necessary to secure passage of the act. This failed to occur, and the Aldrich Plan was replaced by the Glass–Owen Act as "the" banking and currency legislation in 1913. See Broz, *International Origins of the Federal Reserve*, 173–85; deSaint Phalle, *Federal Reserve*, 48–49; Rothbard, *History of Money and Banking*, 257; Bruner and Carr, *Panic of 1907*, 145–47.

31. Glass, *Adventure in Constructive Finance*, 64.

32. The government needed a mechanism to adjust cash flow into the economy to account for fluctuations that occurred during harvest season, when banks needed greater cash reserves to respond to increased demands as crops were bought and sold, and nonharvest times, when the lack of crops created less demand for cash in circulation. See Bruner and Carr, *Panic of 1907*, 50; deSaint Phalle, *Federal Reserve*, 54; and Rothbard, *History of Money and Banking*, 240–43.

33. Paul Warburg summarized the most critical aims of the Fed in a 1915 address: "The member banks and the businessmen of the United States will thus derive the greatest benefits from the Federal Reserve System by, first, the safety from acute panics of the old familiar kind, and, second, the greater ability of the member banks to uninterruptedly extend legitimate commercial credit facilities at reasonable and fairly stable rates." Warburg, *Federal Reserve System*, 338.

34. "In New York City and other major financial centers, many traditional banks had formed associations through which its members would pay cash, or 'clear,' in exchange for any checks submitted by other member banks. . . . It would serve as a lender of last resort in the event of any financial emergencies. In effect, the clearing houses would essentially pool the risk that any individual member would not be able to honor

THE FEDERAL RESERVE, A STRATEGIC ALLIANCE · 121

individual checks. In such cases the clearing house would issue 'clearing house certificates,' a kind of currency backed by all members of the clearing house. There was no uniformity to clearing house organizations and practices; in some geographic areas, no clearing houses existed at all." Bruner and Carr, *Panic of 1907*, 59.

35. Ibid., 59. Lawrence J. Laughlin, an academic from the University of Chicago and the chairman of the National Citizens League for the Promotion of a Sound Banking System, advocated the importance of a clearinghouse feature. He says, "The situation of 1907 brought clearly to the front that our reform must supply the essentials of what was provided by the clearing house in granting a means of payment by clearing-house certificates. All other schemes must be makeshifts." Laughlin, *Federal Reserve Act*, 4.

36. Kemmerer and Kemmerer acknowledge the role Morgan played in the crisis but argue that he may have had the ability to wield too much power. They argue, "That Morgan acted with considerable wisdom and contributed greatly to stopping the panic does not change the fact that the vast power he held over the welfare of his fellow men was not compatible with the principles of a democratic society." Kemmerer and Kemmerer, *ABC of the Federal Reserve*, 32. For more about the "money trust," see Bruner and Carr, *Panic of 1907*, 148.

37. This sentiment is reflected in the democratic platform for the presidential elections of 1912. Woodrow Wilson said to the Democratic rallies in 1912 that "currency and banking questions must be discussed and settled in the interests of those who use credit, produce the crops, manufacture the goods, and quicken the commerce of the nation, rather than in the interest of the banker and the promoter and the captain of finance, who if set off by themselves in the management of such things too easily lose sight even of their own intimate and inseparable relation to the general needs and interests of the rank and file." Link, *Papers of Woodrow Wilson*, 25: 502.

38. Glass, *Adventure in Constructive Finance*, 236.

39. Broz, *International Origins of the Federal Reserve*, 166.

40. In 1910 the *New York Times* reported that "President Taft advocates a still further extension of the principles of impartial scientific study by experts before any legislation is undertaken." Taft is quoted as saying, "A comparison of the business methods and institutions of our powerful and successful business rivals with our own is sure to be of immense value. I urge upon Congress the importance of a non-partisan and disinterested study and consideration of our banking and currency system." *New York Times*, "Taft's Message Asks for Little," December 7, 1910.

41. The following texts are examples of works that explore currency and banking reforms between 1907 and 1912 and that either fail to mention President Taft or that mention him very briefly: Broz, *International Origins of the Federal Reserve*; Livingston, *Origins of the Federal Reserve*; Rothbard, *History of Money and Banking*; Rowe, *Public–Private Character*; and Shull, *Fourth Branch*.

42. Pringle, *Life and Times of William Howard Taft*, 167.

43. Broz, *International Origins of the Federal Reserve*, 174–76.

44. The Aldrich Plan was the result of the findings of the National Monetary Commission and was drafted following a set of secret, week-long meetings at Jekyll Island, Georgia. The meeting was attended by Aldrich and the nation's foremost elite bankers

including Paul Warburg; Henry Davison of J. P. Morgan; Frank A. Vanderlip of National City Bank of New York; and A. Piatt Andrew, the assistant secretary of the Treasury. While some contend that the Jekyll Island meeting and the resulting Aldrich Plan was the backbone of what became the Federal Reserve (see Bruner and Carr, *Panic of 1907*, 145–46), Carter Glass—the author of the Federal Reserve Act—and others strongly disagree, saying that the Aldrich Plan was written "by bankers for bankers," and the structural suggestions for an institution were commonly agreed knowledge. Glass states, "Some of the essential ideas of the Federal Reserve Act had been, in different guise, considered and discussed long before either the Aldrich Plan or the Federal Reserve Act was projected. . . . So manifestly dangerous and contrary to the genius of democratic institutions was the Aldrich scheme of monetary reform that the Republican party, with President Taft as its leader, failed to accept it; the Democratic party, with Woodrow Wilson for its nominee, openly rejected it, and the Progressive party . . . denounced it. . . . Not a member of either House of the Congress ventured to propose the Aldrich bill as a substitute for the federal reserve bill"; Glass, *Adventure in Constructive Finance*, 240–41. See also Rothbard, *History of Money and Banking*, 252–54; and Broz, *International Origins of the Federal Reserve*, 183–84.

45. Link, *Woodrow Wilson and the Progressive Era*, 44.

46. A congressional investigation called the "Pujo hearings" occurred in 1912 as a result of fear that a so-called money trust was funneling money to a few elite private-sector businessmen who would use these funds to "control the country." The aims of the Pujo hearings were to "determine the existence of a 'money trust,' a financial analogue to the large industrial trusts—like Standard Oil—that had been formed in the late nineteenth century." J. P. Morgan testified in the Pujo hearings. No substantial evidence was found during the hearings against the business community indicating collusion among financiers. See Bruner and Carr, *Panic of 1907*, 148.

47. Shull, *Fourth Branch*, 42–43. In addition to Aldrich's close work with many private-sector bankers on currency issues, he was also the son-in-law of John D. Rockefeller, one of the most powerful (and some argue most hated) men in America at the time. This further served to undermine his legislation. See Kemmerer and Kemmerer, *ABC of the Federal Reserve*, 33. The ties between presidents Roosevelt and Taft to major financial industrial groups at the time are outlined in Rothbard, *History of Money and Banking*, 263.

48. Broz writes of the negative sentiments toward the Aldrich Plan. He says, "The Aldrich Plan became the subject of a slow, creeping, deadly hostility. Neither party would have anything of it, nor does any politician seeking votes dare to speak a good word for it. President Taft, a previous backer of the Aldrich plan, had his treasury secretary announce that reporters had 'misquoted' his earlier statements of support"; Broz, *International Origins of the Federal Reserve*, 192.

49. Link, *Woodrow Wilson and the Progressive Era*, 45.

50. "The Aldrich bill for a national reserve association proved to be a lightning rod for the opposition that saw it as the product of the 'money trust'"; Shull, *Fourth Branch*, 41–43. See also Rothbard, *History of Money and Banking*, 254.

51. See Woodrow Wilson election speeches during 1912 in preparation for the presidential elections, Link, *Papers of Woodrow Wilson*, 25: 14, 203, 343, 478–79, 502.

52. Ibid., 25: 478.

53. Broz, *International Origins of the Federal Reserve*, 167.

54. Quoted in Glass, *Adventure in Constructive Finance*, 75.

55. Rothbard, *History of Money and Banking*, 257; Bruner and Carr, *Panic of 1907*, 146.

56. Glass began reaching out to Wilson regarding banking and currency reform immediately after the election. The pair communicated regularly while Glass drafted the legislation and sought its passage through the House. For instances of interaction between Glass and Wilson to discuss the act, see Glass, *Adventure in Constructive Finance*, 75, 83–89, 105, 113–17, 131–32, 141, 167, 227–33.

57. Ibid., 112.

58. Broz, *International Origins of the Federal Reserve*, 167.

59. Link discusses the role Wilson took in swaying opposition to the bill. He says, "By the middle of June [1913] it was plain the controversy would continue for months unless [Wilson] could find a workable compromise and reconcile the opposing factions." Link, *Woodrow Wilson and the Progressive Era*, 47; For press statements, see Link, *Papers of Woodrow Wilson*, 27: 150–51, 351, 364–65, 378–79, 558–64. For more on Wilson gaining support of the private sector and Congress, see Glass, *Adventure in Constructive Finance*, 112–26, 141, 196; and Link, *Woodrow Wilson and the Progressive Era*, 47–49, 150–51.

60. Glass, *Adventure in Constructive Finance*, 126.

61. Ibid., 227. Wilson was inaugurated as president of the United States on March 4, 1913.

62. This is not to imply that the passage of the legislation was in any way easy. Livingston describes the legislative processes that resulted in the Federal Reserve Act as "insanely complicated struggles over the various drafts of banking legislation." Livingston, *Origins of the Federal Reserve*, 215.

63. Kemmerer and Kemmerer, *ABC of the Federal Reserve*, 32.

64. For more on the work of Warburg during this period, see Warburg, *Federal Reserve System*.

65. Rowe, *Public–Private Character*, 52–53.

66. See Warburg, *Federal Reserve System*.

67. H.R., "Banking and Currency Reform Hearings, pt. 1–13," HR62A-F2.1 to F2.3.

68. Warburg, *Federal Reserve System*, 313.

69. Link, *Papers of Woodrow Wilson*, 25: 343. See also H.R., "Banking and Currency Reform Hearings, pt. 1–13," HR62A-F2.1 to F2.3.

70. For specific private-sector viewpoints about how legislation should be written, see the testimony of James E. Furgeson (president of Temple State Bank, Temple, Texas) on January 14, 1913, Part 4, 239–73; and Edmund D. Fisher (deputy comptroller of City of New York) on January 15, 1913, Part 5, 322–35, both in H.R., "Banking and Currency Reform Hearings, pt. 1–13," HR62A-F2.1 to F2.3.

71. Federal Reserve Act of 1913, Pub. L. No. 63-43, 38 Stat. 251 (1913).

72. Although the Federal Reserve Act was signed on December 23, 1913, it did not come into effect until November 1914. See Wells, *Federal Reserve System*, 21.

73. Shull, *Fourth Branch*, 60.

74. The twelve Federal Reserve Banks are located in Boston, New York, Philadelphia, Richmond, Cleveland, Atlanta, Chicago, St. Louis, Minneapolis, Kansas City, Dallas, and San Francisco. Board of Governors, *Federal Reserve System*, 8.

75. The board of governors was originally called the Federal Reserve Board. The name of the board was officially changed in the 1935 Banking Act to the "Board of Governors of the Federal Reserve System." I refer to them by their contemporary name or simply as the "board."

76. Board of Governors, *Federal Reserve System*, 4.

77. Federal Reserve Board, "Frequently Asked Questions: Board of Governors." www.federalreserve.gov/faqs/faq.htm.

78. Shull, *Fourth Branch*, 49.

79. The desire for diversity in the Federal Reserve Board of Governors is reflected in Wilson's first appointees, who included William P. G. Harding (banker from Alabama), Frederic A. Delano (president of Chicago, Indianapolis, and Louisville Railroad), Adolph Miller (economist from the University of California), and Paul Warburg (New York banker and central banking expert). Wells, *Federal Reserve*, 26.

80. Bankers are known as "class A" directors, commercial representatives are known as "class B" directors, and the public-sector representatives are known as "class C" directors. Class A and B directors are selected by the member banks of each individual reserve district. Class C directors are appointed by the board of governors in Washington. The chairman and deputy chairman are chosen from the class C directors by the board of governors in Washington. For more on classifications of appointees, see Shull, *Fourth Branch*, 50; Kemmerer and Kemmerer, *ABC of the Federal Reserve*, 29; and Board of Governors, *Federal Reserve System*, 11.

81. Rowe writes that the major private aspects of the Fed are "the inclusion of member-bank-elected directors on the boards of the Reserve Banks, the compulsory stock subscriptions required of member banks, and some modest flexibility in the management of the System's internal operations." Rowe, *Public–Private Character*, 177.

82. Kemmerer and Kemmerer, *ABC of the Federal Reserve*, 28.

83. The board of governors refer to the Fed as "independent within the government" in its overview of the organization. Board of Governors, *Federal Reserve System*, 3.

84. Federal Reserve Board, "Who Owns the Federal Reserve?" 2007, www.federalreserve.gov/faqs/about_14986.htm.

85. Ibid.

86. Rowe, *Public–Private Character*, 65.

87. Ibid., 67.

88. Laughlin comments that in writing the Act, "his [Glass's] point mainly was to get a measure so drawn that it would not antagonize the Democratic platform or call up objections." Laughlin, *Federal Reserve Act*, 115.

89. deSaint Phalle, *Federal Reserve*, 60.

90. Board of Governors, *Annual Report*, 1915, quoted in Meltzer, *History of the Federal Reserve*, 132.

91. Shull, *Fourth Branch*, 166–67.

92. Rowe, *Public–Private Character*, 176–77.

93. Shull, *Fourth Branch*, 26–27; and Bruner and Carr, *Panic of 1907*, 59.

94. Shull, *Fourth Branch*, 27.

95. Bruner and Carr, *Panic of 1907*, 9. Clearinghouse certificates were used in every financial crisis until the Federal Reserve Act. See Shull, *Fourth Branch*, 27.

96. Bruner and Carr, *Panic of 1907*, 154.

97. Shull, *Fourth Branch*, 27.

98. Bruner and Carr, *Panic of 1907*, 59.

99. Trust companies, for example, were not included in clearinghouse associations because the bankers did not trust this type of financial institution. Ibid., 66–67.

100. Several private-sector bankers discussed the importance of clearinghouses in the avoidance of panic when testifying before Congress in early 1913. S. M. Wilhite, of Louisville, Kentucky, testified before the subcommittee of the Committee on Banking and Currency representing the National Association of Comptrollers on January 15, 1913. In his testimony, Wilhite advocates the importance of clearinghouses in small cities. He also points out that the NYCH did not help small banks in small cities during the panic. In addition, prominent banker and former head of the NYCH William A. Nash used his time before the subcommittee to advocate the permanency of twenty national clearinghouse systems across the country because they were so effective. For Wilhite testimony, see H.R., "Banking and Currency Reform Hearings, pt. 1–13," Part 5 (319–22); for Nash testimony, see H.R., "Banking and Currency Reform Hearings, pt. 1–13," Part 6 (337–54).

101. For details on how the NYCH tried to avoid the panic, see Bruner and Carr, *Panic of 1907*, 57–70, 102.

102. It should be noted that a central bank typically serves a clearinghouse function, and because the United States did not have any form of centralized banking system during this period, clearinghouse associations grew to fill this gap. In the United Kingdom, for example, the Bank of England had a clearinghouse function managed by the bank.

103. Bruner and Carr, *Panic of 1907*, 59–60; and Shull, *Fourth Branch*, 29.

104. Bruner and Carr, *Panic of 1907*, 60.

105. After nearly two days of runs where the bank was kept afloat only through the funds of the NYCH, the clearinghouse took "its most drastic measure to date" and ordered the immediate elimination of Augustus Heinze and his business associate Charles W. Morse from all banking interests in New York City. Ibid., 62.

106. It is important to note that some of the larger trust companies, like Knickerbocker, were able to benefit indirectly from clearinghouses. As Bruner and Carr explain, "certain trust companies in larger markets often forged relationships with individual clearing-house member banks; those partner banks then agreed to clear for certain favored trust companies, thereby giving the trust companies indirect access to

clearing-house protections." This is not to say it was part of the clearinghouse. When runs on the Knickerbocker ensued, the NYCH declined assistance. Ibid., 67.

107. Ibid., 85.

108. Ibid., 169.

109. This function would normally be carried out by a central bank, but since the United States did not have one during this period, clearinghouses adopted this function. At the height of the crisis in 1907, clearinghouse certificates constituted roughly 14 percent of the total currency in circulation. Member banks used these certificates in times of crisis in place of currency so that they could then use currency to pay claims made by depositors. Ibid., 135; and Broz, *International Origins of the Federal Reserve*, 29.

110. Bruner and Carr, *Panic of 1907*, 107.

111. Federal Reserve Act of 1913; and Glass, *Adventure in Constructive Finance*, 337.

112. Federal Reserve Act of 1913, Sec. 13, 16 and 18; Glass, *Adventure in Constructive Finance*, 368–74, 377–86, 390–92; and Shull, *Fourth Branch*, 49–52.

113. The legislation says, "Wherever the word 'bank' is used in this Act, the word shall be held to include State bank, banking associations, and trust company, except where national banks or Federal reserve banks are specifically referred to." See Federal Reserve Act of 1913; and Glass, *Adventure in Constructive Finance*, 337.

114. Nash, "Emergency and Asset Currency."

115. Bruner and Carr, *Panic of 1907*, 92, 99–103, 111–12, 115–19, 131–33; and Shull, *Fourth Branch*, 30–32.

116. H.R., "Banking and Currency Reform Hearings, pt 1–13," HR62A-F2.1 to F2.3.

117. Chernow, *House of Morgan*, 127.

118. Ibid. For more on Morgan's involvement in the takeover of Tennessee Coal and Iron, see Bruner and Carr, *Panic of 1907*, 115–19, 131–33, 185.

119. See Records of the US House of Representatives, 60th Congress, "Committee on Banking & Currency, Currency & Banking Reform," NARA, Washington, DC, RG 233, HR60A-H4, boxes 667–71; and Records of the US House of Representatives, 62nd Congress, "Committee on Banking & Currency, Currency & Banking Reform," NARA, Washington, DC, RG 233, HR62A-F2.1–F2.3, box 523. These boxes include extensive letters from private-sector representatives throughout the United States lobbying Congress either for or against specific aspects of banking reforms. Box 523, in particular, contains transcripts of congressional hearings held to engage with the private sector and learn their opinions prior to the drafting of the bill that became the Federal Reserve Act.

120. Senator James Reed, quoted in Glass, *Adventure in Constructive Finance*, 220.

121. President Woodrow Wilson, *New Freedom*, quoted in ibid., 81.

122. This statement was made while Warburg served on the Federal Reserve Board. Warburg, *Federal Reserve System*, 501.

123. Quoted in Bruner and Carr, *Panic of 1907*, 77.

124. As Warburg stated in a 1910 essay, "A modern system must be so constructed that a demand for cash caused by distrust shall be absolutely impossible, or the system is not safe." Warburg, *Federal Reserve System*, 165. For more on the Fed as a safety mechanism to strengthen public confidence, see Bruner and Carr, *Panic of 1907*, 77.

125. Willis comments that the Federal Reserve was able to offer safeties to the public by "insuring against banking suspension and by tending to 'smooth out' and unify rates of discount the country over; and it was particularly a safeguard to the interests of the agricultural population," Willis, *Federal Reserve System*, 524.

126. Warburg, *Federal Reserve System*, 313.

127. DeSaint Phalle further argues that adaptability was "in part through legislation but more often through the necessary filling of a vacuum." See deSaint Phalle, *Federal Reserve*, 60–61.

128. Shull, *Fourth Branch*, 2. These three instances are studied in great detail by Shull, who explores each of these as examples of instances in which the "Federal Reserve was strengthened in periods of economic distress." He argues that this is noteworthy because in each instance "the institution was under severe attack from a host of influential critics who blamed its flawed policies for causing or exacerbating economic problems that it was intended to prevent or ameliorate." Despite this, however, the Federal Reserve adapted, or as Shull puts it, "survived and grew." Ibid.

129. Moore writes, "Goals of the system were not firm, and policies were uncertain. Lacking clear direction, confusion was bound to prevail." Moore, *Federal Reserve*, 59.

130. Glass, *Adventure in Constructive Finance*, 272.

131. Moore, *Federal Reserve*, 59. The war began in Europe in 1914 and was entered by the United States in 1917. It is interesting to note that Carter Glass was secretary of the Treasury during much of this period, serving from 1918 to 1920. His successors to this post were Andrew Mellon and David Houston. See Meltzer, *History of the Federal Reserve*, 107.

132. Meltzer writes that "wartime (and prewar) changes made the System more like a central bank. . . . Independence was sacrificed to maintain interest rates that lowered the Treasury's cost of debt finance. The system became subservient to the Treasury's perceived needs." In addition, Shull describes the Fed's support of the Treasury during the war by selling securities at below-market rates to help the Treasury in fundraising. The member banks of the Federal Reserve System were encouraged to "borrow in order to purchase Treasury securities and to extend credit to customers to do so." In this way Shull describes the reserve banks as bond-distributing organizations and says the "credit facilities of the Federal Reserve Banks were placed at the disposal of member and non-member banks in order that they might lend freely on bonds for which the subscribers were unable to pay." This was highly contentious among many economists who felt this practice was unacceptable. The Department of the Treasury, however, praised the Fed with the comptroller of currency going so far as to say that it was "one of the most potent means for saving this country and the world during the war." Meltzer, *History of the Federal Reserve*, 64; Shull, *Fourth Branch*, 64–65. See also Meltzer, *History of the Federal Reserve*, 84–90.

133. Shull, *Fourth Branch*, 66. Prices increased nearly 17 percent from March 1919 to March 1920.

134. Shull comments that at the end of the war in 1918, the Treasury continued to insist on the support of the Fed. He argues that Reserve officials were alarmed and were "convinced that the System was contributing to inflation and feeding a speculative

bubble that would ultimately collapse into crisis and panic. They, nevertheless, felt their hands were tied. The Treasury vigorously opposed any monetary restraint involving higher interest rates." Shull, *Fourth Branch*, 63, 68.

135. Ibid., 71.

136. Ibid., 73. The recession resulted in a drop of prices on farm products that ultimately contributed to the failure of between five thousand and six thousand banks, most of them in rural areas. Most of these banks were state or private banks that were not members of the Federal Reserve System. An additional nine thousand banks failed between 1929 and 1933. As Meltzer points out, however, despite the fact that more banks failed in 1921 than in earlier recessions, there was no banking panic, which indicated at least a small-scale success by the institution. Wells, *Federal Reserve System*, 41; and Meltzer, *History of the Federal Reserve*, 134.

137. Shull, *Fourth Branch*, 63.

138. Ibid., 80, 87.

139. Ibid., 81–82. Meltzer agrees, saying, "The early postwar years is principally the story of the Federal Reserve's struggle for independence from the Treasury.... It made several mistakes, some avoidable, some unavoidable in the circumstances." Meltzer, *History of the Federal Reserve*, 90.

140. Meltzer, *History of the Federal Reserve*, 429.

141. The crash of the stock market was the result of prosperity in 1928–1929, which created an "exuberant stock market" that the Federal Reserve could not contain. New industries such as telephone communications, films, and automobiles were emerging and the economic outlook was excellent. Many in the Fed suspected that the economic "bubble" could not be sustained, but the Fed was in conflict about how to manage the growth without reducing prosperity. The Fed's inability to control the stock market or prevent its collapse enhanced the economic downturn already under way. Shull, *Fourth Branch*, 95–97, 158; and Wells, *Federal Reserve System*, 47.

142. Shull, *Fourth Branch*, 98. Wells describes the bank runs of the period as "contagious" and says the public were losing confidence in the banking system. "People were withdrawing their deposits in currency and hoarding this currency in safe deposit boxes or in cookie jars at home." Wells, *Federal Reserve System*, 49.

143. For more on bank holidays, see Shull, *Fourth Branch*, 99; and Kemmerer and Kemmerer, *ABC of the Federal Reserve*, 115–17.

144. Kemmerer and Kemmerer, *ABC of the Federal Reserve*, 117.

145. Meltzer, *History of the Federal Reserve*, 430.

146. Centralization of authority and control of open-market operations was a significant and important aspect of the Banking Act of 1933 and was designed specifically to control the ability of the New York Reserve to engage in independent action without the permission of the Fed, as had occurred under the leadership of Benjamin Strong (president of the New York Federal Reserve Bank) throughout the 1920s.

147. Meltzer, *History of the Federal Reserve*, 430–31.

148. Shull, *Fourth Branch*, 83; Kemmerer and Kemmerer, *ABC of the Federal Reserve*, 106–7; and Rothbard, *History of Money and Banking*, 371. See also Moore, *Federal Reserve*, 57; and Wells, *Federal Reserve System*, 27.

149. Shull, *Fourth Branch*, 83.

150. Kemmerer and Kemmerer, *ABC of the Federal Reserve*, 106–7; see also Moore, *Federal Reserve System*, 57.

151. Shull, *Fourth Branch*, 116; and Rowe, *Public–Private Character*, 76–77. The Banking Act of 1935 also instituted changes in terms and titles. Members of the Federal Reserve Board were given the title "governor," and the head of the board was designated "chairman." Additionally, the heads of the reserve banks (previously called the "governors") were given the new title of "president." Term limits for the board were reestablished to allow governors to serve nonrenewable fourteen-year terms. The chairman of the board of governors, however, was designated to serve a renewable four-year term. The reserve bank presidents were given five-year renewable terms, by the approval of the board of governors. Through this mechanism the board was able to secure even greater control over the actions and leadership of the reserve banks. See Shull, *Fourth Branch*, 116.

152. Meltzer, *History of the Federal Reserve*, 115–17. It is important to note that despite the removal of the secretary of the Treasury from the board, the influence of the Treasury over the Fed did not stop. During World War II, the Fed again relinquished its independence in order to support war finance. Independence from the Treasury, enabled and encouraged by the act of 1935, was eventually realized, although not until after the Korean War. See Meltzer, *History of the Federal Reserve*, 739–40; and Shull, *Fourth Branch*, 115.

153. Shull, *Fourth Branch*, 116.

154. Friedman and Schwartz, *Monetary History*, 437; and Kemmerer and Kemmerer, *ABC of the Federal Reserve*, 126–27, 135.

155. Shull, *Fourth Branch*, 160.

156. Ibid., 171.

CHAPTER FOUR

The War Industries Board, a Responsive Alliance

Responsive alliances are created as a reaction to a particular crisis and are established not to resolve the cause of the crisis itself but to face a national challenge that has developed because of crisis. In the case of the World War I crisis, the War Industries Board (WIB) was established as a responsive cross-sector partnership to harness industry and the military together to ensure that the United States was mobilized for war and able to provide for its citizens and troops.

The WIB lasted a very short time and was fully functional for less than one year, from March to November of 1918. This case study tracks the history of the organization to understand it as a public–private alliance. The WIB was one of a number of emergency agencies created by President Woodrow Wilson's administration during World War I. A great deal of writing explores Wilson's actions and the politics of the period in terms of the tendency to "statism" during the period, as well as the degree to which the actions of the Wilson administration were in keeping with the principles of a democratic, capitalist society. Some authors even go so far as to describe Wilsonian statism as essentially fascist.[1] While such discussions are beyond the scope of this particular work, they are worth noting.

Because the WIB was such a short-lived agency, only a limited amount of work is published on this subject. Many of the more historical accounts are written by individuals who were intimately involved in the mobilization effort and, while hugely informative, are often laced with bias and personal agendas. The chairman of the WIB, Bernard Baruch, wrote extensively on the WIB in two books, one of which was published after he was asked to testify before Congress during the Nye Committee hearings of 1935 regarding the WIB and his conduct as chairman.[2] While Baruch and the WIB were exonerated, and some even praised Baruch for his conduct, his account of the period is not objective. Perhaps the most famous historical WIB account, *Industrial America in the World War: The Strategy behind the Line 1917–1918* by Grosvenor Clarkson, is an excellent reference but must also be handled with caution and has been criticized as a "promotional tract to keep alive in peacetime the mobilization lessons of the first world war." Critics said the work "publicized the organizational philosophies of WIB director Baruch, who had paid for the study and its publication."[3] Accordingly, this chapter relies most heavily on the work of academic and historian Robert D. Cuff, whose extensive research and writings about the organization offer the least biased, most critical and thorough resource on the WIB published to date. While numerous additional sources are employed in this case study, including journal articles as well as papers, congressional reports, and letters drawn from the US National Archives, Cuff's work is by far the most important.

This chapter explores the WIB using the same seven critical factors used to assess disaster-oriented PPPs and the Fed. These seven factors—crisis, leadership, organizational structure, information sharing, shared benefits, trust, and institutional adaptability or sustainability—have been identified as crucial to the development and success of disaster-oriented PPPs. The WIB is explored in these terms to determine the degree to which these factors are relevant to a responsive cross-sector partnership in order to assess whether any relevant parallels emerge that make these historic partnerships relevant to disaster-oriented PPPs.

THE CRISIS OF WAR

> The twists and turns of American prewar diplomacy came to an end on April 2, 1917. On that day Woodrow Wilson asked a hushed Congress for a declaration of war. . . . The challenges that now confronted the Wilson administration were enormous. Manpower, shipping, credit, trade, munitions—a whole range of problems came crashing in on an administrative structure ill-equipped to meet them. . . . An emergency crisis was upon the United States, but the obstacles to a systematic response remained.
>
> Robert D. Cuff, *War Industries Board*

Crisis in the WIB was crucial to achieve the backing of public and private leaders and to convince the nation that a cross-sector alliance was necessary. Although the WIB was established as a result of World War I, to fully understand the important role that crisis played in the creation of the institution, it is necessary to begin a few years before the war began.

The United States was ill prepared for World War I. Although the United States was neutral when the war erupted in Europe in 1914, and it did not enter the conflict until 1917, the nation was "shocked into a realization of the inadequacy of her defense measures in event of becoming involved."[4] World War I marked a new kind of war with new technologies, such as chemical weapons, armored cars, telephones, aircraft, tanks, and submarines, all of which changed the way of war. For the first time, the United States had to completely mobilize its economy for war.[5] The Germans swiftly defeated the Allies in the early days of the conflict, making it clear that "war was no longer a conflict between armies but between nations," and that war could be won only if "all the nation's resources of men, money, materials, and morale mobilized behind them."[6]

In contrast to the Americans, the Germans were well equipped for war. As early as 1870, Germany had begun developing a war economy by instituting what was referred to as the "Teutonic formula," which was a method of mobilizing industry in support of the military.[7] In testimony before Congress in 1935, Baruch described the German advantage and their physical and economic preparation for war. He held that defeating the Germans required the Americans and Allies to undergo a "similar conversion of manpower and resources."[8] The Allies were forced to focus beyond military coordination and began to realize the importance of creating an administrative body to facilitate the relationship between the public and private sectors.[9]

Soon after the outbreak of World War I in Europe in June 1914, discussions began in public and private circles about how to incorporate American industrial know-how into the government's preparedness strategy.[10] From the late spring of 1915 until the creation of the WIB a year later, no fewer than three official administrative bodies attempted to coordinate public and private industrial preparedness. As the failings of one organization became apparent, an offshoot would evolve. This trend continued until the outbreak of war generated a crisis of sufficient magnitude to create urgency and jar the public and private sectors into action, which resulted in the WIB. The organizations that preceded the WIB and aimed to facilitate cross-sector cooperation for industrial mobilization were the Naval Consulting Board, the Council of National Defense and Advisory Commission, and the General Munitions Board.

Instructed by President Wilson to develop a national defense strategy, Secretary of the Navy Joseph Daniels created the Naval Consulting Board (NCB) in July 1915.[11] One of the new board members of the NCB, Howard E. Coffin, became a key figure in the preparedness campaign. Coffin was known for his success in the organizational restructuring of the Society of Automobile Engineers and was the president of that organization as well as of the Hudson Motor Car Company.[12] Coffin sought to standardize the committee system and encourage the NCB to include all branches of the armed services. He suggested dividing the board into committees in which board members were assigned based on their professional expertise.[13] Coffin was appointed to chair the NCB's Committee on Industrial Preparedness.[14]

By the spring and summer of 1917, Coffin had recruited numerous private-sector volunteers, including Grosvenor B. Clarkson, a former newspaper reporter turned public relations expert, and Walter S. Gifford, an executive from telephone company AT&T.[15] Together these men drafted a model for industrial preparedness that included plans to collect a national inventory from manufacturers to assess the country's capacity for munitions production and ways to increase it, teach manufacturers how to produce the munitions most suited to their factory, and exempt factory workers from the military draft to ensure that the mobilization process would not be disrupted by labor transfer if the war began.[16] Coffin's belief in preparedness can be seen in his comment that "twentieth century warfare demands that the blood of the soldier must be mingled with from three to five parts of the sweat of the man in the factories, mills, mines and fields of the nation in arms."[17]

Support from both the private and public sectors was necessary to enact this plan. To collect inventories, the Committee on Industrial Preparedness needed manufacturer acquiescence. Legislative support was also required to get permission to show manufacturers how their factories could be used for alternative purposes to support the war effort.[18] After much lobbying, Coffin managed to convince the secretaries of War and the Navy as well as the chair of the Senate Committee on Military affairs to support his plan, and section 120 of the National Defense Act passed on June 3, 1916.[19] In addition to authorizing the collection of inventories, the legislation gave the president the authority to appoint a "nonpartisan Board on Mobilization of Industries Essential for Military Preparedness."[20]

Despite the political victory achieved by section 120, the Committee on Industrial Preparedness had very little real effect. As one state chair wrote to Coffin, "voluntary support has not proven a success; the lethargy and procrastination of the manufacturers has been irritating and the deliberateness of the Field Aides embarrassing."[21] Although inventories had been taken of nearly eighteen thousand plants by 1916, the information was never put into effect to prepare the United States for war.[22]

By the spring of 1916 Germany stopped trying to appease or negotiate with the United States, indicating that a war crisis might soon be upon the nation and industrial mobilization would prove necessary.[23] As the impending crisis loomed on the horizon, it became clear that the NCB, with its Committee on Industrial Preparedness, simply lacked the organizational scope and institutional authority to coordinate a national preparedness strategy. As Paul Koistinen describes, Coffin's committee was composed of "unofficial industrial consultants" and was generally unequipped to handle such "grandiose responsibilities" as the oversight of industrial mobilization.[24]

Prewar preparedness efforts were significantly strengthened when Congress passed the Army Appropriations Act on August 29, 1916, which included a provision to create a Council of National Defense (CND).[25] The CND ultimately absorbed the NCB's Committee on Industrial Preparedness and was an advisory body composed mainly of private-sector volunteers.[26] The council was authorized only to "investigate, advise, and recommend policies to the president."[27] Dr. Hollis Godfrey was responsible for writing the CND legislation and facilitating its inclusion in the Army Appropriations bill.[28]

Disorganization, decentralization, and ambiguous lines of authority plagued the CND and its advisory commission as world events unfolded and war looked increasingly imminent. Baruch says in his autobiography, "Neither the Council of National Defense or the Advisory Commission were suitably organized or sufficiently empowered to meet the demands made upon the national economy by the needs of the expanding navy and the much more rapidly expanding army."[29] Curtice Hitchcock agrees with Baruch but argues that the failure of the CND highlighted a much larger organizational flaw within the government: "The fundamental weakness in the whole situation was not so much the individual incapacity . . . as the lack of cohesion in the whole governmental system which prevented the adoption by all bureaus of a single policy toward industry."[30] On January 31, 1917, Germany declared it would engage in unrestricted submarine warfare, an action that rapidly resulted in the United States breaking all diplomatic ties with that nation on February 3, 1917.[31]

The possibility that the United States might soon be entering the war generated a sense of urgency and led to an unexpected surge of patriotism in US manufacturers. The CND soon found itself overwhelmed with offers from the private sector.[32] Like the industry experts who served on the CND, these men came to Washington as volunteers. Although this new interest in the CND could be used to achieve greater cooperation from the private sector, increased volunteerism only added to the general confusion by stressing an already disorganized, decentralized, and unsupported agency.[33] There was little connection between formal agencies for mobilization, like the CND, and the actions of small groups of private individuals offering to lend their expertise and support.[34] Feverish debates were held among the commissioners of the CND about how the organization should adapt to cope with the growing crisis, but the lack of agreement led to further internal polarization.[35] Cuff calls mobilization efforts in the spring of 1917 "simply a disjointed collection of independent feudalities."[36] By the end of March it was clear that a coordinating agency was needed to manage the relationship among government agencies, within the industrial sectors, and, most importantly, the interplay of the industrial sectors with the government.[37]

In addition to structural flaws within the CND, several external factors further limited the agency's ability to withstand the crisis. First, the United States was not yet engaged in war. This is significant because the appetite of Congress and the administration to concentrate seriously on industrial mobilization, or to grant the CND greater authority, was limited until the country was at war and there was an urgent need to mobilize.[38] Second, the CND lacked significant external support from political- or private-sector leadership, which served to further undermine its effectiveness and enhance the general disarray of the organization. Third, the major industrial players were not motivated to work with the CND. While they did not oppose their efforts, they did not actively support them either. Field writes that "these new bodies faced a very tough problem in obtaining fair prices for the government, because the Allies had been bidding against each other to get the needed war supplies and were still heavily in the market."[39] With international buyers paying high prices for their products, what would motivate American manufacturers to volunteer in an organization that would ask them to accept a lower price at home?

The General Munitions Board (GMB) was established in March 1917 as a subordinate to the CND.[40] The primary aim of the GMB was to act as a "coordinating agency to draw the various departments and bureaus together for common planning."[41] The creation of this board was another attempt to create a cross-sector partnership to facilitate mobilization and represented an important step toward the WIB. The GMB sought to prevent competition between government agencies, and since it lacked the authority to negotiate or sign contracts, it was intended to serve as a facilitator between the public and private sectors for industrial preparedness.[42]

Baruch described the GMB as a direct reaction to the impending war crisis. He refers to the munitions board as "consciously an emergency procedure, adopted in an absence of sufficient organization or experience both in industry and in the governmental agencies themselves to do otherwise."[43] Like its predecessors, the GMB struggled for authority. Hitchcock illustrates how the continued lack of authority bestowed on the agency plagued the GMB. He says that the "War Department Bureaus were told to consult the Munitions Board 'where time permitted,' in order that their orders might be 'coordinated' with those of the navy, but bureau heads were reminded . . . that their responsibility was in no way detracted from by this requirement."[44]

On April 6, 1917, three days after the first meeting of the GMB, the United States entered the war. Despite these early attempts at preparedness, the nation was ill prepared and the physical requirements of the war were enormous. Baruch quantified this lack of preparedness:

On April 6, 1917, the Army of the United States comprised about 200,000 men, organized in no higher units than regiments, without substantial equipments in artillery, aircraft, or any of the lately developed instruments of war, and without reserves of food, clothing, ammunition, or equipment for a considerable expansion. Between it and the battlefield of France were 3,000 miles of ocean rendered precarious by submarines. There were no ships for transports, and both the Army and the Nation were without experience in the mobilization, organization, and supply of armies of the size engaged in the European struggle.[45]

To put these numbers into perspective, by the time the war was over nineteen months later, in November 1918, the army consisted of 3.6 million men. Troops and supplies had been sent overseas at a rate of roughly 225,000 per month, and "practically the entire manufacturing capacity of the nation had been converted to direct or indirect war work."[46] With the pressing demands of a war crisis upon the nation, the American response was summarized by one scholar as "a very chaotic interaction of the federal government as a whole, the industrial community, and the military services."[47] Finally, the necessary urgency had been created by the war to prioritize the mobilization effort. "What was not possible during peace became imperative during war. . . . The federal government lacked the personnel, the information, or the experience necessary for the massive economic regulation World War I demanded."[48]

In the spring and summer of 1917, in the midst of this disorder and while the GMB was struggling to find its feet, Baruch and others sought to develop the "cooperative committees of industry" as yet another voluntary mechanism designed to facilitate better government–private sector cooperation. Baruch sought to get industry more actively involved in the mobilization efforts by making them more than informants and advisors to the committees. He believed that the private sector was best equipped and qualified to mobilize the economy most efficiently and should provide far more than just information and advice.[49]

Baruch's efforts in forming the cooperative committees of industry greatly informed the WIB because they were able to demonstrate that the private sector could serve a much more active, useful role in war mobilization. For example, the zinc committee was able to secure 25 million pounds of zinc at two-thirds the normal market price for the US government.[50] Like other attempts to create a cross-sector alliance to mobilize, the committee struggled. Their success depended upon military acknowledgment of their role and authority, on the one hand, and the willingness of the private sector to cooperate with the committee, on the other. This was no easy feat because the committee had no authority to compel either side to participate, and in many cases either the military or the private sector were not motivated to engage. "The whole committee network, as well as Baruch's place in it, rested on the insubstantial basis of volunteerism. Baruch could compel neither businessmen nor the military services to cooperate with him."[51]

The cooperative committees of industry and the GMB were the last in a progression of agencies, shaped and adjusted as the war crisis became more pressing, that resulted in the WIB. By the summer of 1917, the GMB and cooperative committees of industry had shown both their merits and their flaws. GMB had become simply a tool of the military rather than an instrument able to harness the military together with the private sector to develop a cooperative scheme for national mobilization.[52] Despite this, the GMB had attempted to coordinate purchasing; this was an advance over the previous systems and demonstrated it could act as an intermediary to achieve cooperation with the military and private sector. Ultimately, both organizations lacked the legal authority and political legitimacy to act on a comprehensive scale. The crisis of war made resolution of these shortfalls a priority.[53]

As a direct result of "a crisis in business–government relations," President Wilson created the WIB on July 28, 1917, and appointed Frank Scott as its chairman.[54] The WIB absorbed the GMB and was established as a subordinate to the CND. The authority to control purchasing centrally was left with the War Department.[55] This meant that although there existed a specific agency to coordinate the mobilization program, it lacked the technical or legal authority to productively manage the mobilization effort, making its powers only advisory at best.[56]

Scott resigned as chairman on October 26. A *New York Journal* article about his resignation highlighted the internal bureaucratic crisis of the organization. The article states, "The WIB has been uneasy under its lack of authority to meet directly the pressing needs of the nation. . . . It has been hampered by lack of legal ability to obtain unlimited production of war supplies."[57]

By early 1918 the United States was fully engaged in the war, and the effect of poor industrial mobilization heightened the economic, social, and political crisis. The WIB was politically paralyzed and suffered from a lack of congressional and presidential backing. Economically, "uncontrolled procurement overloaded the Northeast" with contracts that exceeded factory production capabilities and businesses found themselves economically at risk because of chaos in government. Additionally, the severity of the winter of 1917–18 meant that fuel supplies were low.[58] The situation was so dire that some argued "the mobilization effort, indeed the whole economy, appeared on the brink of collapse."[59] The president and Congress were forced to either strengthen the WIB as America's mobilization agency or face the very real possibility that the United States could not provide the supplies needed for the war.[60] On one side, the WIB "fought against internal chaos," while on the other, "against the external cross currents of military, business, and Congressional pressures—and the furious pace of war itself."[61] Thus, the crisis created the political momentum necessary to drive organizational change in the framework for American mobilization.

On March 4, 1918, President Wilson appointed Bernard Baruch as chairman of the WIB and provided the agency the independence and authority that Baruch envisioned. The WIB became independent of the CND and would report directly to the president of the United States.[62] At long last, with the economy on the brink of collapse, the president had given the agency the authority necessary to coordinate the mobilization effort. Crisis held the organization captive, however. The impact of crisis on the WIB must be understood in the context of the "tension between traditional, peacetime impulses and the imperatives of a nation in modern war," on the one hand, and the "forces of rationalization, centralization and bureaucratization inherent in capitalism and war [that] accelerated rapidly in the crisis," on the other.[63]

Although several attempts had been made before the outbreak of World War I to build an effective cross-sector partnership to mobilize the nation for war, it took the crisis and urgency generated by the US entry into the conflict to prioritize and sufficiently empower the organization. It was only after the nation was engaged in war and the economy was on the brink of collapse that public- and private-sector leaders collectively backed the WIB.

PUBLIC- AND PRIVATE-SECTOR LEADERSHIP

Once the crisis of war prioritized mobilization efforts in both sectors, it was up to public and private leaders to ensure that cooperative efforts were successful and the nation was mobilized. In the public sector, this required consistent presidential backing, whereas in industry it required the continued efforts of a small, dedicated vanguard of American businessmen.

Public-Sector Leadership

President Wilson faced a significant political challenge from 1915 to 1917. It was his responsibility to prepare and mobilize the nation for the possibility of entering the war, but the mood among the American people favored peace. With Wilson's campaign centered on his ability to keep America out of the conflict, the president could not be seen as actively supporting preparedness initiatives.[64] Suspicion of the private sector also prevailed in the office of the president and in the public at large, and many wondered about the ability of private industry to put national interests above self-interest.[65] Thus, the period is marked by executive leadership that sought to look responsible but not eager in its involvement with and support of preparedness agencies.

Wilson began to formulate a plan for national defense in the summer of 1915 and asked Secretary of the Navy Daniels to create a national defense strategy. Daniels returned with a proposal, coauthored by Thomas Edison, to create the NCB.[66] The president made preparedness a key issue in his annual message in December 1915, and in January 1916 he undertook a speaking tour on behalf of his defense proposals, which included cross-sector alliances to mobilize industry for the possibility of war. By June 1916, in a "zig-zag pattern characteristic of presidential politics," Wilson was hailed at the Democratic convention as the man who had "kept America out of war," and active presidential support of preparedness initiatives ground to a halt.[67]

After Wilson was reelected on November 7, 1916, he spent much of the next five months focused on Europe, trying to broker peace.[68] If Wilson were successful in Europe, industrial mobilization would be unnecessary. Even if he were not successful, the president would not be seen to advocate peace while simultaneously preparing the nation for war. Baruch says that there was little appetite for preparedness initiatives during this period and argues that, when the CND began, "public opinion and the president's policy were directed toward keeping us out of what was generally considered Europe's quarrel."[69] With these pressures influencing this strategy, Wilson gave little leadership, support, or direction to the CND and left it to find its own way.[70] The absence of the president's open public support, directional advice, and leadership significantly reduced the ability of the WIB to organize centrally or gain legitimacy in Washington, and it resulted in confusion and disorder in the CND during the winter of 1916–17.[71]

The president, Congress, and the public began to openly support preparedness-focused initiatives that involved the private sector once the United States entered the war in April 1917.[72] The WIB did not benefit from executive action, however, until the spring of 1918, when the mobilization program was on the verge of collapse and the need for a WIB organization could no longer be ignored.[73] The urgent need for war materials and congressional action forced Wilson to empower the agency.

While congressional leadership had little direct bearing on the WIB, its actions significantly impacted the willingness of the president to lend his support. The degree to which Congress influenced the president was particularly evident in late 1917. With the war crisis growing, the Senate Military Affairs Committee, led by Sen. George Chamberlain, launched an investigation to explore the ways to address the crisis. The Chamberlain Committee found that "chaos in the army supply" had a direct effect on the US economy.[74] Relying upon suggestions from the US Chamber of Commerce and many senior private-sector executives, the committee suggested that the United States should mirror the United Kingdom and place procurement in the hands of a civilian-controlled ministry of munitions.[75] The committee also suggested that a war cabinet should be created to oversee the war effort.[76]

Wilson took great exception to the assumption of the Chamberlain Committee that he was inadequately organizing his cabinet for the war. To circumvent passage of the two bills presented by the Chamberlain Committee in January 1918 and to address some of the major concerns that emerged in the

Senate investigation, Wilson reformed the WIB and gave it (and its chairman) the direction and authority it previously lacked.[77] Hitchcock wrote in 1918 that "the president, far more definitely and emphatically than before, has thrown the vast prestige of his office behind the agency."[78] Baruch and the WIB continued to benefit from full executive support until the war ended in November 1918.[79] As a result of the competing factors influencing the president, Cuff argues that organizational changes within the WIB "must be seen in the context of a presidential strategy designed to cope with the larger political crisis of these months."[80]

Congressional influence had four significant impacts on the development of the WIB. First, congressional criticism of preexisting arrangements for mobilization led to the establishment of the WIB. Wilson hoped that, in keeping the WIB within the CND, he could appease Congress and use the organization as a buffer between competing public and private interests that could reassure Congress and the public that "private industrial power was accountable to public authority."[81] Second, Congress indirectly fueled bureaucratic battles for power and authority within the government by undermining WIB and its predecessors by regularly voicing its skepticism about the aims and patriotism of business volunteers. This served to provide the army and navy a legitimate reason not to cooperate with the agencies. Third, a chorus of congressional discord about the creation of an organization of this nature influenced Wilson and gave him further encouragement to maintain a distance from the mobilizers until the economic crisis of war turned public support in their favor.[82] By the time the public and Congress were ready to accept the idea of private involvement in industrial preparedness (in the spring of 1918), the United States was deeply involved in the war, and the need for a coordinated, centralized, empowered agency was urgent. Finally, the WIB was revised and empowered as a direct result of both Congressional acquiescence that the private sector had a critical role to play in mobilization efforts, and executive action culminating from the president's anger at the Chamberlain Committee's insinuation that his war government was on the brink of collapse.

Private-Sector Leadership

While presidential backing was the linchpin that secured the place of the WIB in the clique of key Washington war agencies, there would have been no WIB without the flood of private-sector volunteers who began focusing on the industrial preparedness campaign in 1915 and sustained the effort through the spring of 1918, when the organization received presidential support. Private-sector leadership was fundamental to the establishment and operation of the WIB for two primary reasons.

First, the predecessor organizations to the WIB (NCB, CND, and early WIB) were wholly reliant on private-sector experts who volunteered their time and expertise. "Committed to industrial self-regulation through cooperation between government and industry, businessmen believed that they had the best working knowledge of the industrial side of war and set their sights on a dominant role for themselves in industrial mobilization."[83] These volunteers became known as the "dollar-a-year men" because they earned so little for their work and many even paid their own expenses, including office space and clerical help.[84] Largely inspired by the officer training camps for business executives held by Gen. Leonard Wood, commander of the eastern department of the army in the summer of 1915, these men became the backbone of advisory councils and committees aimed at industrial preparedness.[85] Baruch praises the efforts of the dollar-a-year men. He argues, "The men were willing at all times to work long hours without holidays and without pay, forgetting personal anxieties and personal fortunes in a patriotic effort of each to do his part to win the war."[86]

The CND and WIB were totally dependent upon the dollar-a-year men to inform committees and serve as expert advisors.[87] Since the WIB was such a decentralized agency, the sixty-odd commodity chiefs played a significant leadership role because they determined how cross-sector cooperation within their sector would function. While there was much debate about the motives driving the volunteerism of these men, Cuff argues that the volunteers felt that, by engaging with the government, they could benefit both the public and private interest. He argues, "These men believed that they could most effectively aid the war effort by protecting and stabilizing industry."[88] The dollar-a-year men continued to advocate plans for preparedness and mobilization when presidential backing was absent and congressional scrutiny was intense.[89] Had it not been for their volunteerism and consistent urging to the president, the United States would have been even more ill prepared for the war. These volunteers became a vanguard for industrial mobilization and sought to legitimize the role of private-sector industry experts in Washington by making them part of the war machine rather than simply advisory "volunteers" who had no legal standing.[90]

Second, the breadth of industries involved in mobilization was vast (including everything from steel and wool to ammunition and chewing gum), and the dollar-a-year men brought two important attributes with them: direct access to private leaders and understanding of specific industrial sectors. The government simply had no employees as specialized or knowledgeable as the dollar-a-year men. Not only were these private volunteers able to use their expertise in a way that was palatable to industry and beneficial to government, but they could also apply organization and efficiency techniques, learned in the private sector, to help develop a partnership framework for their commodity sector within the WIB to support the war effort.[91]

The dollar-a-year men also served as lobbyists, an important role that allowed the cross-sector collaboration to survive before Wilson backed the agency. For example, volunteers in the WIB, including Baruch and Coffin, testified before the Chamberlain Committee to advocate a more centralized, empowered public–private structure to oversee mobilization. One executive pled, "We are at sea without a chart. . . . There must be some kind of leadership in this situation. We have a very great fear with regard to industry."[92]

Of the dollar-a-year men, Baruch stands out as the most influential and historically significant.[93] He was a Wall Street speculator and a self-described patriot who saw the preparedness campaign as being of such critical national importance that he became involved very early, offering his services and insights to General Wood in 1915 and to President Wilson by the spring of 1916.[94] He served important leadership roles on a committee with other "dollar-a-year men," but he stands out for his consistent lobbying of the White House for better, more centralized control over the preparedness and mobilization plans, as well as for his charismatic leadership while chairman of the WIB. Baruch was known and applauded for his ability to recruit excellent men, earn their respect and loyalty, and use them to inform his decisions.[95] Cuff describes Baruch's leadership style while chairman of the WIB: "Baruch operated by means of a group of experts who provided him with expertise and distilled opinion without which his efforts could never have been so effective, nor his reach so wide."[96]

Prior to assuming the chair of the WIB in the autumn and winter of 1917–18, Baruch worked in the CND on the advisory commission and GMB, and he held responsibility for the raw materials sector. At this period in the war, the pressure on the Allies was great and the United States faced a shortage of nitrate—a critical ingredient of gunpowder, which was imported primarily from Chile. The shortage was so severe that, Baruch says, "I had nightmares in which I pictured our boys going into combat using blank cartridges because we had no nitrate with which to make gunpowder."[97] In the midst of this growing crisis, Baruch received intelligence from the navy that the Chilean government was trying in vain to retrieve the gold reserves it held in Germany. Baruch, acting on instinct, made the Chileans an offer: "If Chile would seize the 235,000 tons of German-owned nitrate in Chile and sell it to us, we would pay for it in gold."[98] Chile agreed and the United States obtained its much-needed nitrate.

As a final point on leadership within the private sector, it is important to note that the dollar-a-year men did not represent the majority of private businessmen and certainly did not represent the corporate powerhouses of the day.[99] Some of the most important private-sector manufacturers for industrialization, such as United States Steel, Standard Oil, and International Nickel, were focused on conducting business with the Allies and profiting from the war in

Europe. They had no incentive to participate in the preparedness movement before the war because they were making profit by selling much-needed supplies to the Allies at higher-than-market prices.[100] While they did not oppose the efforts of preparedness advocates such as Baruch, Godfrey, and Coffin, neither did they support them.[101] Like Congress and the public, until the United States actually engaged in the war, these suppliers had little reason to involve themselves in preparedness initiatives.[102] Once the war began, it was up to Baruch and his committee leaders to negotiate and coerce these executives to cooperate with the government and provide supplies at affordable rates. While there were pockets of significant private-sector leadership, which were critical to the formation and success of the WIB, many of the most powerful corporations were not part of this vanguard. It was simply too lucrative for them elsewhere.

Presidential backing was critical to the authority and perceived legitimacy of the WIB. Congress, while doubtful about the organization, did not interfere with the executive empowerment of the agency because the need to mobilize outstripped more intangible concerns about the public–private nature of the organization. Thus, in the ad hoc, emergency environment in which the WIB developed, direct presidential support was crucial to the organization's survival while the leadership of a few private executives drove the agency itself.

THE EVOLUTION OF THE ORGANIZATIONAL FRAMEWORK FOR COOPERATION

There were many defects and many shortcomings and many bases
for criticism, but we must realize that we were in the position of
a railroad with a single-track bridge over which a huge amount
of traffic had to go. We could not pull up that single track until
we had built a new one. We were trying to build new ones and
straighter ones beside the old one.

Bernard Baruch, describing the evolution of the
WIB organization and its continued attempts
to adapt to the changing needs of war[103]

The organizational framework of the WIB may be best understood as an emergency system that grew organically and developed as the war crisis worsened. It started initially with the NCB, developed further within Coffin's Committee on Industrial Preparedness, then morphed into the CND with its various committees including the GMB and the advisory council, and finally resulted in the WIB. While the mobilization framework evolved with each institutional progression, the basic tenets of how public–private interaction would be facilitated changed very little. In Baruch's report on the WIB published in 1941, he argues that this evolution permitted the organization to meet the needs of war as they developed.[104] Randall Kester appears to agree with this assessment, describing the WIB as "ad hoc—developed in response to immediate needs, without a predetermined and comprehensive plan."[105] This section explores the organizational structure of the WIB, focusing primarily on the WIB post–May 1918 (when Wilson designated Baruch as chair and provided the agency with the authority to mobilize American industry). All references to the WIB, unless specifically indicated otherwise, refer to the period after May 1918, when the WIB became independent of the CND.

At its strongest, the WIB was able to facilitate American industrialization for World War I as a direct result of a presidential directive that centralized the agency and provided it with the authority to control mobilization. In a letter to Baruch sent on March 4, 1918, Wilson asked that Baruch assume the chairmanship and laid out a revised and more definitive role for the WIB and its new leader.[106] Through the Overman Act, passed in May 1918, and Executive Order 2868, issued a few days later, the president was able to reorder the executive agencies of the government as he deemed necessary to respond to the war crisis.[107] Using the Overman Act, Wilson made the WIB independent of the CND and restructured the organization to give it the centralized, more authoritative structure that the private-sector volunteers had so long advocated.[108]

The lack of congressional involvement in the WIB's remit led to grumblings on Capitol Hill about Wilson's use of power to create such authority in the WIB.[109] Baruch biographer Carter Field writes that while there were "grave wonderings" about all the authority granted to the WIB during the war, no one in Congress ever tried to change the organization or formally oppose it. He argues that "this unwillingness of Congress to rock the boat, despite the obvious encroachment on its prerogatives, was astonishing."[110]

At the same time, it was the very informality and flexibility of the structural framework that appealed to many private-sector partners. "The very flexibility of which an informal emergency agency like the WIB offered business interests as a protective device during the crisis was one of its great appeals to business synthesizers" because it prevented the organization from being perceived as "the strong arm of a regulatory state" and allowed it to operate as a flexible agency run by volunteer businessmen.[111]

The physical structure of the WIB and the way the organization facilitated military and industry cooperation changed very little once it became independent of the CND. The CND was designed to include an advisory commission composed of seven industry experts appointed by the president of the United States to represent various key sectors of industry.[112] The council represented the following industrial sectors: transportation, labor, general industry, finance, mining, merchandise, and medical.[113] Baruch and Coffin were appointed to serve on the advisory commission.[114]

In the early days of the CND, the organization struggled to find its footing and was left to fend for itself with little guidance, authority, or focus. As a result, the committees naturally focused inward on their own areas of expertise. In some regard this autonomy gave the committee leaders the space and flexibility to mold their sector of the CND as they saw fit to maximize their efficacy.[115] Overall, however, the lack of central coordination and internal cohesion reduced the legitimacy of the organization and made a coordinated multisector response impossible. Not realizing that the war would soon be on the council's doorstep, the lack of consensus about how the organization should function, combined with the general peacetime mood of the nation, left the council with a mistaken lack of urgency.[116] As the war crisis rendered the CND, the advisory commission, and the GMB insufficient, political and economic realities paved the way for the WIB. The WIB was designed to be a "clearing house for the war industry needs of the Government."[117]

The board was meant to respond to production requirements, create or expand industries as "demanded by the emergency," and assess the urgency of the needs of the government services.[118] Baruch further summarized the functions of the board as "(1) To analyze the needs of our Government, of the Allies, and of the civil population; (2) to study the extent to which the resources could meet those needs; (3) to provide means and encouragement for increasing production; and (4) to promulgate rules and suggestions for preventing waste and unnecessary use."[119]

To accomplish these aims, the WIB adopted a committee structure like those established by predecessor organizations to facilitate mobilization and public–private cooperation. The WIB was divided into committees based on industry sector and led by volunteers with specialist knowledge in each field. The division heads were responsible for prioritizing orders, negotiating contracts between the manufacturers and military, determining the price of goods, and generally serving as a broker between the sectors.[120] As the number of commodity sections within the WIB grew, they found it challenging to coordinate directly with the numerous private corporations in each industry. Therefore, a series of groups was created that could "represent before the commodity sections and the functional divisions of the board the interests of all members of the respective trades to be affected by war regulation."[121] To ensure that the committees represented entire sectors, including both large and small companies, the WIB worked in cooperation with the US Chamber of Commerce to identify and organize the key industries of the country so that each industry was represented by a war service committee of the Chamber.[122] Eventually 350 industrial sectors were represented.[123]

Few structural changes were made to the organization when Wilson rewrote its charter in his March 1918 letter to Baruch. Wilson's letter empowered the organization to oversee and enforce the mobilization of industry and to be independent of the CND. Baruch was appointed as chair and led the board alongside his vice-chair, a representative from the army and one from the navy, six committee heads (who held responsibility for sixty commodity sections), a general counsel, and the secretary.[124] These ten board members oversaw the twelve key functional sections of the WIB.[125] This structure, while slightly adapted, was similar to that of the CND, but the WIB was still unable to make contracts or to determine the type or quantity of materials that would be needed. This was left to the permanent agencies of government, the army, and the navy.[126]

Other than the committee designations, the organizational structure of the WIB was loose, at best. While the very lack of specificity within the organizational framework was a great asset in some regard, allowing the WIB the flexibility to change and develop as necessity demanded, it was also a great hindrance.[127] No legislation was passed to establish or empower the WIB, and, without statutory backing, the organization was reliant on the support of the president and cooperation from the private sector and military. The board's decisions were made by holding a series of meetings between the WIB, private-sector sellers, and government purchasers until a satisfactory agreement was reached. Once this occurred, the agreement was then made a "ruling of the board," and all parties agreed to adhere to the decision. Thus, the mandates of the board were based on consensus rather than legal standing.

There are four key areas where the WIB's lack of statutory authority significantly impacted the organization. First, without an act of Congress designating the roles and responsibilities of the WIB and its chair, the organization was dependent upon the president of the United States for the organizational direction and political support necessary to survive. The power of the president grew as the war crisis developed.[128] These gradually accumulated powers meant that by the time the Overman Act was presented and passed, granting the president the authority to reorganize the executive agencies as he wished, there were already statutory measures in place to allow the president to commandeer production facilities, food, and fuel as necessary to support national defense measures.[129] Wilson used these powers to strengthen the WIB. As one of the emergency agencies reporting directly to the president, the WIB was reliant upon the administration for organizational direction and political support. Wilson removed the WIB from under the CND and made the organization report directly to him.[130] In his letter to Bernard Baruch, Wilson provided both the organization and the chair with the authority they lacked.[131] Final decisions would be made by the chair, rather than the board as a whole, and the board would finally have some powers to secure cooperation with private and public partners through its new authority to commandeer factories and prioritize supply orders.[132]

Second, the authority bestowed on the chairman of the WIB by the president illustrates the important role the leader of the WIB played as ultimate decision maker and figurehead. A more authoritative chair was meant to signify the centralization of decision-making within the WIB as a tool to avoid the bureaucratic turf wars and confusion that had previously dominated mobilization efforts.[133] The understanding that Baruch had the president's full support was an important enhancement to the organizational fabric of the WIB.[134]

Despite the symbolic authority bestowed on Baruch, the WIB remained a highly decentralized agency that continued to struggle for "external power and internal cohesion" throughout its existence.[135] Baruch could not have successfully run the organization as an authoritarian leader even with his presidentially designated powers because the success of the WIB continued to rely upon the ability of the organization to balance public and private interests.[136] These varied on an issue-by-issue basis and, as Cuff points out, "neither the Board nor any single man could control all of these factors at once."[137] Baruch was required to continue to rely on his division heads and leave them to interact with each industrial sector based on their specialist knowledge, run a decentralized organization, and use his role as chair to project an image of strong leadership, unity, and control.

Third, the relationship between the WIB and the public and private sectors is noteworthy because, in lieu of an act of Congress to cement the involvement of the sectors, the WIB relied upon voluntary cooperation driven by the shared urgency of the crisis to ensure success. Without a legislative act creating the WIB and designating the roles and responsibilities of the agencies and its partners, the organization struggled for power and authority until the end of the war. "Only as the military services on the one hand and the business groups on the other could be relied upon to cooperate with the board did it achieve meaningful power." [138] Baruch and his section heads spent a great deal of energy proving themselves "friends" to business and developing trust within the business community to ensure their continued cooperation. At the same time, they continued to struggle with the military to streamline purchasing and obtain lower prices to ensure that the needs of war were met. The military was a further challenge to the WIB because the military worked its way into the administrative fabric of the organization and thereby managed to "upset WIB plans for organizational coherence and control" to such an extent that the WIB was just as dependent upon military cooperation as it was on the good will of the private sector.[139]

Finally, the legal standing of the WIB as an executive agency was opaque at best—a fact that may have facilitated its success in the short term but ultimately limited the sustainability of the organization in the long term. As the WIB's legal counsel told Baruch when he assumed the chair, any decision he made was "*ultra vires*," or beyond his authority, and Baruch could be personally sued for a loss suffered by anyone who carried out his orders.[140] While Baruch found this legal opinion "paralyzing" at first, he argues "since I had already issued enough orders to have my fortune swallowed up many times over, there was nothing to do but go ahead as I had been doing."[141] While the organization's opaque legal standing initially created a degree of confusion, the board was able to sustain a place for itself within Wilson's war administration. In lieu of legal authority compelling cooperation from the private sector and military, the WIB was forced to work closely with both parties to earn their trust and respect and obtain their cooperation. In the case of the private sector in particular, Baruch spent a great deal of time and energy maintaining private-sector good will. Baruch took private complaints very seriously and championed many issues on behalf of industry because anything that Baruch could do to make industry more effective only supported the war effort and increased his prestige with the business community.[142]

In cases in which the private sector could not be compelled by good will and friendly negotiation, the WIB had the power to prioritize war orders (or, as Baruch explains, "the power to determine who gets what and when"[143]). Still, priority decisions could be controversial and "often caused anguish and outrage in the armed services and procurement agencies and even more among industrialists, neither of whom were accustomed to interference in their own affairs."[144] Additionally, the WIB had the power to commandeer factories in lieu of volunteer cooperation if absolutely necessary.[145] Baruch says, "Although the WIB acted primarily through its power over priority, we also relied on our power of persuasion to elicit the cooperation from industry.... When priorities and persuasion failed, we had one instrument of last resort to enforce our will: the power of commandeering—the power to seize property."[146]

An instance in which Baruch used the threat of commandeering to obtain private-sector support occurred in 1918 in a conflict with the automobile industry. Baruch became aware of a large offensive that would require armored troop and weapons carriers. Because of the steel shortage in the United States, Baruch asked the car manufacturers to reduce production in the United States by 75 percent to allow for the production of the war equipment. When the car manufacturers, including John Dodge and Henry Ford, refused, Baruch called Secretary of War Baker and instructed him to take over the steel from several of the factories. Using this threat and additional political pressures, the executives eventually agreed.[147] The power to commandeer was a strong tool, but it had to be used cautiously and only in the case of absolute necessity because it could backfire and cause a widespread revolt among industry partners and dissuade cooperation from other industrial sectors. The relationship of the WIB with the private sector, in lieu of clear and legitimate legal standing, can best be described as "a gaming process marked by loose, informal understandings, ad hoc arrangements, calculated risks of infringement, and pervasive bargaining."[148]

The WIB was developed "on the hoof" in the midst of the crisis and was an entirely ad hoc, emergency institution with an inherited framework, no direct legislative authority, and no mechanism to facilitate either short- or long-term cross-sector cooperation. A combination of factors allowed the WIB to function effectively despite its loose organizational framework. including confusion within government driven by the war crisis, the urgent need to mobilize industry, the private-sector preference for a loose organizational structure, and organizational empowerment from the president of the United States.

INFORMATION SHARING

As with every aspect of the WIB, the sharing of information between public- and private-sector partners was ad hoc, conducted in the midst of crisis, and plagued by the questions of power and authority. In the WIB context, "information sharing" refers to the ability of the private and public sectors to communicate with the agency to facilitate the supply orders needed to support the war. Communication between all parties was most successful when the agency was empowered by the president to take decisive action, which gave the WIB coercive power. Even then, information sharing was a significant challenge.

The WIB shared information with industry through the sixty commodity sections of the agency, which represented more than 350 industries. Clarkson describes communication between the WIB and industry as a two-way flow where information about production flowed into the board from industry at the same time requests and orders of the board flowed from the agency to the private sector.[149] There was no structured method for sharing information. Baruch was keen to allow each commodity division head to run his section based on his expertise.[150] This meant that each commodity chief gathered and relayed information as he deemed most appropriate for his particular sector. Just as Baruch had used his contacts, leadership skills, and wit to resolve the crisis of US nitrate supplies while he was head of the raw materials committee of the CND, so also the commodity chiefs were each engaged in brokering deals for their own industrial sectors. In the chaos of war in which the WIB operated, it is safe to say that priority was placed on collecting the raw information, fulfilling orders, and supplying the needs of the military. Little, if any, time was spent considering how that information was collected and if it was consistent across the agency. From their perspective, so long as the orders were being fulfilled, they cared little about the process. A war was on.

Before the war, industry had been reluctant to cooperate with the WIB or share information for two significant reasons. First, it was much more profitable to sell directly to the Allies.[151] Second, the military's poor handle on its supply requirements led to constantly shifting assessment for goods.[152] This was a cause of extreme frustration in the private sector, costing them both time and money. "It was difficult enough for business advisors to lure American businessmen from a relatively established and highly profitable Allied munitions market; unreliable information on government requirements made the task even harder. Could business advisors expect business to cooperate . . . with a purchaser who never knew his own mind?"[153]

The military was equally unenthusiastic about sharing information with the mobilization agencies. The army and navy did not want to relinquish any power or authority to the WIB or to each other, and both agencies were eager to maintain their "turf" and sole responsibility for the procurement of war materials. Clarkson says that the army and navy supply departments saw the WIB as "a sometimes helpful but usually meddlesome agency" whose advice it occasionally sought but generally "felt no imperative necessity of yielding to it as the central clearing-house of the business activities of war."[154] Therefore, the WIB struggled to maintain a cooperative spirit with the military, who felt no inherent desire to work with them.

US entry into the war significantly changed the willingness of both sectors to share information. The urgency of war and the sheer pace required to meet war demands forced the sectors together out of both absolute necessity and patriotism. In addition, war was big business, and government contracts could be very lucrative for some industries. The authority of the WIB after May 1918, including presidential backing and the power to commandeer plants, also offered coercive encouragement for the sectors to cooperate.

The WIB's new authority and political backing gave the army and navy little choice but to fall in line (although they did retain a foothold in the agency by having a military representative on the board). The private sector also cooperated readily with government, albeit begrudgingly at times, once the WIB had real authority to serve as a broker and the power to seize plants if necessary. It is important to note that one of Baruch's priorities was to work closely with industry to win their trust and respect so that cooperation came from shared understanding rather than coercion.[155] Even then, there is little doubt that the willingness of the private sector to find such a shared understanding was largely based on the fact that action could be taken by the WIB if they failed to cooperate. Clarkson argues, "While it was not necessary for the WIB to draw its gun very often, the fact that it had a high-powered one in its holster was of immense value in invigorating its administration, after many months of more or less ineffectual attempts to borrow powers it had no right to command."[156] Thus, the agency was only able to share information effectively once it had the authority to attract and compel partners to participate.

The WIB shared information in an ad hoc institutionalized structure. Very much reflective of the emergency environment in which it operated, the WIB tried to use charm whenever possible to encourage cooperation but resorted to threats and presidential intervention if necessary to achieve its aims. There was no single channel or method through which information was shared: communication methods varied by sector as determined by each commodity chief within the WIB. The WIB had no means to continue cross-sector cooperation or share information after the war and was equipped to function only in an emergency environment where shared urgency generated mutual prioritization and a willingness to cooperate.

BENEFITS TO BOTH SECTORS

For any cross-sector collaboration to function effectively, it is critical that both sectors perceive some benefit from participation, otherwise there is no motivation to stay involved. World War I provided both sectors sufficient reason to engage in the WIB for a very short time. The economy was on the brink of collapse, and the ability of the public and private sectors to meet production demands was an urgent necessity that could decide the outcome of the war.

Industry was not motivated to participate with the WIB prior to May 1918 because participation had distinct financial disadvantages. As the war in Europe worsened, the needs of the Allies for raw materials and manufactured goods grew to such an extent that normal principles of supply and demand no longer applied, and American manufacturers could charge higher than normal prices for goods.[157] "The fact that American business reaped huge profits from Allied munitions orders after 1915 reduced still further the incentive among American industrialists to develop a systematic relationship with such an impoverished customer."[158] The private sector earned far more from the Allies than they would have earned as a partner of the US government. Prewar preparedness initiatives in the United States were, after all, largely designed to secure lower prices from American manufacturers.

After the United States joined the war, private industry became far more motivated to respond to calls for industry–government cooperation. Patriotism played a significant role in this shift, and many industrial heads made business compromises to assist with the war effort. Baruch discusses how many industrialists bowed to the will of the government during this period. He recalls that the president of the powerful Aluminum Corporation did anything he asked during the war and contends that "the Aluminum Company was virtually placed at the disposition of the government." [159]

At the same time, business imperatives remained; for many industrial leaders, war was big business, and this factor superseded any patriotic impulses. It was clearly in the best interests of the Aluminum Corporation, for example, as a supplier of a material that would be in huge demand during the war, to cooperate fully with the government. Being a cooperative partner would likely help secure more government contracts, earning the corporation more money in the long term. This is in sharp contrast to the situation faced by the auto industry, described earlier in the chapter. In that instance, the automobile market in the United States was booming as many Americans bought their first car. The interests of national defense and the car manufacturers did not align. To make tanks and other equipment for a major offensive planned in Europe, the government needed the steel that the car manufacturers planned to use to build cars. The strength of the domestic automobile industry left manufacturers unwilling to slow production to enable the military to build the necessary equipment. They agreed only reluctantly when Baruch threatened to commandeer steel plants. [160] Baruch himself acknowledges, "it would be misleading to suggest that all industry leaders were motivated by altruism or that their cooperation was spontaneous. Had this been so, the history of the WIB would not have been filled with so many instances of conflict. If some men accepted without question the intrusion of government into their affairs, others resented it and fought tooth and nail." [161] When industry and the WIB did not agree, decisions were eventually reached as a result of extensive negotiation, bargaining, and coercion, if necessary. [162]

Private-sector volunteers also gained no significant benefit by lending their expertise to the WIB. Not only were the dollar-a-year men paid very meager salaries (if any), the lack of statutory authority in the agency meant they could be held legally liable for actions they took as members of the organization. [163] While this was certainly true during the CND, the risk that private volunteers could be held legally liable remained throughout the conflict because of the lack of statutory authority in the agency. While Baruch would be the most likely target of legislation, there was no guarantee that other private volunteers would not also be at risk.

Like the private sector, the army and navy did not see any compelling reason to cooperate with the WIB prior to the United States' engagement in the war. Both services sought to maintain their own power and authority over purchasing and saw the WIB as a nuisance. Despite the military's strong desire to maintain individual control of purchasing, by the time the war began, it was apparent that the military was uncoordinated and badly organized. There was "congestion in some manufacturing areas, while others were not being fully utilized" and at the same time "the filling of orders was unbalanced, so that one department might succeed in overstocking itself while others could not secure necessities."[164] This chaotic, decentralized process spiraled out of control as the war reached its climax. Wilson placed a representative of the military on the board of the WIB to ensure that the interests of these permanent agencies were represented, and he gave the WIB full authority to oversee industrial mobilization. With a strong foothold in the agency through a military representative, it was in the best interests of the military to relinquish some of its authority to the WIB so it could focus on the war.

After the armistice, it was no longer mutually beneficial for the military and the private sector to participate in the WIB. Baruch acknowledges that at times the actions of the agency caused military and private industrial partners "anguish" and "outrage" since neither partner was "accustomed to interference in their own affairs."[165] With the war over, there was no longer any need to tolerate interference from an outside body. The patriotism and urgency created by the war were no longer motivating factors; the military no longer had urgent demands of industry and, with orders from the government drastically reduced, the private sector had no real motivation to provide the government any special price considerations or treatment. Perhaps most importantly, with the conclusion of the war, Wilson's war powers were diminished and he could no longer provide his emergency agencies with the backing and authority he had during the war. It was simply not in the best interests of either sector to continue.

The degree to which a cross-sector partnership is beneficial to both parties is critical to the longevity of the partnership structure. The WIB was beneficial to both sectors only during the apex of the war crisis. This responsive organization was designed to mobilize the nation for war, and once peace was achieved, there was no longer any significant incentive to continue working together.

TRUST

The relationship between the president, Congress, military, industry, and the WIB was built on self-interest and a sense of urgency, not trust. The sectors were driven together by a national defense crisis that at times risked becoming a national economic crisis. A shared desire to avoid these crises, combined with the urgency of war, allowed the partners to overlook their distrust for one another in the interest of meeting their shared objectives. The public and private sectors' mistrust of one another, combined with a shared lack of trust in the WIB as an institution, limited the long-term prospects of the agency.

Lack of trust between the sectors undermined public–private cooperation because neither party felt secure about the long-term reliability and motives of the other partners. Congress distrusted the private sector in general, and members were suspicious of the motives of private volunteers in particular. They worried that the dollar-a-year men acted in private, rather than national, interests.[166] In addition, Congress was hesitant to endorse a civilian-led mobilization agency and conceded only reluctantly that a cross-sector collaboration was needed when the crisis was at its worst. Because of the urgency of the situation, they overlooked the questionable legality of the WIB and Wilson's use of his wartime presidential powers to enable it. The likelihood was small that they would continue to do so without the compelling urgency of war.

At the same time, the private sector did not trust that Congress and the president would not use the war as a means of regulating and controlling free trade and private industry after the war. They feared increased government involvement in industry and were hesitant to relinquish too much power. In addition, because the government, as a partner, consistently failed to take into account the varied interests of the private sector, the government was a risky partner that could cost private-sector corporations a great deal of money.

The military did not trust either the WIB or the private sector. As discussed previously, the military distrusted the agency, seeing the WIB as a potential threat to their own power and authority in Washington. In addition, the military had no faith that either the WIB or industry at large would work in their best interests unless compelled to do so.

Finally, beyond the partners' lack of trust in one another, there was a further lack of trust in the WIB as an institution. All parties knew the shaky legal ground the organization rested upon, its dependency on the president, and the organization's status as a wartime construct. The president and Congress had been hesitant to support the WIB until forced to, and the likelihood that either one would back the agency in peace was small. Without a solid institutional structure, the WIB relied on informal networks of trusted personal contacts. The dollar-a-year men were invaluable in this regard because they represented and furthered the interests of the WIB with their industry knowledge and personal relationships. Baruch was a champion of this method, realizing the importance of relationship building in developing trust and encouraging cooperation. He worked hard to "cultivate good relations with corporate executives themselves" because he realized that they were the ones who "possessed the most direct access to economic control."[167] The agency was able to survive the war despite a general lack of institutional trust because it was able to rely on interpersonal trust to win over private executives.[168]

Without embedded institutional trust, the WIB relied upon individual trust and the shared bonds created by the crisis of war to sustain its relationships. Since the organization was responsive and was created and equipped only to last the course of the war, there was no sense of it having a future in ongoing crisis avoidance. Public trust was simply beyond the emergency, reactionary remit of the organization.

ADAPTABILITY OR SUSTAINABILITY

Prior to 1918 America's preparedness and mobilization strategy adapted quickly to meet national needs as the country entered the war. From 1915 to 1917 no fewer than four organizations adapted to meet the growing crisis, and these agencies eventually evolved into the WIB.

World War I ended on November 11, 1918, and on November 27 Baruch sent a letter to President Wilson suggesting that the WIB be decommissioned as of January 1, 1919.[169] Clarkson says, "The WIB died with the war and the magnificent war formation of American industry was dissipated in a day; the mobilization that had taken many months was succeeded by an instantaneous demobilization."[170] Baruch was quick to recognize that the organization was not adaptable. He argued, "Only a national emergency could sustain the momentum and mask the inadequacies of a mobilization program so fundamentally dependent upon voluntary administration and the private cooperation of corporate interest groups."[171] In his letter to the president, Baruch said, "The American people would resent . . . the continuance of apparent war powers" and added that if the WIB were to continue as a powerless agency, this would only "create a lack of respect for the government."[172]

While it may be true that Baruch was concerned with how the American people would perceive the agency and the government if it continued after World War I, it is more likely that Baruch's greatest concern was that the fabric that held the WIB together would quickly unravel without the bonding thread of crisis. The WIB's relationship with the president, Congress, and its military and private-sector partners was all held together by a shared desire to facilitate mobilization. With the war over, this would no longer be the case. Although Congress had turned a blind eye to the lack of statutory authority held by the agency during the war, they would not continue to do so.[173] Wilson empowered the WIB by using the enhanced wartime authority that allowed him to act quickly and decisively. Once the war was over, Congress would no longer overlook the legal grey area within which the WIB operated, and the president would no longer have the authority to support the agency. The only way around these issues would be to make the WIB a legitimate agency established through an act of Congress. Remembering that both the administration and Congress had been hesitant to support the WIB until forced by the war crisis to do so, it was very unlikely that either one would support making the WIB a statutory agency.[174] There was a further worry that if the WIB was made permanent it might "very easily fall prey to politicians or unsympathetic government officials."[175] Politically speaking, justifying why the organization was necessary after the war was over would be difficult, and the WIB simply remained too controversial and lacked the organizational coherence to sustain itself.

Volunteerism and the willingness of the private sector and the military to continue working together through the WIB waned rapidly during the armistice. The crisis had ebbed, the nation was recovering, and normality would soon return. Many of the dollar-a-year men, originally driven to volunteer in the WIB by a combination of power lust and patriotism, were being pulled by industry to return to the private sector.[176] This desire to leave Washington was also fueled by the legal ambiguity and organizational chaos under which the agency had operated during the war.[177] WIB member E. E. Parsonage wrote in a letter on November 16, 1918, "No one wants the responsibility of the clean-up. It is a question of getting out from under and going home."[178] Private-sector corporations who had engaged with the WIB out of a combination of patriotism, financial incentive, political gain, and coercion were no longer motivated to participate.

The military was also not as eager to cooperate after the war. The end of the war meant that army and navy contracts decreased significantly, and working with the WIB was far less beneficial. The military, often coerced into compliance with the WIB because of its wartime power to prioritize military supply orders, was no longer bound by the agency.

In both the private sector and the military, without the urgency of war as a driver, there was no significant incentive to partner. The WIB lacked any legal standing and had an ad hoc and structurally weak organizational framework. Therefore, when national circumstances changed, the WIB lacked the legal and structural tools to adapt and was not sustainable. The partners engaged with the agency were motivated by the crisis of war; once the armistice arrived, it was not in the interests of either sector to continue.

The inability of the WIB to adapt or be sustainable is not a condemnation or an assessment of its relative success or failure. It is important to remember that WIB as a responsive organization was designed to be a reactionary agency able to respond to the immediate needs of war. The WIB was not created with the intention of a permanent existence, and it may be argued that having met the needs of war and accomplished its primary objectives, the organization came to a natural end.

TABLE 4.1: Summary of the Seven Critical Factors in the War Industries Board

Critical Factors	Key Elements of Public–Private Cooperation in the Development and Establishment of the WIB
Crisis	The chaos of operating within a crisis culture underscores every aspect of the WIB. Conceptually developed when World War I began, the organization was wholly oriented toward addressing a national defense need that developed as a result of the war crisis—the pressing need to mobilize American industry for war.
Leadership	The WIB was able to accomplish its tasking because of strong executive leadership. The president served to empower and support the WIB in lieu of an act of Congress that would provide it statutory authority. The leadership of the dollar-a-year men was also instrumental. These men formed the backbone of the WIB, kept it afloat when it was politically unpopular, and used their industry experience and contacts to achieve the objectives of the agency.
Organizational Structure	The WIB was an ad hoc emergency institution with a very loose organizational framework, no specific mechanism to facilitate cross-sector cooperation, and tenuous legal standing. The organization was not created by an act of Congress and relied upon the office of the president for authority and support.
Information (Reserve) Sharing	The ad hoc organizational framework of the WIB meant that information sharing in the WIB was informal and varied according to the style of individual commodity chiefs. The WIB used a combination of negotiation, cooperation, and coercion to obtain the information it needed to support mobilization.
Shared Benefits	During the war, a combination of patriotism and urgent necessity drove the partners together, and during this period both derived some benefit from engaging with the WIB. The reasons not to cooperate were so compelling, however, that without the urgency of war pulling them together, there was little reason to sustain a partnership.
Trust	The looseness of the WIB organizational framework led to a lack of institutional trust in the agency. The dollar-a-year men were able to overcome this during the crisis by using their own trusted network of private contacts to establish relationships within their sector on the basis of individual trust.
Adaptability/ Sustainability	The WIB was designed to address national needs of war. It was not intended to survive in the long term and did not have the legal or structural tools to adapt after World War I ended.

CONCLUSION

The WIB was an ad hoc organizational structure that was the product of evolutionary development and inconsistent public- and private-sector support. As a responsively oriented partnership, the WIB was designed and equipped to address the problems the United States faced in terms of industrial mobilization, a smaller aspect of the larger war crisis faced by the nation. Once the war had reached its conclusion, the need to mobilize was eliminated and the partnership reached its natural conclusion.

The WIB operated within an environment of chaos. Externally, the nation was scrambling to meet the demands of the war. This created a sense of urgency in the military, Congress, and private sector that had previously been lacking and made each of these parties willing, for the first time, to empower and seriously engage the WIB as a coordinating intermediary. Internally, the organizational structure of the WIB was dynamic and operating at fever pitch in an effort to accomplish its remit. The focus was on fulfilling orders by any means possible, and little thought was given to process or consistency. There simply was not the time. While this allowed the WIB to move quickly and flexibly, it also meant that there was no consistency between commodity sections in terms of how information was shared, who shared that information, and how orders were processed and coordinated. The WIB was effectively treading water in the midst of a maelstrom, and it struggled to facilitate US mobilization between a large number of actors in an environment characterized by urgency and chaos.

While the loose, ad hoc organizational structure of the WIB allowed it to avoid bureaucratic delays, this flexibility came at a cost. First, the questionable legal authority of the organization and its ability to issue orders placed significant liability on the private-sector volunteers working within the agency. Second, the loose organizational structure, empowered primarily by the president, was not sufficiently solid for public or private partners to develop any sense of institutional trust in the WIB as an organization. The sectors participated out of a shared sense of need and urgency driven by the war, and they saw the WIB as expedient in the short term.

This chapter's case study of the WIB demonstrates that the seven critical factors—crisis, leadership, organizational structure, information sharing, shared benefits, trust, and adaptability or sustainability—are important factors in responsive partnerships such as the WIB. The next chapter compares and contrasts the three partnerships to understand which structure may be the most appropriate model for disaster-oriented PPPs and identifies any lessons from these strategic and responsive alliances that may be applied to contemporary efforts at developing a partnership framework.

NOTES

1. See, for example, Goldberg, *Liberal Fascism*.

2. Baruch testified before the Nye Committee in 1935, and his two primary works discussing the WIB were published in 1921 and 1960. Baruch, *American Industry*. For full testimony of Bernard Baruch to the Nye Committee, see Senate, Special Committee to Investigate the Munitions Industry. *Munitions Industry: Final Report of the Chairman of the United States War Industries Board to the President of the United States, February 1919*, 74th Cong., 1st sess. (1935), NARA, RG 287, box no. Y 5932.

3. Dorwart, *Eberstadt and Forrestal*, 44.

4. Kester, "War Industries Board," 655.

5. Koistinen, "Industrial-Military Complex," 379.

6. Baruch, *American Industry*, 21.

7. Bernard Baruch argues that "the resources of Germany were accurately known, the requirements of war had been carefully computed, and the whole economic structure was systematized for concentration on a single national purpose. With us [the United States] the case was quite otherwise. Senate, *Munitions Industry: Final Report*, 1–2.

8. Ibid.

9. Clarkson, *Industrial America*, 18.

10. Kester, "War Industries Board," 655.

11. In 1915 President Wilson called upon the secretaries of War and Navy to make sure that programs were in place to ensure adequate national defense. Secretary Daniels was primarily informed by inventor Thomas Edison, who helped brainstorm how to structure the new organization. Daniels contacted Edison after his article "Edison's Plan for Success" appeared in the *New York Times* on May 30, 1915. Edison was the first head of the NCB, and he helped Daniels formulate a "department of invention and development" within which the navy could "evaluate suggestions by either military or civilian inventors." For more on Edison's role, see Daniels to Edison, July 7, 1915, reprinted in Scott, *Naval Consulting Board*, 286; and Senate, *Munitions Industry: Final Report*, 3.

12. Cuff, *War Industries Board*, 16; and Koistinen, "Industrial-Military Complex," 382.

13. Clarkson, *Industrial America*, 13; and Cuff, *War Industries Board*, 17.

14. Cuff, *War Industries Board*, 17–19.

15. Ibid., 20. Both Clarkson and Gifford worked diligently on preparedness issues for years. Both men would also serve as the director of the Council of National Defense, a later evolution of the General Munitions Board.

16. Senate, *Digest of the Proceedings of the Council of National Defense during the World War.* Franklin H. Martin, 73rd Cong., 2nd sess., Doc. No. 193 (1934), 512; see also Clarkson, *Industrial America*, 13–14; and Koistinen, "Industrial-Military Complex," 382.

17. Senate, *Digest of the Proceedings*, 512.

18. Cuff, *War Industries Board*, 24.

19. Sen. George E. Chamberlain was the chair of the Senate Committee on Military Affairs, and at the time Coffin spoke to him, he was also focused on preparedness issues. After Coffin had convinced Secretary of War Newton Baker and Secretary of the Navy Joseph Daniels of his position by arguing that it would allow munitions to be produced "at a moment's notice," Chamberlain finally agreed to include the amendment in the Hay Bill. Section 120 "gave the president power, exercised through his department heads, to place obligatory orders directly with any manufacturers who produced or could produce war material." It also authorized the secretary of War "to make complete lists of all private plants equipped to manufacture arms and ammunition as well as those plants that could be converted to munitions production." Ibid.

20. US Statues at Large, vol. 39, part 1, 213–14, quoted in Cuff, *War Industries Board*, 24.

21. A. O. Powell (the chair of the engineering committee in the state of Washington) to Coffin, September 14, 1916, quoted in Cuff, *War Industries Board*, 25.

22. Senate, *Munitions Industry: Final Report*, 3. Cuff writes that by the spring of 1917, some thirty thousand inventories had been taken, but the inventories were of "little practical value" and "did not prepare industry for war." Cuff, *War Industries Board*, 26.

23. Ibid, 36.

24. Koistinen, "Industrial-Military Complex," 382.

25. The act is also referred to by Grosvenor Clarkson as the Military Appropriations Act of 1916; however, because it is most often called the Army Appropriations Act, that is the name used here. Clarkson, *Industrial America*, 19. Those who refer to the act as the Army Appropriations Act include Cuff, *War Industries Board*, 39; Koistinen, "Industrial-Military Complex," 383; Hitchcock, "The War Industries Board," 548; and Field, *Bernard Baruch*, 146.

26. Koistinen, "Industrial-Military Complex," 382.

27. Ibid., 385.

28. Godfrey was a consulting engineer for the Bureau of Gas in Philadelphia who became president of the Drexel Institute of Philadelphia and was an ardent supporter of preparedness. He spent time in Europe in 1906 and returned convinced that war was inevitable, and further convinced that the United States should create a Council of National Defense (CND), modeled after the British Council of Imperial Defense. Godfrey lobbied legislators, the secretaries of War and Navy, and others to try to create a CND, and he began writing articles to this effect as early as 1910. Although Coffin had his own plans for expanding preparedness through his committee, he supported Godfrey's initiative. As one member of Coffin's committee put it, "We [Coffin's team] begin where he [Godfrey] leaves off. He finds out the sources of a product which may be useful in war and we take that product as it is and record and coordinate it." William Saunders of the Industrial Preparedness Committee, quoted in Saunders to Redfield, January 20, 1916, in Cuff, *War Industries Board*, 28; and Koistinen, "Industrial-Military Complex," 382. See also Cuff, *War Industries Board*, 27, 35.

29. Baruch, *American Industry*, 43.

30. Hitchcock, "War Industries Board," 551.

31. Cuff, *War Industries Board*, 46.

32. Cuff writes that Wilson's decision to break diplomatic relations "trigger[ed] a countrywide flood of patriotic service offers, including promises by manufacturers to turn over their plants to the government in the event of war." An emergency meeting of the CND was held to discuss how to handle the private-sector outpouring of support and offers of assistance. The commissioners decided to hold a series of conferences with leaders from every industry to ask them to cooperate and begin to develop centers of support and cooperation. As a result of these meetings, the CND divided itself into seven permanent committees that were assigned to commissioners based on their expertise, very much like the NCB. The committees were medicine, labor, transportation and communication, science and research, raw materials, minerals and industrial relations, and supplies. Each commissioner became "master of his domain," which gave each section head the independence to react quickly and coordinate his sector, but this also "ruled out the possibility of organizational coherence" because the commissioners tended to "proceed according to their own ideas and opportunities" rather than as a cohesive unit. Ibid., 46–47.

33. Ibid., 47.

34. Ibid., 69.

35. While some, such as Coffin and Godfrey, favored a standardized approach to industry, others, like Baruch, pushed for a more flexible method that would favor forming ties with the most powerful personalities in key industries as an access point into a particular sector. Ibid., 48.

36. Ibid., 69.

37. Ibid., 47, 61, 65.

38. Ibid., 65.

39. Field, *Bernard Baruch*, 149.

40. The board was originally called a "purchasing board" because many felt that a name involving the word "munitions" was too controversial until the United States engaged in the war. One day after Wilson asked Congress for a declaration of war, on April 3, 1917, the purchasing board had its first meeting. Frank Scott, the chairman of the board, changed the name of the board to the General Munitions Board. This was done largely to secure legitimacy. The GMB was overseen by the CND and the secretary of War (Baker). See Cuff, *War Industries Board*, 66.

41. Hitchcock, "War Industries Board," 555.

42. Field, *Bernard Baruch*, 149; Koistinen, "Industrial-Military Complex," 390; Cuff, *War Industries Board*, 66.

43. Senate, *Munitions Industry: Final Report*, 6.

44. Hitchcock, "War Industries Board," 556.

45. Senate, *Munitions Industry: Final Report*, 1.

46. Ibid.

47. Koistinen, "Industrial-Military Complex," 379.

48. Ibid., 380.

49. Cuff, *War Industries Board*, 69–70.

50. Ibid., 70.

51. Ibid., 73.

52. Ibid., 80.

53. Hitchcock, "War Industries Board," 556.

54. In June of 1917 Secretary of War Baker sent President Wilson a proposal to create a War Industries Board and by the end of July the WIB was established. Cuff, *War Industries Board*, 102, 110.

55. Kester, "War Industries Board," 659.

56. Ibid.; Koistinen, "Industrial-Military Complex," 394; Hitchcock, "War Industries Board," 558.

57. *New York Journal*, "Reorganization Near as Scott Resigns," October 27, 1917. NARA II, College Park, MD, RG 61, File 21 A-A1, Box 2. Daniel Willard (the head of the CND advisory commission) replaced Scott in mid-November 1917 but subsequently resigned in January 1918. Judge Robert S. Lovett led the WIB temporarily between Scott and Willard, and again after Willard resigned. Koistinen argues that Willard "quit in disgust over the board's impotence" while Scott, he claims, had "his health broken through agonizing months spent in government service." Scott resigned from the WIB for health reasons, assumed to have occurred because of the strain of his task. Lovett agreed to chair the WIB, but only on a temporary basis because he wished to return to the private sector and look after his railway company. Lovett was a Texas lawyer who served as general counsel and eventually president of Union Pacific and Southern Pacific Railroad. Lovett volunteered with the Red Cross when the United States entered the war, and he joined the WIB in August of 1917. For more on Lovett, see Cuff, *War Industries Board*, 119. For more on Scott's resignation and Lovett's appointment, see Cuff, *War Industries Board*, 110. For more on Willard's resignation and quote by Koistinen, see Koistinen, "Industrial-Military Complex," 394; Hitchcock, "War Industries Board," 560; Cuff, *War Industries Board*, 139.

58. See Koistinen, "Industrial-Military Complex," 395.

59. Ibid.

60. Cuff writes that during the winter of 1917–18 "never had the powerlessness of the WIB been so apparent. The entire war machine seemed to be grinding slowly to a halt." The situation was so dire that many in the WIB wondered if the organization would last the winter. Cuff, *War Industries Board*, 135–36.

61. Cuff, "Bernard Baruch," 124. Baruch describes the period as a "hopeless tangle" where mobilization efforts were so unorganized that "men who were offered positions refused to take them and many who were connected with the civilian side of the war were leaving or expressed a desire to leave." Bernard Baruch in the Nye Committee hearings, part 22, 6264, as quoted in Cuff, *War Industries Board*, 135.

62. The appointment of Baruch and all of the changes made to the War Industries Board were laid out in Baruch's appointment letter of March 4, 1918; however, they were made legal by Executive Order on May 28, 1918, following the passage of the Overman Act on May 20, which gave the president the authority to reorganize executive agencies as he saw fit to meet the demands of war. See Kester, "War Industries Board," 660; Koistinen, "Industrial-Military Complex," 396.

63. Cuff, *War Industries Board*, 148.

64. Koistinen writes that Wilson was not alone in his lack of support for prepared-ness during this period. He says, "Neither the Wilson administration, Congress, nor prominent American industrialists, financiers and the firms they represented ap-peared excessively concerned about the economics of warfare between 1914 and 1917." Koistinen, "Industrial-Military Complex," 380. See also Cuff, *War Industries Board*, 25.

65. See Koistinen, "Industrial–Military Complex," 397.

66. By May 30, 1915, nearly two years before the United States engaged in World War I, the *New York Times* published Thomas Edison's "Plan for Preparedness." In this piece Edison outlined his views about how the United States should be preparing for the war effort and discussed how the military and government should partner with private-sector manufacturing and engineering experts to ensure industrial readiness for war. Edison's article struck a nerve and marked the beginning of what would become a turbulent and extensive experiment in public–private cooperation. Marshall, "Edison's Plan"; Clarkson, *Industrial America*, 12; Cuff, *War Industries Board*, 15–16.

67. Cuff, *War Industries Board*, 25.

68. Ibid., 45.

69. Baruch, *Baruch: The Public Years*, 35.

70. Cuff, *War Industries Board*, 45.

71. "While the president searched for peace abroad, the council [of national defense] and [advisory] commission drifted along with little sense of a national defense policy, or even a sense of how they might manage their own limited activities." Ibid., 45.

72. Cuff writes in an article about Bernard Baruch, "The vast majority of the Ameri-can people were reluctant to enter World War I, but once President Wilson reached his decision, they responded to the crisis with an outburst of patriotic fervor and a deluge of voluntary activity." Cuff, "Bernard Baruch," 117. See also Cuff, *War Industries Board*, 67.

73. Cuff writes that "only after America became deeply immersed in the maelstrom of war itself would the president moderate his caution toward governmental innova-tion. Only then would influence swing more positively to the men anxious to break down the walls of traditional government on behalf of a new kind of war system." Cuff, *War Industries Board*, 67. See also Koistinen, "Industrial-Military Complex," 386.

74. Koistinen, "Industrial-Military Complex," 395–96.

75. Ibid., 395; Cuff, *War Industries Board*, 138.

76. Koistinen, "Industrial-Military Complex," 395.

77. Cuff writes that Wilson, "stung by the attacks of his critics . . . denounced charges of organizational collapse in Washington and publically opposed proposals for a war cabinet and munitions industry." Cuff, *War Industries Board*, 141.

78. Hitchcock, "War Industries Board," 547.

79. Ohl, "Navy, the WIB, and the Industrial Mobilization," 20.

80. Cuff, *War Industries Board*, 141.

81. Ibid., 104.

82. Many in Congress felt that these preparedness experts were embedding them-selves in Washington in an attempt to drive purchase prices up (at public expense) to benefit industry, and many business volunteers struggled to work in an environment

where congressional inquiries "looked for and expected the worst." This congressional distrust made the WIB a politically hazardous topic and significantly reduced Wilson's willingness to engage or actively support the organization. This caused the president and legislature to avoid "facing issues of economic mobilization whenever possible" because of the political sensitivity of public–private cooperation. Ibid., 85; Koistinen, "Industrial-Military Complex," 386.

83. Ohl, "Navy, the WIB, and the Industrial Mobilization," 17.

84. Koistinen, "Industrial-Military Complex," 387.

85. General Wood is referred to as the "official drill master for the preparedness crusade" and was a driving force behind educating and inspiring many private-sector participants in prewar preparedness cross-sector partnerships. Cuff, *War Industries Board*, 29. For more on the private-sector role on councils and committees, see Clarkson, *Industrial America*, 12; Cuff, *War Industries Board*, 29.

86. Baruch, *American Industry*, 28.

87. Kester, "War Industries Board," 657.

88. Cuff, "Dollar-A-Year Man," 420.

89. During 1917, for example, the dollar-a-year men "came under repeated attack" as Congress sought to "prohibit the use of industrial advisory committees and government officials serving on a nominal salary." This effort by Congress was thwarted by the Wilson-backed Overman Bill that rejuvenated the WIB. Koistinen, "Industrial-Military Complex," 397–98.

90. Cuff, *War Industries Board*, 83.

91. Howard Coffin, for example, was recruited as a volunteer for the NCB largely because of his corporate leadership experience in standardizing the Society of Automobile Engineers. Cuff, *War Industries Board*, 16; Koistinen, "Industrial-Military Complex," 382.

92. Cuff, *War Industries Board*, 138.

93. "Baruch emerged in the process of industrial mobilization as the best known of the 'dollar-a-year men,' the major symbol of business–government cooperation during World War I." Cuff, "Bernard Baruch," 115.

94. In his memoir, Baruch describes meeting Wood at a bridge game hosted by Henry Frick in New York. He explains his early support of Wood during this first meeting: "We began to discuss the war in Europe and the problem of American preparedness. He told me of the citizens' military training camp at Plattsburg, New York. If the camp was to be opened that year, Wood said, he would have to raise $10,000. . . . When I pledged the money on the spot, General Wood was as surprised as he was grateful." Baruch, *Public Years*, 20. Baruch's involvement in Wood's training camps is further seen in Cuff, *War Industries Board*, 32.

95. "He [Baruch] was good at getting men, backing them and keeping this equanimity." Cuff, "Bernard Baruch," 119–20.

96. Ibid., 120.

97. Baruch, *Public Years*, 45.

98. Ibid.

99. Prior to the outbreak of war, the CND could not manage to secure cooperation from the nation's major industrial players. "The huge industrial bureaucracies that stood astride the American economy had not yet allied themselves with these organizational entrepreneurs." Cuff, *War Industries Board*, 26.

100. Ibid., 42. For more on profits earned by industry by selling to the Allies, see Kester, "War Industries Board," 661; Field, *Bernard Baruch*, 149.

101. Cuff, *War Industries Board*, 42.

102. As Cuff points out, "Until America actually entered the war they had no need to merge their preparedness activities with the work of those professionals now moving into public life." Cuff, *War Industries Board*, 42.

103. Senate, *Munitions Industry: Final Report*, 6265.

104. Baruch argues in his report on the WIB that "the war was constantly developing new needs so that a comprehensive undertaking in war manufacture, inaugurated five years before we entered the war, might have been largely wasted." Baruch, *American Industry*, 17.

105. Kester, "War Industries Board," 683.

106. For full reproduction of letter to Baruch, see Baruch, *American Industry*, 24–25.

107. The Overman Act was presented in February 1918 and passed on May 20, 1918. This was reinforced on May 28 by Executive Order No. 2868. Kester, "War Industries Board," 660. See also Hitchcock, "War Industries Board," 547; Koistinen, "Industrial–Military Complex," 396; Cuff, *War Industries Board*, 142; Paxson, "American War Government," 62.

108. The Overman legislation, while inspired by the war crisis, was also inspired at least in part by political pressure placed on the president through two bills being presented by the Senate Military Affairs Committee led by Sen. George Chamberlain. The Overman legislation was a way for the president to maintain control, circumvent passage of the Chamberlain bills, and at the same time address some of the major concerns that emerged in the Senate investigation. While the act led some congressional critics to label Wilson a "dictator," the urgency of the crisis overshadowed these concerns and the Overman Act passed Congress. The *New York Times* reported that the Overman bill caused "the most profound sensation of the entire legislative sessions, in which sensations have been frequent." *New York Times*, "President Seeks Blanket Powers for War Period: Bill to Give Him Authority to Coordinate and Consolidate All Governmental Activities," February 7, 1918. See also Koistinen, "Industrial-Military Complex," 395–96; Cuff, *War Industries Board*, 138, 141, 142.

109. Field holds that the legality of the WIB was the cause of great speculation by Congress. He says, "Never had the senators and representatives seen so much power exercised without their having made the grants of authority, approved the appropriations to exercise them, and had something to say about the personnel. There was criticism in the cloakrooms, not of the actual deeds of the War Industries Board, but of this method of governmental functioning." Field, *Bernard Baruch*, 155.

110. Ibid., 155–56.

111. Cuff, *War Industries Board*, 248.

112. On October 11, 1916, President Wilson announced his appointments to the advisory commission. He said: "The Council of National Defense has been created because the Congress has realized that the country is best prepared for war when thoroughly prepared for peace." Wilson went on to acknowledge the institution as a cross-sector alliance in saying that the council "opens up a new and direct channel of communication between business and scientific men and all departments of the Government." "President Names Defense Advisors: Board of Seven to Act with National Council Is Headed by Daniel Willard. Samuel Gompers a Member. Bernard Baruch and Julius Rosenwald among Others Appointed—Executive Explains Their Duties," in *New York Times*, October 12, 1916, 10. For more on organizational design of the advisory committee of the CND, see Clarkson, *Industrial America*, 21; Koistinen, "Industrial–Military Complex," 383.

113. Cuff, *War Industries Board*, 39.

114. The advisory commission was made up of Daniel Willard, president of the Baltimore and Ohio Railroad; Samuel Gompers, president of the American Federation of Labor; Howard Coffin, president of Hudson Motor Company and head of the NCB Preparedness Committee; Bernard Baruch, Wall Street speculator; John Ryan, Anaconda Cooper Company; Julius Rosenwald, president of Sears Roebuck; and Franklin Martin, a distinguished surgeon. Cuff, *War Industries Board*, 33, 39, 49; *New York Times*, "President Names Defense Advisors.

115. Cuff writes, "The very absence of formalized patterns and complicated structures afforded them a wide field for creative action." Cuff, *War Industries Board*, 43.

116. Cuff argues that the "vast majority of the American people were reluctant to enter World War I"; Cuff, "Bernard Baruch," 117; Cuff, *War Industries Board*, 44–45.

117. Baruch, *American Industry*, 21. Dorwart calls the WIB a "policy-centralizing clearing house and coordinating agency linking government to industry"; Dorwart, *Eberstadt and Forrestal*, 45.

118. Baruch, *American Industry*, 21.

119. Ibid.

120. Dorwart describes the committee system: "Industrial divisions and commodity sections, each run by a director, board of experts, and government representative from the purchasing agency interested in that particular commodity, exerted control over conflicting interests. Division directors authorized and prioritized contracts. They translated central policies to private industries through regional advisors and the war service committees of the Chamber of Commerce." Dorwart, *Eberstadt and Forrestal*, 45.

121. Baruch, *American Industry*, 22.

122. Ibid.

123. Clarkson, *Industrial America*, 299.

124. In addition to Baruch, the members of the WIB included Alex Legge (vice-chair), Rear Adm. F. F. Fletcher (navy representative), Major Gen. George W. Goethals (army representative), Robert S. Brookings (chair of the price-fixing committee), Edwin B. Parker (priorities commissioner), George N. Peek (commissioner of finished products), Hugh Frayne (labor representative), J. Leonard Replogle (steel administrator),

L. L. Summers (technical advisor), Albert C. Ritchie (general counsel), and H. P. Ingels (secretary). Baruch, *American Industry*, 26; Field, *Bernard Baruch*, 156. For a detailed organizational chart of the WIB, see Baruch, *American Industry*, 14–15, 29.

125. The twelve functional sections of the WIB that were overseen by the WIB were the priorities section, the clearing office, the conservation division, the resources and conversion section, the industrial inventory section, the facilities division, the advisory committee on plants and munitions, the labor division, the technical and consulting section, the purchasing commission for the Allies, the division of planning and statistics, and the price-fixing section. Clarkson, *Industrial America*, 61.

126. Baruch, *American Industry*, 27.

127. Kester, "War Industries Board," 662.

128. Other legislative measures that enhanced the power of the president include the National Defense Act of June 3, 1916, which gave the president the power to request corporations to produce specific products that might be needed to support the war. This was further enforced in the Naval Emergency Fund Act of March 4, 1917, the Deficiency Appropriations Act of June 15, 1917, and the Navy Appropriation Act of July 1, 1918. The Food and Fuel Control Act of August 10, 1917, gave the president the authority to "requisition food, feeds, and fuels and other supplies necessary to the army or navy, or any other public use connected with defense." Finally the Esch Car Service Act of May 29, 1917, and the Preferential Shipments Act of August 10, 1917, allowed the president to control and suspend traffic or shipments as necessary to support national defense. Ibid., 676–77.

129. Ibid., 677. Hitchcock wrote in May 1918 that "the passage by Congress of the so-called 'Overman' bill, of which there now seems little doubt (this article is written in early May [1918]) giving the president power to redistribute the powers of the executive departments in any way which he may wish, will undoubtedly make available to the president the power to remove any existing legislative obstacles to the assumption of full control over governmental industrial policy by the War Industries Board and its investment with any or all necessary prerogatives now held by the several existing production and contracting bureaus and departments." Hitchcock, "War Industries Board," 547.

130. Cuff, *War Industries Board*, 147.

131. Hitchcock writes that the WIB, "backed by the power of the president to commandeer, to withhold fuel, and in other ways to force the halting into line . . . can mold the country's industrial system almost as it will." Hitchcock, "War Industries Board," 565. For a full reproduction of the letter to Baruch, see Baruch, *American Industry*, 24–25.

132. Hitchcock, "War Industries Board," 547, 565.

133. Hitchcock describes the significance of this change: "The president practically delegates to the chairman of the War Industries Board his own authority so far as it extends to the supervision of the industrial needs." Ibid., 563

134. Ibid.; see also Ohl, "Navy, the WIB, and the Industrial Mobilization," 20.

135. Cuff, "Bernard Baruch," 126.

136. Baruch is praised by Grosvenor Clarkson for his leadership, ability to trust his staff, and run an effective decentralized agency. Robert Cuff, while recognizing Baruch

as a charismatic and capable leader, is less forthcoming with his praise. He argues that Baruch had no choice but to run the WIB as a decentralized organization in which he was an independent chair because his power was more perceived than real. He contends that Baruch was "bounded by power relationships on all sides, with private industries, the military departments and his own internal organization," which governed the degree to which he could centrally manage the agency. Baruch was able to "gather good men around him," gain their trust and loyalty, and, he argues, it was this ability more than anything that facilitated his success as chairman. Regardless of whether Baruch's power was real or perceived, or a little of both, it is clear that he managed to sustain an important place for himself as ultimate decision maker and figurehead. Cuff, "Bernard Baruch," 127, 130, 131. See also Clarkson, *Industrial America*, 75.

137. Cuff, "Bernard Baruch," 126.

138. Ibid., 125, 127.

139. Cuff, *War Industries Board*, 268.

140. Baruch, *Public Years*, 79.

141. Ibid., 79.

142. Cuff, "Bernard Baruch," 121.

143. Baruch, *Public Years*, 55.

144. Ibid., 56.

145. Kester holds that while "the Board had no legal sanction for enforcing its rulings . . . the threat of commandeering or withholding priority or preference proved sufficient to keep recalcitrants in line." Kester, "War Industries Board," 662.

146. Baruch, *Public Years*, 58.

147. For Baruch's full account of the incident, see Baruch, *Public Years*, 59–62.

148. Cuff, *War Industries Board*, 266.

149. Clarkson, *Industrial America*, 299.

150. Baruch describes how he managed his section chiefs after receiving his letter from President Wilson. He says, "Authority for all principal controls except price fixing had thus at last been centralized in the new Chairman. He in turn took immediate steps to decentralize the execution of his powers, making each of his colleagues fully responsible for a particular field"; Baruch, *American Industry*, 27. Cuff and Clarkson also comment on Baruch's approach and the freedom left to the commodity chiefs to manage their sectors; Cuff, "Bernard Baruch," 120; and Clarkson, *Industrial America*, 74–75.

151. Cuff, *War Industries Board*, 10. See also Field, *Bernard Baruch*, 149; and Kester, "War Industries Board," 661.

152. Kester, "War Industries Board," 662; Paxson, "American War Government," 57.

153. Cuff, *War Industries Board*, 69.

154. Clarkson, *Industrial America*, 41.

155. For more on Baruch's role to increase his credibility with the private sector to encourage cooperation, see Cuff, "Bernard Baruch," 121–22.

156. Clarkson, *Industrial America*, 99.

157. Kester explains, "Normally, a rising price is self-defeating, because, beyond a certain point, demand will begin to fall off. But a war demand is absolute, and that

potential ceiling is removed when the government must have the supplies regardless of the price." Kester, "War Industries Board," 661.

158. Cuff, *War Industries Board*, 10.

159. Baruch also cites a case where a Boston chemical manufacturer who stormed into his office because of a WIB ruling relented after Baruch explained the national defense reason that compelled the board's action. Baruch, *Public Years*, 58.

160. Ibid., 59–62.

161. Cuff agrees with Baruch's assessment and asks, "How could one rationalize the obvious reluctance of many business groups to accept WIB policy without extended negotiations and hard bargaining? If businessmen were so patriotic why could the board not secure lower prices?" Ibid., 59; Cuff, *War Industries Board*, 267.

162. Baruch's famous clash with the American auto manufacturers is an excellent example of an instance where the imperatives of the public and private sectors were not aligned.

163. In writing about the risk to private volunteers of the Council of National Defense, Cuff says, "without legally constituted authority, business volunteers remained vulnerable to legal suits from both the Attorney General's office and private manufacturers who objected to committee plans for pooling contracts and prorating production." Cuff, *War Industries Board*, 82.

164. Kester, "War Industries Board," 662.

165. Baruch is referring particularly to the decisions of the priority committee, which were the most controversial and impactful of those made by the board. Baruch, *Public Years*, 56.

166. Cuff says that "business–government cooperation required a legitimizing tactic. . . . The administration had to reassure the general public that their interest remained beyond the reach of selfish privateers." Cuff, *War Industries Board*, 154.

167. Ibid., 50.

168. Koistinen says that Baruch felt that "successful mobilization depended upon winning industry's voluntary cooperation and maintaining the existing power structure." Agranoff's exploration of public management networks also identifies the use of the known and established contacts as a factor in the development of cross-sector networks as a common mechanism of establishing trust. Agranoff, *Managing within Networks*, 119–20; and Koistinen, "Industrial-Military Complex," 399; see also Cuff, *War Industries Board*, 50.

169. Cuff, *War Industries Board*, 259.

170. Clarkson, *Industrial America*, 486–87.

171. Cuff, *War Industries Board*, 264.

172. Ibid., 259.

173. Baruch biographer Carter Field writes that while there were "grave wonderings" on Capitol Hill about all the authority granted to the WIB during the war, no one ever tried to change the organization or formally oppose it. He says "this unwillingness of Congress to rock the boat, despite the obvious encroachment on its prerogatives, was astonishing"; Field, *Bernard Baruch*, 155–56.

174. Cuff, *War Industries Board*, 248.

175. Ibid.

176. In a piece written about WIB industrial representative George Peek as a dollar-a-year man, Robert Cuff argues that "to join public work cannot only confirm one's patriotic motives but can also satisfy any number of personal desires from gaining public acclaim to being near famous people." Cuff, "Dollar-a-Year Man," 418.

177. In a memorandum for the WIB's priority committee, legal concerns loomed large. It states: "It would seem that so intricate a system of priority, involving much inconvenience and financial sacrifice on the part of a large number of producers and manufacturers, could hardly be effectively administered without a firm legal basis." "Memo, for Consideration of Priority Committee," *Records of the War Industries Board* (undated), NARA, College Park, Maryland, RG 61, File 21A-A4, Box 1163.

178. E. E. Parsonage. "Correspondence to C. S. Brantingham," In *Records of the War Industries Board*, November 16, 1918, NARA, College Park, Maryland, RG 61, File 21A-A4.

CHAPTER FIVE

Comparing the Frameworks and the Identity Crisis of Disaster-Oriented PPPs

The previous chapters explore disaster-oriented PPPs, the Fed, and WIB in depth. This chapter compares and contrasts each of the organizations to one another to determine whether disaster-oriented PPPs are more suited to a strategic or responsive framework and to establish the degree to which the seven critical factors are applicable to all three organizations. The chapter concludes by highlighting the most important points that emerged in the comparison of each cross-sector alliance and assessing what these findings imply for contemporary disaster-oriented PPPs.

COMPARING THE PARTNERSHIP FRAMEWORKS

In chapters 2, 3, and 4, contemporary disaster-oriented PPPs, the Fed as a strategic public–private collaboration, and the WIB as a responsive alliance are individually explored in terms of the seven critical factors: crisis, leadership, organizational structure, information sharing, shared benefits, trust, and adaptability or sustainability. Those same factors are used here one final time to compare and contrast the partnership models to determine if the seven critical factors are able to function as a mechanism to assess public–private collaborations, if modern day disaster-oriented PPPs bear more in common with strategic or responsive cross-sector alliances, and if any lessons from the WIB and Fed may be relevant to disaster-oriented partnerships.

Crisis

Whether it was the beginning of a world war (as in the case of the WIB), a calamitous economic panic (as in the case of the Fed), a shocking terrorist attack or a devastating natural disaster (as in the case of disaster-oriented PPPs), the role played by crisis was the same in all three partnerships. Crisis, and the shared desire of the public and private sectors to minimize disruption and mass panic, served as a focusing event to highlight the benefits of cross-sector collaboration, prioritize cooperation, create a strong sense of urgency to act, and illuminate a role for the private sector that had previously been underestimated or unrecognized.

For disaster-oriented PPPs, the crisis of 9/11 had two significant impacts. First, it demonstrated the extent to which critical infrastructure in the United States is owned and operated by the private sector, and made it clear to business leaders and policymakers alike that safeguarding the United States would require enhanced cross-sector cooperation. Second, the attacks of 9/11 forced the US government to recognize how the private sector's unique insight and knowledge of global systems and networks could make them an invaluable partner in attempts to avoid future attacks. The value of disaster-oriented PPPs was further underlined after Hurricane Katrina, when the rapid response of corporations such as Ford, Walmart, and FedEx made it apparent that cross-sector collaboration was an important aspect of all types of disaster response and resilience, whether the disaster was caused by man or by nature. For disaster-oriented PPPs, these crises demonstrated the benefits of cooperation, prioritized them in the minds of public and private leaders, and prompted policymaking.

The crisis caused by the economic panic of 1907 had a similar effect on the public and private sectors. After several years of bank runs and financial panics, the 1907 incident was the most severe and nearly brought the nation's economy to its knees. The actions of a few New York bankers led by J. P. Morgan averted economic collapse. The severity of the crisis and potential for disaster were so great during the crisis of 1907 that both sectors agreed unequivocally on several priorities: first, that a flexible system must be established to adjust to currency fluctuations; second, that it was important to create a centralized mechanism (clearinghouse) to facilitate the sharing of reserves between the banks; and third, that both sectors should be involved in the leadership of these mechanisms.

The WIB was established in the midst of a crisis. The WIB is a particularly interesting case because although a small pocket of public and private leaders foresaw the need to mobilize the public and private sectors in advance of World War I and tried to develop a formalized federal cross-sector collaboration to prepare, these preemptive efforts met with little success. It was not until the United States entered World War I that the war crisis created the urgency necessary to drive the public and private sectors together to cooperate, mobilize the nation, and adjust to a wartime economy. The WIB was created, prioritized, and provided with the necessary support to function effectively only after the crisis of war set in.

The importance of a significant national crisis as an ignition point in the development of cross-sector collaboration cannot be overstated. In the Fed, WIB, and disaster-oriented PPPs, national crises generated a widespread realization that cooperation was a priority, awakened both sectors to the value of working together, and established the urgency necessary to spur policymaking.

Public and Private Leadership

In the midst of crisis and in its immediate aftermath, the role of public and private leaders had a significant impact on the development of the Fed, the WIB, and disaster-oriented PPPs. In all three cases, cooperation was effective only when the leaders of both sectors provided focused, unwavering support. While leadership by private-sector leaders helped the nation survive each period of crisis, it was as a result of leadership in the public sector that partnership frameworks were eventually organized and formalized to maximize effective collaboration.

Public leadership played an influential role in all three cross-sector alliances. In each instance public-sector leaders were behind the formalization of partnership efforts and were the driving force in providing the partnership structure with the necessary authority to be effective. Partisanship also emerges as an influential aspect that both draws in and repels public leaders toward partnership efforts based on the political popularity of cross-sector partnerships. The role played by partisanship in all three partnerships makes it clear that, in terms of the willingness of public-sector leaders to support cross-sector partnerships, timing is everything.

Public-sector leadership in disaster-oriented PPPs is distinguished primarily by the extreme gap between the creation of ambitious policies for disaster-oriented PPPs by the president and Congress, on the one hand, and the implementation of those policies, on the other. In the immediate aftermath of both the 9/11 and Katrina crises, there was a distinctive surge in policymaking driven by the president (in the form of Presidential Directives and Executive Orders) and from Congress (with the passage of measures such as the Homeland Security Act of 2002, Implementing Recommendations of the 9/11 Commission Act of 2007, and the Post-Katrina Emergency Management Reform Act of 2006). As time passed with no other disasters of equal or greater scale, the attentions of public-sector leaders began to drift away from disaster-oriented PPPs and onto the most pressing issues of the day, including external wars, economic crises, and elections. As the tyranny of the inbox pushed disaster-oriented PPPs further down the list of priorities, DHS was left with the difficult task of implementing the lofty, vague policy objectives that were crafted in the aftermath of significant national crises without the continued focused support of the president or Congress. Because the president and Congress ultimately control and direct the activities of DHS, the agency's priorities invariably echo those of its leaders. Thus, when the urgency from the crises waned, making disaster-oriented PPPs less urgent in the minds of Congress and the president, the implementing agency (DHS) to some extent mirrored this response.

DHS has also been limited by partisanship and regular administration changes. Partisanship can impact PPP efforts when the private partners see the public sector acting in their own political interests rather than toward the shared best interests of the partnership. The effectiveness of disaster-oriented PPPs has also been limited by the fact that the private sector's primary contacts in government change every time a new president is elected and new agency leaders are appointed. This regular shift in leadership is disruptive and essentially forces private partners to "start at zero" each time a new president is elected, reestablish working relationships, and rebuild the partnership with newly appointed leaders.

Political leadership was the driving force behind the drafting and passage of the Federal Reserve Act in 1913. Similar to the process for disaster-oriented PPPs, after the crisis of 1907, a flurry of policymaking (during which the Aldrich–Vreeland Act was passed in 1908) was followed by a lull in efforts to promote cross-sector cooperation as banking reform and cooperation with industry were deemed politically unpopular. This changed in 1910 when a different political party seized control of Congress and adopted banking reform as a key platform of the 1913 presidential elections. When Wilson won the presidency, the interests of the executive and legislative branches aligned and the development of banking and currency legislation became a priority. As in disaster-oriented PPPs, partisanship played an important role in the establishment of the Fed by stifling the development of collaboration in the years immediately following the crisis and ultimately driving the passage of legislation once the political parties changed. After the political parties backed banking reforms that included cross-sector cooperation and collaboration, public leaders lent their support and the Federal Reserve Act was written, debated, and passed into law in less than nine months. Congressional leadership ensured that the legislation was successfully passed while the president used the authority of his office to influence legislators when troubles arose during the passage of legislation.

As it had for the Fed and disaster-oriented PPPs, partisanship had a significant impact on public leadership of the WIB. Creating the WIB was politically unpopular before the war. As a result, the president did not fully support the organization until the United States entered World War I and the looming threat of economic collapse made mobilization (and the creation of the cross-sector collaboration) a priority that was backed by Congress. Although there had been a sense for several years that this type of organization would be necessary if the

United States were to enter the war, suspicions about the motives of the private sector as an honest partner and the fact that most Americans did not want the United States to enter into the war prevented political leaders from supporting the WIB until the war crisis gave them little choice. Once the priorities of Congress and the president were aligned, the WIB was established.

Private-sector leaders played a very similar role in the Federal Reserve as they do in disaster-oriented PPPs. During the panic of 1907, J. P. Morgan coordinated the most powerful American bankers to ensure that the nation passed through the immediate emergency without total economic collapse. Congress and the president had a more secondary role. Similarly, during 9/11 and Katrina, corporations such as Verizon and Walmart restored critical services and proved themselves able to provide goods to the public faster and more effectively than the government. The financial crisis of 1907 and the disasters of 9/11 and Katrina were so significant that cross-sector cooperation to rapidly restore normality created an incentive for leaders of both sectors to work together. When the crisis was over, the private sector assumed the backseat as Congress and the president began to formalize cooperation by generating policy to continue the partnerships.

In contrast, for the WIB, it was in the financial interests of many of the larger businesses not to partner with the government. Despite this, a group of business leaders led by charismatic executives such as Bernard Baruch helped to steer the government toward an ad hoc structure (the WIB) that could serve as a broker between the private sector and government and meet the needs of the war.

In evaluating the role played by public and private leaders in the Fed, WIB, and disaster-oriented PPPs, it is clear that the backing of the president and Congress is a key factor in formalizing cross-sector collaborations and creating policy. In all three cases, when legislative and executive backing was strong and consistent, policy objectives were realized. In the case of the Fed, because the Federal Reserve Act cemented cross-sector collaboration, the organization was able to survive when national priorities shifted the attention of the president and Congress away from issues related to banking reform. In contrast, because disaster-oriented PPPs and the WIB lacked this mechanism to sustain cooperation, both organizations rely on the continued, focused support of public-sector leaders to survive. This is clearly seen in disaster-oriented PPPs, where DHS has been left unable to implement many policies in the way they were originally envisaged, and it is evidenced in the WIB, where the ability of the organization to harness the necessary authority to conduct mobilization was based entirely on the backing of the president.

The role played by private-sector leaders is noteworthy for two reasons. First, in observing the role played by the private sector in all three cases, it becomes clear that although the private sector plays a pivotal role in the heat of the crisis, its ability to formalize collaborative efforts after the crisis is limited. Second, the variation in cross-sector participation seen in the WIB highlights the importance that corporate self-interest plays in the decision-making of private-sector leaders and their willingness to participate.

Organizational Structure

While the role played by public and private leaders is influential, examining the organizational framework that houses each collaboration is the best possible way to assess the effectiveness and long-term viability of each partnership. For a cross-sector collaboration to remain viable during times of crisis and calm, the organizational framework must be able to sustain the priorities and interest of both sectors even without the focused support of the president.

Of the three organizations, the Federal Reserve System is the only one where the public–private nature of the organization is legally and institutionally fortified through an act of Congress. The Federal Reserve Act clearly laid out the goals of the organization. It was designed to be quasi-public in nature to ensure that it was not wholly owned or influenced by any one agency or political party. The Fed is independent within the government, meaning that it is not held accountable by Congress (Congress does not control its appropriations), but the Fed is responsible for reporting to Congress. The president is responsible for appointing the seven members of the board of governors (including the chairman), and the US Senate then ratifies appointees. While these appointments are often politically motivated, terms last for fourteen years and are staggered so that one term expires every even-numbered year. The terms are intentionally designed this way to minimize the degree to which partisanship, administration changes, and appointments can disrupt monetary policy in the Fed.

In addition, ongoing private-sector involvement at all levels of the organization is ensured by designating key leadership positions (including the chair of the system) at the national and regional levels for private-sector leaders. The top seven leadership positions at the federal level are specifically for private-sector leaders, as are six of the nine positions of leadership at the regional level. The Act also specifies that private-sector participants must be geographically and industrially diverse to represent the broadest possible range of insights and opinions. In this way, the Fed ensures that it involves not only the public and private sectors but also a range of industries within the private sector.

While the strategic objectives for the organization were laid out fairly specifically, little tactical direction was provided to the founders of the Fed about how the system should be operated and managed. This intentional vagueness was politically expedient in the short term because a more general text would be easier to pass through Congress, and it gave the public- and private-sector leaders of the Fed the ability to have a hand in designing the inner workings of the organization. Because the experts in the field not only would be working within the Fed but also knew and understood banking and currency issues far better than the legislators, this was an important aspect in the early development of the organization. In addition, as the organization aged, the vagueness of the Federal Reserve Act had a further benefit of endowing the organization with the institutional flexibility to adapt as the US economy, global markets, and demands on the Fed changed. The priorities of the Fed at the time it was established in 1913—its focus on currency elasticity, the need to develop a national clearinghouse mechanism for banks to avoid panics, and the importance of incorporating the private sector—are not the same priorities the organization faces today. The Fed has been able to develop and adapt accordingly because of its institutional capacity to evolve.

The WIB, in sharp contrast, was never granted statutory authority and developed in an ad hoc manner in the midst of crisis. The framework that eventually became the WIB began as the NCB and was then transformed and adapted into the CND before undergoing a further evolution to become the WIB. The organization was not created with any long-term plan in mind but was designed to address a pressing need facing the nation as a result of entering World War I—the need to mobilize. Unlike the Fed, which was independent within the government, the WIB was a wartime agency residing wholly in the public sector. Whereas the Fed gained its authority through an act of Congress, the WIB relied upon the backing and support of the president for authority, on the one hand, and the voluntary cooperation of the private sector and the military, on the other.

Without an act of Congress to provide the organization legitimacy, centralize authority, cement cross-sector collaboration, and provide an organizational framework, the WIB was much more malleable and vulnerable than the Fed. Without statutory authority backing the organization's existence and giving the chairman the power to execute his remit, the WIB relied upon the president for backing, authority (with both sectors), and organizational direction. The legal standing of the WIB was tenuous at best, and without an act of Congress making the actions of the board and its leaders legal, ongoing questions arose about their accountability. Ultimately, these questions limited the long-term sustainability of the WIB.

In addition, the WIB facilitated partnerships across a number of industrial sectors. Without an organizational mechanism to facilitate cooperation, the leaders of each commodity section organized their sphere of influence as they deemed most appropriate. Cross-sector cooperation was not established in any formalized, consistent manner but was ad hoc. The organization relied largely on interpersonal relationships and individual trust, and participants engaged with the organization on the basis of shared need and a sense of urgency that developed because of the war. The WIB's organizational structure developed organically as war became imminent and was more fragmented than that of the Fed. With the United States at war, the priority was to ensure that American industry was making and selling the supplies the military needed. How that collaboration occurred mattered far less in the end than the fact that boots were on soldiers' feet, bullets were in guns, and food was available to feed the troops.

In observing the organizational structures of the Fed and WIB, their strategic and responsive nature is readily apparent. The Fed was purposefully and methodically established for the long term to ensure ongoing public and private cooperation and to address existing and future problems that the nation might have faced in matters of banking and finance. The aims of the Federal Reserve Act were strategic, aiming to not only react and respond to crises when they occurred but to avoid them altogether if possible. The WIB, in contrast, developed in the maelstrom of war and grew out of necessity. There was little thought about the viability of the structure or the long-term relevance of the organization. It lacked the organizational structure or legal backing to be sustainable and was equipped to respond to the needs of a single crisis.

The organizational framework for disaster-oriented PPPs remains in its developmental stages, and the strategic or responsive orientation of the organization is not yet apparent. The current framework for cooperation was developed by the DHS, on the orders of Congress and the president, and is outlined in the NIPP. Both public- and private-sector leaders agree that the existing mechanisms of cross-sector cooperation are imperfect, and they cite a number of challenges directly relating to the fact that the framework "resides" within DHS and lacks centralization. A number of structural shortcomings within DHS are largely beyond its control but have nonetheless limited the ability of the agency to develop the best possible organizational structure to facilitate disaster-oriented PPPs. These are largely due to the relative newness of DHS and the regular power struggles and organizational changes that invariably occur during the developmental years of a massive new agency in Washington.

When DHS was created, the facilitation of disaster-oriented PPPs was one congressional and presidential assignment given to the agency on a very long "to do" list. The NIPP, the organizational framework designed to facilitate cross-sector collaborations, reflects the chaotic, organizationally confused environment in which the plan was created. It is ad hoc, borrows heavily from past partnership structures (specifically the largely ineffective ISACs), and was hurriedly assembled under the guiding principle that "something is better than nothing." Taking into account the regular shifting priorities of Congress and the administration and the lack of sustained focus on PPP initiatives, this response is not surprising.

While the existing organizational structure is not yet fully evolved, thus far it most closely resembles the responsive framework of the WIB. Like the structure of the WIB, the organizational structure created to facilitate disaster-oriented PPPs lacks statutory authority, is highly decentralized, and is hindered by internal governmental overlap in private-sector outreach efforts and by inter-agency power struggles. While the Fed is a quasi-public agency, both the WIB and disaster-oriented PPP organizational structures are wholly managed by the government, thus limiting the degree to which the private sector is involved in decision-making and limiting the ownership felt by private-sector participants.

Despite the number of parallels between the organizational structures of the WIB and disaster-oriented PPPs, there is one very significant difference dividing them: disaster-oriented PPPs, while arguably structurally flawed and highly decentralized, survived the crises of 9/11 and Katrina, and partnership efforts continue to this day. This is in sharp contrast to the WIB, which collapsed soon after the end of the war. Therefore, although disaster-oriented PPPs have struggled without the prioritization and focus of a crisis to sustain them, the partnership has survived. In this regard, disaster-oriented PPPs bear some similarity to the early years of the Fed and reflect a key characteristic of a strategic partnership structure: sustainability after the immediate crisis.

Just as the public sector worked after the panic of 1907 to pass the Aldrich–Vreeland Act in 1908 and the Federal Reserve Act in 1913, the president and Congress created policy after both 9/11 and Katrina to develop more formal mechanisms to facilitate cross-sector cooperation. There was a sense that these PPPs must be created to enhance preparedness, resilience, and national security. This did not occur with the WIB after World War I. The primary difference between the organizational structure established in 1913 and the one established by the NIPP in 2009 is that disaster-oriented PPPs are not equipped or endowed with statutory authority to centralize their power, ensure their long-term sustainability, provide the organizational structure legitimacy within Washington, or definitively establish the key aims of public–private cooperation. As a result, while the existing disaster-oriented PPP organizational structure was originally intended to be strategic, it has been built as a largely responsive framework.

There is one substantial difference between the organizational framework for disaster-oriented PPPs and the frameworks of the Fed and WIB. The Fed and WIB were both established as independent agencies that were designed specifically to facilitate cooperation between the public and private sectors to achieve their institutional goals. This is in sharp contrast to disaster-oriented PPPs. The organizational framework for disaster-oriented PPPs is more conceptual than actual, and there is no specific, stand-alone agency focused solely on the facilitation of these alliances. The plan for cross-sector cooperation is housed deep within a large DHS manifesto outlining the overarching national plans to protect infrastructure (the NIPP). No designated physical disaster-oriented PPP "organization" exists in the way that there is a Federal Reserve System or that there was a War Industries Board. DHS, as an agency, is theoretically responsible for overseeing the actualization of public–private partnerships—one of a multitude of responsibilities. In contrast, for the Fed and the WIB, facilitating cross-sector cooperation was the primary, not subsidiary, mission of the organization. Under the current organizational structure, however, it remains unclear how long efforts to sustain disaster-oriented PPPs may continue. The cooperative framework is plagued with problems and lacks the statutory authority that has sustained the Fed.

Information Sharing

In comparing the Fed, WIB, and disaster-oriented PPPs in terms of crisis, leadership, and organizational structure, and assessing the way the three institutions interact and share information, trends begin to emerge. One of the most significant is that the statutory authority bestowed on the Fed not only provides institutional stability for the organization but also allows it to avoid many of the problems that plague contemporary efforts to develop disaster-oriented PPPs, such as the lack of centralization in governmental coordination of PPPs.

Sharing information (monetary reserves) in the Fed has become such an intrinsic aspect of the organization that it is no longer a significant concern. The development of a clearinghouse mechanism to facilitate the sharing of information (reserves) was prioritized in the Federal Reserve Act and institutionalized between the public and private sectors as well as at the national and regional levels. The organizational structure of the Fed facilitated information (reserve) sharing on a centralized, streamlined platform. This platform for sharing information created consistency in the system, increased public and private confidence, reassured the public that measures were in place to avoid financial crisis, and reduced the likelihood that panic would spread in the event of a future banking crisis.

In contrast, information sharing in the WIB was ad hoc, carried out in the midst of crisis, and plagued by struggles for power and authority. Unlike the Fed, the WIB lacked a centralized structure to streamline cross-sector information sharing and each commodity chief organized information sharing based entirely on individual sector preferences. There was little consistency in information-sharing methods and practices between commodity divisions. Members of the WIB used charm, where possible, to encourage information sharing but resorted to threats and coercion if necessary. The sheer pace required to mobilize for war required cooperation. The methods of communication mattered far less than the fact that it occurred at all and that it aided mobilization efforts. After the war, the coercive power of the organization dissipated, as did the need (and willingness) of the partners to share information.

Information sharing also presents a number of obstacles for disaster-oriented PPPs that relate directly to the loose structure of the organizational framework. These include problems relating to US government classification standards, a largely one-way flow of information (from the private sector to the government and not vice versa), antitrust laws, customer privacy concerns, and the maintenance of competitive advantage. Without a more centralized organizational structure, the methods and guidelines used for information sharing are inconsistent and vary by industrial sector. Like the WIB during World War I, cross-sector information sharing is ad hoc and the sector-specific agencies have developed their own methods for sharing information based on the preferences of particular industrial sectors. This lack of consistency may provide some short-term expediency, but it exacerbates rather than resolves greater information-sharing impediments, such as the development of a consistent method to avoid duplication in governmental outreach or address the problems associated with classification barriers. The current organizational structure also lacks the ability to ensure that governmental outreach with the private sector is consistent and coordinated across industrial sectors.

The Fed's institutionalized organizational structure is the primary reason that information sharing in the Fed is more streamlined than in the WIB or disaster-oriented PPPs. Because information sharing was prioritized in the formative years of the Fed, the problems caused by banks failing to share reserves were soon eliminated as a concern. Because the WIB and disaster-oriented PPPs grew in a more organic manner, information sharing between the sectors has been based less on centralization and more on individual relationships forged as a result of national crisis.

Perceived Benefits of Cooperation

For collaborations to be a partnership rather than a mandate, cooperation must serve some benefit to both sectors, otherwise there would be no incentive to engage. In the Federal Reserve, WIB, and disaster-oriented PPPs, a significant national crisis drove the sectors together and made cooperation in their shared best interests. In all three cases, the private sector had clear financial incentives to become a partner of government, whereas the public sector needed private-sector intervention to effectively respond to the crisis and minimize its national impact.

During the panic of 1907 the private sector helped the banking and economic system survive a series of harmful bank runs. The motivation for private-sector participation was simply loss avoidance. A run on one bank or trust company made all the banks vulnerable. As a result, it was mutually beneficial for the banks and the government to cooperate. A stable banking system that avoided panics and promoted economic stability (the Fed) would promote the national economy as well as the health and longevity of banks. The public and private sectors have continued to work together for nearly a hundred years and continue to find cooperation mutually beneficial. Economic stability was—and always will be—in the best interests of both sectors.

WIB differs slightly from the Fed largely because it is a responsive partnership. Because the organization was operational only in a crisis environment, the benefits each sector received as a result of cooperation were immediate and short term. Mobilizing for war was in the shared interests of both sectors only so long as the war was on, demand for goods was high, and the national need so great that the sectors were driven to partner. Unlike the Fed, which aimed to maintain economic stability, the WIB had no broad incentive driving cooperation beyond the crisis.

Disaster-oriented PPPs are also mutually beneficial during a crisis. Both sectors want to restore normality as quickly as possible. The public sector is motivated to engage because a significant amount of critical US infrastructure is in private-sector hands. In the event of a catastrophic disaster, the public sector cannot adequately respond without some level of private involvement. Beyond direct disaster response, the public sector can also benefit from the private sector's knowledge of international networks and new technologies. The private sector also benefits from cooperation. Disasters are bad for business and can result in business closures and network delays that reduce corporate earnings. It is in corporate interests to restore communities and resume normal business practices. Corporations also have the potential to boost their brand image when customers see them assisting with recovery efforts.

Just as the public and private interests aligned in the Fed to promote economic stability, the desire to respond rapidly to disaster is in the shared interests of industry and the government. Knowing this, and understanding that the private sector and government have so much to lose in the event of a disaster, it is in the shared interests of both sectors to cooperate to enhance national resilience.

Despite the benefits of cooperation, both sectors face a number of risks as a result of participating in disaster-oriented PPPs. While the government fears loss of power and authority by partnerships with the private sector for these purposes, and must beware of appearing to practice favoritism, the private sector fears they may encounter legal problems, violate customer privacy and trust, or risk their competitive advantage. These risks, while significant, are largely the result of an organizational structure that lacks centralization and are the primary result of the responsive orientation of the partnership. In applying the Fed as a model, it appears that the existing risks to cooperation could be addressed if a more strategic, institutionalized framework were put into place to address legal concerns and formally establish the roles and responsibilities of each sector.

In comparing the benefits each sector receives through cross-sector cooperation in all three organizations, the Fed and disaster-oriented PPPs most closely resemble one another. Economic fluctuations, like disasters, are inevitable and the long-term interests of both sectors are served by their cooperation in an effort to minimize the disruption that could be caused by a future crisis. Although the public and private sectors face a number of risks by participating in disaster-oriented PPPs, the broad objective of the partnership serves the long-term interests of both sectors and outweighs the potential risks of cooperation. In contrast, cooperation for the WIB was in the interests of both sectors for only a very short period of time and only in the midst of a national crisis.

TRUST

Beyond being mutually beneficial, the development of trust between public and private participants is an important element of partnerships that can indicate long-term viability. Trust represents the belief that the other party will uphold their end of the partnership so that each side can achieve its goals. In comparing the Fed, WIB, and disaster-oriented PPPs, two distinctive forms of trust emerge. While the Federal Reserve Act institutionalized the roles of the public and private sectors, and thus established institutional trust in the Fed's framework for cross-sector collaboration, the WIB and disaster-oriented PPPs rely on individual trust between known and trusted contacts.

Public–private cooperation in the Fed is formally institutionalized through an act of Congress. The roles and responsibilities of both sectors are clearly defined, lines of authority established, and priorities articulated. Because both sectors trust the statutory authority of the Fed, there is little risk that personnel changes, elections, or personality clashes will impact the effectiveness of the partnership. This enhances trust between the partners and the long-term sustainability of the organization. The formalization of the partnership through legislation also enhances public trust and reduces the likelihood of panic. For example, the institutionalization of the Fed's partnership framework provides a broad awareness that the public and private sectors are organized and working to protect them. This knowledge becomes trust when the public believes that the banks and the government are working together, under the quasi-public organizational umbrella of the Fed, to avoid economic crisis by safeguarding against bank collapses and ensuring that customers' savings are secure. After the Fed was created, trust grew with the passage of time as the public observed the institution actively working to preserve stability. As a result of the institutional trust that has developed, when a crisis does occur, this trust in the Fed provides an important buffer against the spread of panic.

In contrast, the WIB and disaster-oriented PPPs, which are less formally institutionalized partnerships, rely on individual trust between known and trusted contacts to facilitate cooperation. This was particularly true with the WIB. The heads of the commodity units were selected based on their expertise, and they used their existing contacts to coordinate between industry and the military. Organizational trust was virtually nonexistent because neither sector was particularly interested in cooperation. Congress and the military distrusted the private-sector dollar-a-year men and feared that they sought to protect private rather than national interests. The army was particularly resistant, perceiving private engagement to be a nuisance, interference, and threat to its own power and authority. Both Congress and the military were weary of endorsing a civilian-led mobilization agency within the government and actively worked to undermine it until the urgency of the war crisis left them with little choice but to cooperate. However, in the midst of the crisis of World War I, when sufficient incentives existed to drive the sectors together, it was the trust between individuals who knew one another that facilitated cooperation.

Disaster-oriented PPPs also rely on individual rather than institutional trust. This is evidenced by the fact that private-sector leaders find changes in administration and personnel so disruptive to partnership efforts and is further demonstrated by the fact that there remains no single overarching national framework to facilitate disaster-oriented PPPs. The NIPP is a guide for cooperation rather than an institutionalized mechanism to facilitate partnerships. Government agencies are hesitant to relinquish direct access to the carefully cultivated private-sector contacts they know personally and trust. At the same time, the private sector is left trying to forge relationships with various agencies and offices across federal, regional, and local governments in an attempt to have the broadest possible range of governmental contacts so they know who to call in the event of a disaster.

There are benefits to establishing cross-sector relationships based on individual rather than institutional trust. First, it allows known and trusted contacts to deal directly with one another. Trust between individuals can develop much more rapidly than trust in an institution. Unlike more institutionalized partnerships, such as the Fed, there is little (if any) bureaucratic red tape limiting interaction between trusted partners; as a result, both sectors are able to act and react to situations very quickly. This is particularly useful when rapid change is required to address very specific problems. Second, the lack of institutionalization allows for a great deal of flexibility in the way partnerships develop between industrial sectors. As a result, each individual sector has more freedom to individualize the partnerships that they deem most appropriate for their industrial sector. For the WIB and disaster-oriented PPPs that by nature require interaction with a number of different industrial sectors, this capability can provide valuable flexibility.

While one-to-one interaction may provide short-term flexibility and expediency, this kind of structure can have negative effects for partnerships designed to last for the longer term. First, because of the reliance on interpersonal relationships and connections, it is more likely that interagency overlap in outreach efforts will occur because the relationships are not centrally coordinated. In disaster-oriented PPPs, this is already an issue as private-sector leaders argue that they frequently receive multiple requests from different government offices for the same information. Because so many individuals within the government communicate directly with the private sector on these issues, they often fail to coordinate with each other within the government before reaching out to the private sector. This creates duplication of efforts for the government and redundancy and frustration in the private sector. In contrast, the clearinghouse mechanism embedded within the Federal Reserve System provides a way for banks to centralize information (reserves) and ensure solvency. Individual banks communicate with the Fed, which then coordinates this service. There is trust in the Fed, as an institution, to be the centralizing agency and to coordinate between the sectors. In contrast, because disaster-oriented PPPs lack this "clearinghouse" to centralize information, uncoordinated one-off negotiations occur regularly.

Second, in partnerships based on individual rather than institutional trust, there is also the real possibility that trust between the partners will dissolve every time there is a personnel change and the chemistry of the partnership is disrupted. This issue emerged in interviews with private-sector leaders who argued that every time a new administration came to power, they were often forced to rebuild the partnership. Relationships built on trusted relationships between individuals can limit the long-term viability of the partnership because the partnership is at risk when personalities change. A private executive from the finance sector argued that one of the benefits of cooperating with the Federal Reserve System rather than the Department of the Treasury or other agencies was that the quasi-public nature of the Fed made it far less disrupted by these changes; as a result, it is a much more consistent partner.[1]

Third, in partnerships based on individual trust, the scope of the alliance is focused but also limited. Although this focus allows these partnerships to affect rapid change and address specific problems, there is little consistency in partnership methods between sectors. In the WIB, this meant that while an immediate issue surrounding a particular commodity (such as aluminum) could be addressed very quickly, if the issue involved a number of commodities (such as aluminum, copper, and steel), negotiations could quickly become complicated

TABLE 5.1: Individual and Institutional Trust

Type of Trust	Individual (WIB, Disaster-Oriented PPPs)	Institutional (Fed)
Advantages	*Confidentiality:* Easier to maintain with fewer people involved *Relationships:* Strong, rely on individual trust between partners *Bureaucracy:* Limited, able to achieve objectives rapidly and effectively	*Scope:* Broad, able to accomplish wider objectives and include more partners. Can go beyond a 1:1 interaction *Fidelity:* High, PPP based on institutional trust and more able to withstand changes in personnel *Overlap:* More avoidable, partnership more centrally organized, should reduce potential for interdepartmental overlap in private-sector outreach
Disadvantages	*Scope:* Narrow, suited for immediate, specific scenarios, not broad security objectives *Fidelity:* Little to none. Strength of partnership relies upon close, trusted relationship. Partnership in danger when personalities change *Overlap:* High, more likely to overlap in private-sector outreach within the government (numerous agencies contacting the same private corporation)	*Confidentiality:* More actors involved making it more difficult to ensure/maintain confidentially *Relationships:* Institutional trust is more difficult to develop than individual trust *Bureaucracy:* Institutional framework, broader scope, and more actors can slow reaction/response times

and muddied as the internal WIB commodity heads negotiated with one another and with their private-sector contacts. Therefore, while relationships built on interpersonal trust can be expedient in the short term and can avoid frustrating bureaucratic delays, they can complicate partnership efforts when trying to coordinate a number of different industrial sectors or when responding to a national crisis that requires more broad communication and coordination to avoid duplication of efforts and ensure consistency across the sectors.[2] During a national disaster, when response and coordination is required across multiple industrial sectors and between public and private partners, this degree of individualization can be problematic as evidenced by the failure of the ISACs in the late 1990s.

Table 5.1 outlines the advantages and disadvantages of cross-sector partnerships based on individual and institutional trust. The comparison reveals that the benefits of one type of trust are the primary disadvantages of the other. Given that the Fed developed institutional trust while the WIB relied upon individual trust, it is apparent that the type of trust a partnership relies upon is a direct indicator of its responsive or strategic nature. Disaster-oriented PPPs' reliance on individual trust is yet another indicator of the "identity crisis" faced by these partnerships as a result of the tension caused by the gap between the development of strategic policies and the implementation of responsive initiatives. Table 5.1 provides further indication that for disaster-oriented PPPs to be more strategic, the partnership should be more centralized to develop the institutional trust necessary to ensure longevity and consistency and to avoid overlapping efforts.

Adaptability or Sustainability

While trust is certainly a strong indicator of the responsive or strategic nature of a cross-sector collaboration, the long-term sustainability of the partnership is an even more significant distinguishing factor. Strategic partnerships are designed to adapt and be sustainable, whereas responsive partnerships are single-event-oriented and are not designed for long-term sustainability. As a result, observing the ability of a partnership framework to adapt and survive over time offers a quick and easy indicator of its responsive or strategic nature.

Adaptability in the Federal Reserve is best demonstrated by the fact that the organization will celebrate its centennial anniversary in 2013. The challenges that faced the founders of the Federal Reserve in 1913—including the need to ensure elasticity in currency and develop a central clearinghouse for sharing reserves—do not reflect the challenges facing the organization today. There is no way the founders of the Fed could have imagined the profound effect of electronic funds transfers, the Internet, and globalization on the way money is managed. The Federal Reserve remains viable because the organization was provided with the institutional flexibility, embodied through an act of Congress, to adapt over time as required by changes in the economy or unforeseen circumstance. This institutional adaptability is a primary characteristic of a strategic cross-sector partnership.

In contrast, adaptation in the WIB occurred only before the crisis, and the organization lacked the institutional strength or organizational flexibility to adapt any further after the end of the war. From 1915 to 1917, no fewer than four organizations adapted to meet the growing crisis, and these agencies eventually evolved into the WIB. Without a solid organizational framework to sustain the organization after the war, outline long-term objectives for cooperation, or drive the partners together when the urgency of war abated, there was no significant incentive to continue cooperation. In addition, the partnership relied upon individual trust rather than institutional trust, and there was a lack of confidence in the WIB as an organization. As a result of all of these factors, the WIB was not able to adapt and essentially "died" with the war. The inability of the WIB to adapt is a key indicator of the responsive nature of the partnership. It was designed to address a single aspect of a larger national crisis, and there was no longer a need for the partnership once the crisis was over. It was simply not designed for long-term sustainability.

The ability of disaster-oriented PPPs to adapt and be sustainable remains to be seen. The existing framework for cooperation, as outlined in the NIPP and enhanced by organizations such as FEMA, has not been recently tested by a calamitous national crisis. This makes it difficult to assess whether improvements have been made in PPP efforts since Katrina, or the extent to which PPPs may need to adapt to address future crises. Like the Federal Reserve System, the NIPP was developed as a result of crisis and continues to function several years later, which indicates that the organization was intended to be strategic and adapt over time. While disaster-oriented PPP initiatives may be leaning toward the strategic in this regard, the fact that they lack a formal mechanism to centralize partnership efforts, to institutionalize trust, and to overcome many of the organizational and information-sharing barriers to cooperation indicates that the partnership is not yet fully strategic. Ultimately, the adaptability or sustainability of the organization will depend upon its ability to overcome the challenges it faces as a strategically designed PPP equipped with a responsively oriented organizational framework.

STRATEGIC OR RESPONSIVE?
THE "IDENTITY CRISIS" OF DISASTER-ORIENTED PPPS

In comparing the Fed, WIB, and disaster-oriented PPPs by the seven critical factors, four key points emerge. First, it is evident that crisis, leadership, organizational structure, information sharing, shared benefits, trust, and adaptability or sustainability are all influential and revealing factors that highlight variations between the three alliances. Second, it is clear that the impediments faced by disaster-oriented PPPs are consistent with those faced by both strategic and responsive collaborations designed to address national policy issues. As a result, the seven critical factors may be best understood as factors that are critical to all cross-sector partnerships designed to address national policy issues and are not unique to disaster-oriented PPPs. Third, through comparing the partnership structures it becomes clear that the most significant differentiating factor between the Fed and the other two organizations is that the organizational purpose and structure of the Fed is cemented through an act of Congress. The institutionalization of the partnership directly influenced the strategic nature of the collaboration. It also ensured the Fed's ability to share information, develop institutional trust, adapt over time, and be sustainable. Fourth, assessing the Fed, WIB, and disaster-oriented PPPs by these same seven factors makes the responsive or strategic nature of the alliance readily apparent. In the case of disaster-oriented PPPs in particular, this evaluation revealed that the organization is facing an "identity crisis" as an organization that is neither strategic nor responsive but that carries attributes of both.

Table 5.2 depicts the responsive and strategic characteristics of current disaster-oriented PPPs. Crisis is a key element in both strategic and responsive partnerships and serves as a driver of cooperation rather than an indicator of the responsive or strategic nature that the partnership will assume. Disaster-oriented PPPs reflect a responsive orientation in terms of the role played by public and private leaders, the organizational structure, the methods used to share information, and the type of trust the partners rely upon to facilitate partnership efforts. Strategic tendencies are reflected in the benefits both sectors derive from cooperation. While it is not yet possible to determine the adaptability or sustainability of disaster-oriented PPPs, the simple fact that efforts to forge these partnerships have survived several years after the crisis that drove their creation indicates they are leaning toward a strategic, rather than responsive, orientation in these areas.

Although disaster-oriented PPPs are currently more responsive than strategic, this chapter has demonstrated that the organizational structure is the most influential of the seven critical factors. In the Fed, the primary goals of the partnership and the roles of public- and private-sector participants were institutionalized and ensured through legislation. This institutionalization immediately impacted the way information was shared and the ability of the organization to adapt, allowed trust to be institutional rather than interpersonal, and equipped the partnership to be sustainable. Therefore, while the "checked boxes" in table 5.2 make it appear that disaster-oriented PPPs are definitively responsive, the Fed model indicates that if the organizational structure were to be institutionalized, almost all of the responsive indicators could easily become strategic. In addition, while crisis and leadership from both sectors are critical elements to the establishment of cross-sector alliances, in comparing the three frameworks, it

TABLE 5.2: Current Characteristics of Disaster-Oriented PPPs

	Responsive Characteristics	*Strategic Characteristics*	*Indeterminate, Leaning toward Strategic*
Crisis	✓	✓	
Leadership	✓		
Organizational Structure	✓		
Information Sharing	✓		
Shared Benefits		✓	
Trust	✓		
Adaptability/ Sustainability			✓

becomes clear that these are facilitating factors that contribute to the formalization of partnership efforts, not indicators of the strategic or responsive orientation of a collaboration.

To determine the strategic or responsive nature of disaster-oriented PPPs, therefore, it is necessary to observe the broad objectives of the collaboration and look closely at the two remaining factors: shared benefits, and adaptability or sustainability. The adaptability and sustainability of disaster-oriented PPPs is noteworthy. Despite the dominant orientation of disaster-oriented PPPs as responsive, which indicates the partnership should not be adaptable or sustainable after the immediacy of a crisis, efforts to build these collaborations have continued to develop several years after the crisis passed (albeit in a rather piecemeal fashion). This indicates there is at least some agreement by both sectors that there is a degree of benefit to long-term, strategic collaboration.

In comparing the benefits derived from collaboration, it has become clear that the Fed and disaster-oriented PPPs share an important commonality: collaboration in both instances was formalized to ensure preparedness and resilience for a significant issue of national concern deemed to be inevitable, reoccurring, and disruptive. As a result, both sectors deemed that their mutual best interests would be served by cooperating to mitigate these events, if possible, and ensuring preparedness and resilience to minimize disruption when such events occur. This is in sharp contrast to the WIB, a responsive PPP designed to address a subsidiary aspect of a larger crisis. When the crisis was over, so too was the need for collaboration. The fact that disaster-oriented PPPs have a broad strategic objective coupled with the ability of collaborative efforts to persist long after the crisis of 9/11 and Katrina passed is a persuasive indicator of disaster-oriented PPPs' strategic orientation.

Disaster-oriented PPPs face an identity crisis. Understanding and recognizing this helps to explain many of the problems that have plagued efforts to develop these partnerships. The organizational structure for disaster-oriented PPPs is not adequately defined as either strategic or responsive but is embedded with crucial elements of both types of partnership. The broad, strategic objectives of disaster-oriented PPPs indicate that the partnerships are intended to be sustainable in the long term and, therefore, strategically oriented. However, the existing framework for cooperation is dominated by responsive characteristics. This creates confusion between the roles and responsibilities of the sector partners and makes the overall aims of the partnership unclear. It also accounts for the troublesome gap currently in place between strategic policies that have been implemented by DHS with responsive solutions. The identity crisis plaguing the partnership framework has made disaster-oriented PPPs neither strategic nor responsive but a little of both.

As it currently stands, unless the identity crisis facing disaster-oriented PPPs is rectified so the aims and methods of the partnership are aligned, these PPPs will not be viable as a national tool of disaster management in the long term. They will be incapable of anything beyond crisis-driven, ad hoc responsiveness.

ASSESSMENT OF FINDINGS

Despite the failings of the current cooperative framework, the comparisons between the partnership structures indicate that if some of the key structural elements of the Federal Reserve model—a successful strategic cross-sector alliance—were applied to disaster-oriented PPPs, the identity crisis of the framework could be rectified. This could occur as a result of just two primary changes.

First, public-sector leaders should *lead*. While the private sector plays an important role during the actual crisis, as the Fed case study demonstrates, it is up to the president and Congress to sufficiently prioritize these collaborations to pass legislation and equip the partnership with the organizational structure, centralized authority, and focus to make it viable in the long term. The foresight and prioritization of PPP initiatives by governmental leaders is a crucial facilitating factor in the development of a strategic partnership.

Second, there are five primary organizational attributes embedded in the Fed through the Federal Reserve Act that have enabled the Fed to survive as a strategic partnership.

1. While political leadership was pivotal as a facilitating factor in the passage of the Federal Reserve Act, the act itself was important because it firmly established leadership roles for each sector within the institution at the national and regional levels.
2. The organizational framework designed for the Fed allowed it to adapt over time, making it sustainable while its quasi-public nature equipped the organization to better withstand the influence of partisan politics and administration changes.
3. The methods for sharing information (reserves)—one of the leading impediments to disaster-oriented PPP efforts today—were specifically laid out with an established central authority to consolidate and distribute information nationally and regionally.
4. The fact that the Fed was created through a legislative act served to centralize authority to avoid overlap and power struggles.
5. The formalization of the organizational structure institutionalized the roles and responsibilities for both sectors and thereby equipped the organization with a mechanism to facilitate long-term institutional trust.

These factors have institutionalized the organizational structure of the Fed and ensured ongoing cross-sector cooperation for nearly a century. Applying them to disaster-oriented PPPs is a proven method of ensuring disaster-oriented PPPs' strategic orientation while employing a tested framework with a clear record of success.

The one area that may require special consideration in reconstructing a disaster-oriented PPP framework relates to the complexity involved in coordinating so many industrial sectors. Although the Fed regional boards include representatives from a variety of industries, the Fed is a cross-sector partnership dominated largely by the relationship between the finance sector and government. Effectively including and coordinating a number of sectors is significantly more complicated. However, in comparing the Fed and WIB, useful clues emerge about how these PPPs could be forged. The WIB sought to coordinate a number of private-sector industries, as did the failed ISACs in the 1990s. In both of these collaborations, partnership efforts became silo-oriented, lacked consistency between industries, and did not coordinate or communicate across sectors. In the event of a calamitous disaster, the simultaneous response and coordination of numerous sectors is required. In addition, this silo-orientation made both of these cross-sector collaborations ineffective in the long-term. Understanding that the Fed model is a different and less complex example of a public-private private collaboration, applying this model to disaster-oriented PPPs could provide a useful means to begin creating an informational clearinghouse mechanism. This mechanism could be carefully applied to centralize communication not only between the public and private sectors but also among industrial sectors. As seen in the Fed, a clearinghouse function that includes representatives from all industrial sectors could also solidify a permanent and institutionalized role for private-sector leaders at the regional and national levels of the organization. In following the model provided by the Fed, precisely how this cooperation should occur to create an "information sharing clearinghouse" should be developed by a coalition of public- and private-sector leaders who would work within the system. As the founders of the Fed realized, these individuals are best equipped to unwrap the complexities of cooperation and understand the needs, risks, and complexities of this form of cross-sector partnership.

Although disaster-oriented PPPs could in theory be transformed into viable partnerships by following the structural model of the Fed and shifting to a fully strategic orientation, in reality this is unlikely without a catastrophic disaster of a magnitude greater than either 9/11 or Hurricane Katrina. It will most probably take an even larger and more devastating disaster to occur before sufficient urgency is created to prioritize these partnerships and develop the necessary organizational structure—backed by an act of Congress—to make them fully sustainable, strategic partnerships.

Cooperation has potential value for both sectors. Although foresight and the proactive development of these initiatives before the next "big crisis" would clearly be advisable, it seems that too much time has passed and too little urgency remains to expect this kind of proactive cooperation.

NOTES

1. George "Gig" Hender, chairman of DHS finance sector SCC 2006–8 and vice-chairman of Options Clearing Corporation (retired), telephone interview with the author from Chicago, April 13, 2010.

2. Although the NIPP, for example, does provide a way for the industrial sectors to meet a few times a year (through the cross-sector coordinating council), there is no mechanism to ensure consistency in communication or coordination between the sectors. For example, while some sectors use HSIN (the Homeland Security Information Network) to communicate, others find it redundant and prefer to use other methods of communication. Nitin Natarajan, Chairman of DHS GCC for Healthcare and Coordinating Director of Health and Human Services/ASPR/OPEO, telephone interview with the author from Washington, DC, May 5, 2010; and Hender, interview.

Conclusion

As an emerging topic of research, this book draws together empirical and historical research to provide the first comprehensive assessment of disaster-oriented public–private partnerships. This book explores, debates, analyzes, and compares disaster-oriented PPPs, the Fed, and the WIB to accomplish two primary objectives. The first is to understand what disaster-oriented PPPs are and to identify the key challenges that this type of collaboration presents. The second is to compare disaster-oriented PPPs to two other cross-sector collaborations developed earlier to address issues of national policy. These objectives aim to determine the extent to which disaster-oriented PPPs are unique, and to identify any parallels with these other partnerships that may inform the structural design of disaster-oriented PPPs. The overall goal is to assess the viability of disaster-oriented PPPs as a tool of disaster mitigation, preparedness, response, and resilience in the United States.

The introduction presents two original frameworks that are used throughout the book to assess and compare the Fed, the WIB, and disaster-oriented PPPs. The first framework differentiates the partnerships by their responsive or strategic orientation. This framework is designed to understand the fundamental nature of these collaborations, to determine whether disaster-oriented PPPs are equipped to function in the long term (strategic), or if they are built as single-incident (responsive) partnerships. The second framework identifies seven "critical factors" that are identified in interviews with public- and private-sector leaders either as necessary conditions for successful collaboration in disaster-oriented PPPs or as challenges that must be overcome for these partnerships to function effectively. These factors are crisis, leadership, organizational structure, information sharing, shared benefits, trust, and adaptability or sustainability.

Disaster-oriented PPPs, the Fed, and the WIB are individually explored in these identical terms to ease the comparison between the organizations, ensure consistency in methods of evaluation between the partnerships, and determine if these seven critical factors are equally relevant to all cross-sector partnerships designed to address national policy dilemmas or if they are uniquely "critical" to disaster-oriented PPPs.

The first objective of this book—to understand disaster-oriented PPPs and identify factors that are problematic—is addressed in chapters 1 and 2. Chapter 1 provides examples from 9/11 and Hurricane Katrina and illustrates how and why disaster-oriented PPPs emerged in the United States and why this collaboration was important during a disaster. In addition, it also summarizes the organizational history of disaster-oriented PPP policy in the United States and lays out the existing federal framework for cooperation.

Chapter 2 critically assesses the partnerships using the seven critical factors. Through this analysis, it emerged that while disaster-oriented PPPs may be viable in principle, the existing framework for cooperation is not viable. Disaster-oriented PPPs have developed in an ad hoc, piecemeal fashion and do not function effectively in the absence of a framework that is centralized and capable of providing guidelines that can ensure a coordinated and cooperative approach. Partnership efforts have been further limited by the fact that as more time passes since a catastrophic disaster in the United States, public- and private-sector leaders have shifted their focus away from disaster-oriented PPPs and toward issues they perceive as more pressing.

To meet the second objective of the book, to compare disaster-oriented PPPs to other cross-sector collaborations designed to address issues of national policy, chapters 3 and 4 provide a critical examination of the Federal Reserve System (an example of a strategic cross-sector collaboration) and the WIB (an example of responsive partnership). As with disaster-oriented PPPs, policymakers during the establishment of the Fed and WIB were plagued by crisis, power struggles, partisan pressures, and divergent opinions about the direction of the proposed reforms and the method for cooperation.

Three noteworthy comparisons emerged in reviewing the Fed and WIB. First, crisis was clearly an important instigating factor in both collaborations. Second, the primary difference between the Fed, as a strategic partnership, and the WIB, as a responsive alliance, was that the organizational structure of the Fed was established through an act of Congress, which served to provide stability and sustainability. Third, in looking at the WIB in particular, it became clear that cooperation must be beneficial to both sectors; otherwise there is little motivation to partner and little chance that an alliance will be sustained.

I compare the three collaborations in chapter 5 with a view toward determining whether disaster-oriented PPPs are strategic or responsive. In closely comparing these frameworks, the relevance of the seven "critical factors" to each national policy collaboration is even more obvious. By comparing each of the organizations in terms of its response to each individual factor, it is possible to both compare and contrast the organizations, and to confirm the strategic or responsive indicator of each factor. This proved to be a valuable assessment tool in demonstrating that although disaster-oriented PPPs have a number of responsive attributes, these partnerships are intended to be strategically oriented. Because of the "identity crisis" that disaster-oriented PPPs face—they are strategically oriented PPPs with predominantly responsive characteristics—they are currently not designed to succeed as a national tool of disaster management. This will continue until the partnership becomes entirely strategic in design and practice. Finally, I argue that while disaster-oriented PPPs could theoretically transition into viable tools of disaster management by adopting many of the attributes of the Federal Reserve model, the lack of urgency presently surrounding these initiatives makes such a transition unlikely without a significant crisis to reprioritize this issue on the agenda of political and private-sector leaders.

This study has advanced the study of cross-sector cooperation by revealing that although disaster-oriented PPPs may be a relatively new type of public–private cooperation, the United States has historically used public–private alliances of other kinds to address and resolve national crises. The relatively small amount of scholarly research that has been published on the topic of disaster-oriented PPPs in general seeks to define and quantify this new form of PPP and to understand why cooperation has proven so challenging. My aim in this book is to advance this discussion by moving beyond "identifying the problem" and toward the development of a solution. To be clear, I do not purport to provide "the solution" but I hope to provide a foundational first step in the development of a comprehensive and viable way forward for disaster-oriented PPPs.

The two frameworks proposed, developed, and tested in this book were designed to assist policymakers and scholars in both the theoretical assessment and conceptual understanding of this unique form of cooperation. The frameworks present a method of differentiating between two distinctive forms of national policy-oriented partnerships (strategic and responsive) to make two very important points: (1) In order to build a successful PPP designed to address an important aspect of US national policy, the long- or short-term goals of the alliance must be clarified and recognized; (2) once determined, the strategic or responsive orientation of the partnership should be accompanied by methods that align with that mission.

The second framework presented in this book tests seven critical factors that emerged in discussions with policymakers and practitioners as key contributing factors to the success or development of disaster-oriented PPPs. Using these factors to examine the Federal Reserve and WIB made it clear that the seven critical factors were equally relevant to all three organizations. As a result these factors may be understood as viable tools of assessment for any form of public–private alliance designed to address pressing new issues of national concern. In addition, using this framework revealed that the seven factors provided a valuable indicator of the strategic or responsive nature of each partnership.

By deploying these two frameworks with a view towards defining and exploring disaster-oriented PPPs, I have advanced the study of this form of cross-sector cooperation substantially and have demonstrated that there is a viable model (the Federal Reserve System) that could be used to develop a more robust framework for these partnerships. This is not to contend that the Federal Reserve System should be applied "wholesale" to disaster-oriented PPPs but to argue that the loose structural framework for public–private cooperation employed by the Federal Reserve System could offer a great deal of insight as to how a similar structure might be adapted, developed, and applied.

I conclude this book, therefore, with a brief assessment of the future implications of this work. It seems likely that the current US disaster-response framework is fundamentally flawed. While the US government knows that 85 percent of critical infrastructure is owned by the private sector, and further recognizes that private-sector involvement after a disaster can significantly boost response capabilities, the nation remains unprepared to respond to a catastrophic natural disaster or terrorist attack within its borders. This problem is not likely to be resolved in the near future, despite the fact that the Fed provides a historically tried and tested structural model that has functioned successfully for nearly a century.

It is easy to understand why federal policymakers may have prioritized the global financial crisis and the wars in Iraq and Afghanistan over domestic disaster-oriented PPP initiatives. At the same time, one hopes that a catastrophic disaster of a scale not yet seen in the United States (such as a nuclear bomb or paralyzing earthquake) will not be needed to generate sufficient urgency and prioritization to prompt policymaking and correct the problems currently facing disaster-oriented PPP initiatives.

I have sought to advance the debate and discussion surrounding the development of these partnerships by suggesting (and testing) two conceptual frameworks that policymakers may use to assist with the structural development of lasting, fruitful partnerships. As a result, I have sought to open the door for scholars and encourage further engagement in this topic of study, particularly in the fields of public administration, public policy, emergency or disaster management, security studies (including cyber security), law, and corporate risk/management. One possible way for scholars to advance this line of inquiry even further is to apply and test the frameworks explored in this study and pursue the development of models for a viable clearinghouse mechanism to facilitate improved information sharing between the public and private sectors, internally among federal offices and agencies, and between the federal government and its regional, state, and local partners. Although the Federal Reserve System admittedly addresses a different and less complex type of PPP, its core structural attributes have a proven track record of facilitating cross-sector collaboration and are worthy of closer examination. A progression of the research in this direction would not only significantly advance scholarship in this underexplored field but would also ensure that when disaster does strike and the US government prioritizes these initiatives, these new models would have been thoroughly considered and would have the potential to be integrated into US contingency planning.

When disaster does strike and policymakers reflect again on disaster-oriented PPPs, it is important for public- and private-sector leaders to remain mindful of both the flaws in the existing framework for cooperation, and of the fact that there is an immediate model (the Federal Reserve) that has the potential to address many of the key issues of cross-sector cooperation on a national and regional level. There has been a great deal of discussion about how to organize effective disaster response, and whether that response is best rooted at the federal level or from the bottom up. The federalist system that guides the United States dictates that the first step is a local response, and that state and federal responders are subsequently involved based on the severity of the disaster. This study has proposed a framework that may be able to provide a mechanism for this elevation to occur seamlessly, simultaneously, and more effectively. Regardless of the structural model ultimately employed, this kind of infrastructure is essential because disasters, especially those of the scale that are the focus of this work, will require rapid national intervention. Fast and effective public–private cooperation is imperative to speeding recovery and ensuring rapid resilience.

This research also highlights the importance of leadership from the executive and legislative branches, as well as from the private sector. While the support of public and private leaders is imperative in the immediate aftermath of a disaster, each case study explored in this book demonstrates that strong leadership is simply not enough if the intent is to ensure lasting, strategic cooperation and prioritization. Policymakers must realize the importance of establishing institutional mechanisms that are able to ensure that when the immediacy of the crisis fades and leaders begin to focus their attention elsewhere, a structure is in place that can sustain the partnership without relying upon either the continued focus of leaders, or the trusted relationships between individuals.

The future implications of this work also extend beyond the borders of the United States. The United States is not the only country in world to realize that cooperation and communication between the government and the private sector is crucial in the event of a catastrophic disaster. The severe floods in Australia and the earthquakes in New Zealand in 2011 and 2012, for example, have made disaster resilience and PPPs a clear priority for these countries. There is tremendous scope for comparative analysis in this field to understand how other nations are organizing disaster-oriented PPPs and learning from applicable best-practices.

Perhaps most importantly, the interconnected world in which we live makes the likelihood of cascading failures in the event of a significant international disaster very high and highlights the need for governments to prioritize disaster-oriented PPPs that are able to function effectively on the international level. Catastrophic events caused by nature or man have little regard for sovereign borders. As the Asian tsunami of 2004 demonstrated, disaster can easily affect a number of nation-states simultaneously. Global terrorist networks have a similar disregard for national borders and are by nature transnational. Simultaneous biological, chemical, or nuclear attacks; large-scale natural disasters; or cyber attacks targeting key international networks require a coordinated, international public–private response. When it comes to transnational disasters, the private sector is a crucial ally that has sophisticated international networks and operates in global rather than national terms. The framework I have developed in this book to facilitate cooperation between the sectors may provide a good starting point for exploring how a global disaster-oriented PPP model might be conceived.

Finally, while this text focuses on partnerships between the public and private sectors, it is important to remember that other nongovernmental actors are also important and influential in US disaster-management strategies. These include the media, academia, and nonprofit organizations. Although excellent work has been done exploring these entities individually, there has yet to be a comprehensive study that explores how to effectively incorporate these actors—in addition to the private sector, government, and military—holistically into national security and disaster-management strategies. Applying the frameworks proposed in this study and specifically exploring the viability of the Fed model in this context would be original, insightful, and potentially groundbreaking.

APPENDIX

Interview Participants

Richard Adkerson: CEO, Freeport McMoRan Copper and Gold

Col. Julie Bentz: Director of nuclear defense policy, National Defense Staff

Robert "Rob" Bolandian: CFO, Brooklyn, NY Holdings

Steve Carmel: Senior executive vice president, Maersk

Clay Detlefsen: Chair, food and agriculture sector coordinating council; vice president of regulatory affairs and general counsel, International Dairy Foods

Archie Dunham: CEO and chair of the board of directors (retired), Conoco; chair (retired) ConocoPhillips; director, Phelps Dodge Corp.; director, Pride International; director, Union Pacific Corps; director, Union Pacific Railroad Company; Americas Advisory Board, Deutsche Bank AG; director, Louisiana Pacific Corporation

Bob Grimaila: Vice president of safety, security, and operations, Union Pacific Railroad

William Hagen: Director, Department of Homeland Security, Domestic Nuclear Detection Office

Douglas Ham: Senior policy analyst, Department of Homeland Security, Office of Policy Development

George "Gig" Hender: Chair, Department of Homeland Security, Financial Services Sector Coordinating Council (2006–8); vice-chair, Options Clearing Corporation (retired); president, Options Industry Council (retired); president, International Options Clearing Association; executive committee member, International Options Markets Association

Mike Hickey: Vice president of governmental affairs and national security, Verizon

Rick Holmes: Assistant vice president for technology, Union Pacific Railroad

Lynne Kidder: Senior executive vice president, Business Executives for National Security

Bryan Koon: Director of emergency management, Walmart (at the end of 2010 Koon was appointed as director of Florida's Division of Emergency Management)

Gen. Charles C. Krulak: 31st Commandant and member of the Joint Chiefs of Staff, US Marine Corps (retired); CEO, MBNA Europe Bank (retired); director, Aston Villa Football Club; board of directors, Freeport-McMoRan Copper and Gold; board of directors, Union Pacific Railroad Corporation; board of regents, Uniformed Services University of the Health Sciences

Bob Liscouski: Assistant secretary of critical infrastructure protection, Department of Homeland Security (2003–5); president and COO, Steel City RE

Capt. George McCarthy: Office of Global Maritime Situational Awareness, US Navy

Erin Mullen: Chair, Healthcare Sector Coordinating Council; director, Rx Response

Nitin Natarajan: Chair, Healthcare Government Coordinating Council; coordinating director, Health and Human Services/ASPR/OPEO

Susan Rosegrant: author, Harvard University Case Study, "Wal-Mart's Response to Hurricane Katrina: Striving for a Public-Private Partnership."

Brian Scott: Deputy director of the partnership and outreach division, Department of Homeland Security, Office of Infrastructure Protection

Paul Stockton: Assistant secretary of defense for homeland defense and America's security affairs, Department of Defense

Benn Tannenbaum: Associate program director of the Center for Science, Technology, and Security Policy, American Association for the Advancement of Science

Frances "Fran" Fragos Townsend: Assistant to President George W. Bush for homeland security and counterterrorism and chair of Homeland Security Council (2004–7), White House; contributor on counterterrorism and homeland security, CNN

Lt. Col. Darryl Williams: Responsible for oversight of Partnership to Defeat Terrorism, US Strategic Command (retired); CEO, Partnership Solutions International

Jim Young: CEO, Union Pacific Railroad

NOTE

The job titles are the positions each individual held at the time of his or her interview in the spring–summer of 2010.

BIBLIOGRAPHY

Agranoff, Robert. *Managing within Networks: Adding Value to Public Organizations.* Washington, DC: Georgetown University Press, 2007.

Alemanno, Albert, ed. *Governing Disasters: The Challenges of Emergency Risk Regulation.* Cheltenham, UK: Edward Elgar, 2011.

Auerswald, Philip. "Complexity and Interdependence: The Unmanaged Challenge." In *Seeds of Disaster, Roots of Response: How Private Action Can Reduce Public Vulnerability*, edited by Philip E. Auerswald, Lewis M. Branscomb, Todd M. La Porte, and Erwann O. Michel-Kerjan, 157–63. New York: Cambridge University Press, 2006.

Auerswald, Philip E., Lewis M. Branscomb, Todd M. La Porte, and Erwann O. Michel-Kerjan, eds. *Seeds of Disaster, Roots of Response: How Private Action Can Reduce Public Vulnerability.* New York: Cambridge University Press, 2006.

———. "Leadership: Who Will Act? Integrating Public and Private Interests to Make a Safer World." In *Seeds of Disaster, Roots of Response: How Private Action Can Reduce Public Vulnerability*, edited by Philip E. Auerswald, Lewis M. Branscomb, Todd M. La Porte, and Erwann O. Michel-Kerjan, 483–505. New York: Cambridge University Press, 2006.

Auerswald, Philip, and Debra van Opstal. "Coping with Turbulence: The Resiliency Imperative." *Innovations: Special Edition for the World Economic Forum Annual Meeting 2009*, 203–18.

Bailes, Alyson J. K., and Otmar Hasler, "Preface." In *Business and Security: Public–Private Sector Relationships in a New Security Environment*, edited by Alyson J. K. Bailes and Isabel Frommelt, xi–xii. Oxford: Oxford University Press, 2004.

Barbaro, Michael, and Justin Gillis, "Wal-Mart at Forefront of Hurricane Relief," *Washington Post*, September 6, 2005, www.washingtonpost.com/wp-dyn/content/article/2005/09/05/AR2005090501598.html.

Baruch, Bernard M. *American Industry in the War: A Report of the War Industries Board.* New York: Prentice Hall, 1941.

———. *Baruch: The Public Years.* New York: Holt, Rinehart and Winston, 1960.

Beaver, Daniel R. "Newton D. Baker and the Genesis of the War Industries Board, 1917–1918." *Journal of American History* 52, no. 1 (June 1965): 43–58.

Berenson, Alex. "After the Attacks: The Markets: Uncertainly, Market Reopens Today," *New York Times*, September 17, 2001, www.nytimes.com/2001/09/17/business/after-the-attacks-the-markets-uncertainly-market-reopens-today.html?scp=1&sq=

After%20the%20Attacks:%20The%20Markets:%20Uncertainly,%20Market%20 Reopens%20Today&st=cse.

Bevan, John L., II, Lixion A. Avila, Eric S. Blake, Daniel P. Brown, James L. Franklin, Richard D. Knabb, Richard J. Pasch, Jamie R. Rhome, and Stacy R. Stewart. "Annual Summary: Atlantic Hurricane Season of 2005." *Monthly Weather Review* 136 (March 2008): 1109–73.

Birkland, Thomas A. *After Disaster: Agenda Setting, Public Policy and Focusing Events.* Washington, DC: Georgetown University Press, 1997.

———. *Lessons of Disaster: Policy Change after Catastrophic Events.* Washington, DC: Georgetown University Press, 2007.

Block, Robert. "Private Eyes: In Terrorism Fight, Government Finds a Surprising Ally: Fed Ex," *Wall Street Journal,* May 26, 2005, www.uniset.ca/terr/news/wsj_fedex _terror.html.

Board of Governors of the Federal Reserve System. *The Federal Reserve System: Purposes and Functions.* New York: Books for Business, 2002.

Bower, Ralph S., Sang O. Choi, Hong-Sang Jeong, and Janet Dilling. "Forms of Inter-Organizational Learning in Emergency Management Networks." *Journal of Homeland Security and Emergency Management* 6, no. 1, art. 66 (2009): 1–12.

Branscomb, Lewis M. "A Nation Forewarned: Vulnerability of Critical Infrastructure in the Twenty-First Century." In *Seeds of Disaster, Roots of Response: How Private Action Can Reduce Public Vulnerability,* edited by Philip E. Auerswald, Lewis M. Branscomb, Todd M. La Porte, and Erwann O. Michel-Kerjan, 19–25. New York: Cambridge University Press, 2006.

Branscomb, Lewis M., and Erwann O. Michel-Kerjan, "Public-Private Collaboration on a National and International Scale." In *Seeds of Disaster, Roots of Response: How Private Action Can Reduce Public Vulnerability,* edited by Philip E. Auerswald, Lewis M. Branscomb, Todd M. La Porte, and Erwann O. Michel-Kerjan, 395–403. New York: Cambridge University Press, 2006.

Breen, William J. "Foundations, Statistics, and State-Building: Leonard P. Ayers, the Russell Sage Foundation and the US Government Statistics in the First World War." *Business History Review* 68, no. 4 (Winter 1994): 451–82.

Brown, Jared T. "Presidential Policy Directive 8 and the National Preparedness System: Background Issues for Congress," *Congressional Research Service,* 7-5700, Washington, DC, October 21, 2011.

Brown, Kathi Ann. *Critical Path: A Brief History of Critical Infrastructure Protection in the United States.* Fairfax, VA: Spectrum Publishing Group, 2006.

Broz, Lawrence J. *The International Origins of the Federal Reserve System.* Ithaca, NY: Cornell University Press, 1997.

Bruner, Robert F., and Sean D. Carr. *The Panic of 1907: Lessons Learned from the Market's Perfect Storm.* Hoboken, NJ: John Wiley & Sons, 2007.

Bull, Benedicte, and Desmond McNeill. *Development Issues in Global Governance: Public–Private Partnerships and Market Multilateralism.* London: Routledge, 2007.

Bult-Spiering, Mirjam, and Geert Dewulf. *Strategic Issues in Public–Private Partnerships: An International Perspective.* Oxford: Blackwell Publishing, 2006.

Burby, Raymond J., ed. *Cooperating with Nature: Confronting Natural Hazards with Land-Use Planning for Sustainable Communities*. Washington, DC: Joseph Henry Press, 1998.

Bush, George W. "We Will Do What It Takes." Address to the nation from Jackson Square, New Orleans, September 15, 2005, http://articles.cnn.com/2005-09-15/politics/bush.transcript_1_americans-first-responders-lake-pontchartrain?_s=PM:POLITICS.

Business Executives for National Security (BENS). *Getting Down to Business: An Action Plan for Public–Private Disaster Response Coordination*. The Report of the Business Response Task Force. Washington, DC: BENS, January 2007.

———. *The Public Benefit Coalition: Building a Resilient America, A Proposal to Strengthen Public–Private Collaboration*. Washington, DC: BENS, March 3, 2009.

Carafano, James Jay. "Resiliency and Public–Private Partnerships to Enhance Homeland Security." *Backgrounder Published by the Heritage Foundation*, no. 2150 (June 24, 2008): 1–9.

Caudle, Sharon L. "National Security Strategies: Security from What, for Whom, and by What Means." *Journal of Homeland Security and Emergency Management* 6, no. 1, art. 22 (2009): 1–37.

Chernow, Ron. *The House of Morgan: An American Banking Dynasty and the Rise of Modern Finance*. New York: Grove Press, 1990.

Chertoff, Michael. *Homeland Security: Assessing the First Five Years*. Philadelphia: University of Pennsylvania Press, 2009.

Clarkson, Grosvenor B. *Industrial America in the World War: The Strategy behind the Line, 1917–1918*. Boston: Riverside Press, Cambridge, 1923.

Cohen, David B., and John W. Wells, *American National Security and Civil Liberties in an Era of Terrorism*. New York: Palgrave Macmillan, 2004.

Cole, David, and James X. Dempsey. *Terrorism and the Constitution: Sacrificing Civil Liberties in the Name of National Security*, 2nd ed. New York: New Press, 2006.

Collins, Pamela A., and Ryan K. Baggett. *Homeland Security and Critical Infrastructure Protection*. Westport, CT: Praeger Security International, 2009.

Congressional Research Service (CRS). *The Economic Effects of 9/11: A Retrospective Assessment*. Report for Congress, RL31617, September 27, 2002.

———. *Federal Emergency Management Policy Changes after Hurricane Katrina: A Summary of Statutory Provisions*. Report for Congress, RL33729, November 15, 2006.

———. *Hurricane Katrina: Social-Demographic Characteristics of Impacted Areas*. Report for Congress, RL33141, November 4, 2005.

———. *Presidential Policy Directive 8 and the National Preparedness System: Background and Issues for Congress*, R42073, October 21, 2011.

———. *The USA Patriot Act: A Sketch*. Report for Congress, RS21203, April 18, 2002.

Cuff, Robert D. "Bernard Baruch: Symbol and Myth in Industrial Mobilization." *Business History Review* 43, no. 2 (Summer 1969): 115–33.

———. "A 'Dollar-A-Year Man' in Government: George N. Peek and the War Industries Board." *Business History Review* 41, no. 4 (Winter 1967): 404–20.

————. *The War Industries Board: Business-Government Relations during World War I.* Baltimore: Johns Hopkins University Press, 1973.

Dalton, Dennis R. *Rethinking Corporate Security in the Post 9/11 Era: Issues and Strategies for Today's Global Business Community.* Oxford: Butterworth-Heinemann, 2003.

Darmer, Katherine B., Robert M. Baird, and Stuart E. Rosenbaum, eds. *Civil Liberties vs. National Security in a Post-9/11 World.* Amherst, NY: Prometheus Books, 2004.

Deloitte Research. *Closing the Infrastructure Gap: The Role of Public–Private Partnerships.* Deloitte Touche Tohmatsu, 2006, www.deloitte.com/assets/Dcom-United States/Local%20Assets/Documents/us_ps_PPPUS_final(1).pdf.

Deparle, Jason. "A Mass of Newly Laid-Off Workers Will Put Social Safety Net to the Test." *New York Times*, October 8, 2001. http://query.nytimes.com/gst/fullpage .html?res=9F00E7DA133CF93BA35753C1A9679C8B63&scp=15&sq=airline +industry+fail&st=nyt.

deSaint Phalle, Thibaut. *The Federal Reserve: An International Mystery.* New York: Praeger, 1985.

Dorwart, Jeffery M. *Eberstadt and Forrestal: A National Security Partnership, 1909– 1949.* College Station: Texas A&M University Press, 1991.

Eaton, Leslie, and Kirk Johnson, "After the Attacks: Wall Street; Straining to Ring the Opening Bell." *New York Times*, September 16, 2001, www.nytimes.com/2001/09/ 16/us/after-the-attacks-wall-street-straining-to-ring-the-opening-bell.html.

The Economist. "When Government Fails: The Pathetic Official Response to Katrina Has Shocked the World. How Will It Change America?" September 13, 2005, www .economist.com/node/4382412.

Ervin, Clark Kent. *Open Target: Where America Is Vulnerable to Attack.* New York: Palgrave Macmillan, 2006.

Faber, David. "The New Age of Wal-Mart," CNBC, original air date September 23, 2009, www.cnbc.com/id/15840232?video=1302753654&play=1.

Faulkner, Bill. "Towards a Framework for Tourism Disaster Management." *Tourism Management* 22 (2001): 135–41.

Feinstein, Jack. "Managing Reliability in Electric Power Companies." In *Seeds of Disaster, Roots of Response: How Private Action Can Reduce Public Vulnerability*, edited by Philip E. Auerswald, Lewis M. Branscomb, Todd M. La Porte, and Erwann O. Michel-Kerjan, 164–93. New York: Cambridge University Press, 2006.

Ferguson, Roger W., Jr. "Remarks by Federal Reserve Board Vice Chairman Roger W. Ferguson Jr." Vanderbilt University, Nashville, Tennessee, February 5, 2003, *Board of Governors of the Federal Reserve Board*, www.federalreserve.gov/boarddocs/ speeches/2003/20030205/default.htm.

Field, Carter. *Bernard Baruch: Park Bench Statesman.* New York: McGraw-Hill, 1944.

Fiscal Affairs Department of the International Monetary Fund. "Public–Private Partnerships." *International Monetary Fund*, March 12, 2004.

Flynn, Stephen. *America the Vulnerable: How Our Government Is Failing to Protect Us from Terrorism.* New York: Harper Collins, 2004.

————. *The Edge of Disaster.* New York: Random House, 2007.

———. "The Neglected Home Front." *Foreign Affairs* 83, no. 5 (September–October 2004): 20–33.

Flynn, Stephen, and Daniel Prieto. "The Neglected Defense: Mobilizing the Private Sector to Support Homeland Security." *Council on Foreign Relations Special Report*, Council Special Report no. 13 (March 2006).

Freudenburg, William R., Robert Gramling, Shirley Laska, and Kai T. Erikson. *Catastrophe in the Making: The Engineering of Katrina and the Disasters of Tomorrow.* Washington, DC: Island Press, 2009.

Frieden, Jeffery A., and David A. Lake, *International Political Economy: Perspectives on Global Power and Wealth*, 4th ed. London: Routledge, 2000.

Friedman, Milton, and Anna Jacobson Schwartz. *A Monetary History of the United States 1867–1960.* Princeton, NJ: Princeton University Press, 1963.

Gilpin, Robert. *Global Political Economy: Understanding the International Economic Order.* Princeton, NJ: Princeton University Press, 2001.

Glass, Carter. *An Adventure in Constructive Finance.* Garden City, NJ: Doubleday, Page & Company, 1927.

Godschalk, David R., Timothy Beatley, Philip Berke, David J. Brower, and Edward J. Kaiser. *Natural Hazard Mitigation: Recasting Disaster Policy and Planning.* Washington, DC: Island Press, 1999.

Goldberg, Jonah. *Liberal Fascism: The Secret History of the Left from Mussolini to the Politics of Meaning.* London: Penguin Books, 2009.

Grunwald, Michael, and Susan B. Glasser, "Brown's Turf Wars Sapped FEMA's Strength: Director Who Came to Symbolize Incompetence in Katrina Predicted Agency Would Fail." *Washington Post*, December 23, 2005, www.washingtonpost.com/wp-dyn/content/article/2005/12/22/AR2005122202213.html.

Hakim, Simon, and Erwin A. Blackstone. "The Role of the Private Sector in Homeland Security." In *Safeguarding Homeland Security: Mayors and Governors Speak Out*, edited by Simon Hakim and Erwin A. Blackstone, 1–21. New York: Springer, 2009.

Hale, Kathleen. *How Information Matters: Networks and Public Policy Innovation.* Washington, DC: Georgetown University Press, 2011.

Harkentt, Richard J., and James A. Stever, "The Cybersecurity Triad: Government, Private Sector Partners, and the Engaged Cybersecurity Citizen." *Journal of Homeland Security and Emergency Management* 6, no. 1, art. 79 (2009): 1–14.

Himmelberg, Robert F. "The War Industries Board and the Antitrust Question in November 1918." *Journal of American History* 52, no. 1 (June 1965): 59–74.

Hitchcock, Curtice N. "The War Industries Board: Its Development, Organization, and Functions." *Journal of Political Economy* 26, no. 6 (June 1918): 545–66.

Holdeman, Eric, and Ann Patton, "Project Impact Initiative to Create Disaster-Resistant Communities Demonstrates Worth in Kansas Years Later." *Emergency Management: Strategy & Leadership in Critical Times*, December 12, 2008, www.emergencymgmt.com/disaster/Project-Impact-Initiative-to.html.

Horwitz, Steven. "Wal-Mart Way in Disaster Preparedness/Response: Policy Implications." *Suburban Emergency Management Project*, November 27, 2008.

Jordan, Alexandra E. "Collaborative Relationships Resulting from the Urban Area Security Initiative." *Journal of Homeland Security and Emergency Management* 7, no. 1, art. 38 (2010): 1–19.

Kahan, Jerome H., Andrew C. Allen, and Justin K. George. "An Operational Framework for Resilience." *Journal of Homeland Security and Emergency Management* 6, no. 1, art. 83 (2009): 1–48.

Kelley, Rob. "Rebuilding Post-Katrina—Follow the $$$: Billions Pledged in Reconstruction Funding—Here Are Some Sectors That May Benefit," *CNN Money*, September 21, 2005. http://money.cnn.com/2005/09/21/markets/katrina_reconstruction/index.htm.

Kemmerer, Edwin Walter, and Donald L. Kemmerer. *The ABC of the Federal Reserve System*, 12th ed. New York: Harper Brothers, 1950.

Kester, Randall B. "The War Industries Board, 1917–1918; A Study in Industrial Mobilization." *American Political Science Review* 34, no. 4 (August 1940): 655–84.

Kettl, Donald F. *System under Stress: Homeland Security and American Politics*, 2nd ed. Washington, DC: CQ Press, 2007.

Koistinen, Paul A. C. "The 'Industrial-Military Complex' in Historical Perspective: World War I." *Business History Review* 41, no. 4 (Winter 1967): 378–403.

Kratz, Ellen Florian. "For FedEx It Was Time to Deliver: Years of Coping with Calamity Have Taught the Huge Shipper to Improvise. That Came in Handy When the Big Storm Hit." *Fortune*, October 3, 2005, http://money.cnn.com/magazines/fortune/fortune_archive/2005/10/03/8356720/index.htm.

Krulak, Charles C. "Ne Cras." Paper presented at the Council on Foreign Relations and provided to the author, New York, New York, September 11, 2007.

Lafferty, Barbara A., and Ronald E. Goldsmith, "Cause–Brand Alliances: Does the Cause Help the Brand or Does the Brand Help the Cause?" *Journal of Business Research*, 58 (2005): 423–29.

Laughlin, Laurence J. *The Federal Reserve Act: Its Origin and Problems*. New York: Macmillan, 1933.

Lee, Elsa. *Homeland Security and Private Sector Business: Corporations' Role in Critical Infrastructure Protection*. Boca Raton, FL: CRC Press, 2009.

Leonard, Devin. "The Only Lifeline Was the Wal-Mart," in *Fortune*, October 3, 2005, http://money.cnn.com/magazines/fortune/fortune_archive/2005/10/03/8356743/index.htm.

Lieberman, Joseph I., and Susan M. Collins. *Letter to the Honorable Janet Napolitano Calling for Long Overdue Disaster Recovery Plan*, Washington, DC, May 31, 2011, http://www.hsgac.senate.gov/media/fema-needs-to-release-long-overdue-disaster-recovery-plan.

Lieberman, Joseph I., Susan M. Collins, Mary L. Landrieu, and Lindsey O. Graham. *Letter to the Honorable Janet Napolitano in Response to the NDRF Draft*. Washington, DC, February 26, 2010, www.fas.org/irp/agency/dhs/fema/ndrf-comments.pdf.

Linder, Stephen H. "Coming to Terms with the Public–Private Partnership: A Grammar of Multiple Meanings." *American Behavioral Scientist* 43, no. 1 (September 1999): 35–51.

Link, Arthur S., ed. *The Papers of Woodrow Wilson*. Vol. 25, *August–November 1912*. Princeton, NJ: Princeton University Press, 1978.

———, ed. *The Papers of Woodrow Wilson*. Vol. 27, *January–June 1913*. Princeton, NJ: Princeton University Press, 1978.

———. *Woodrow Wilson and the Progressive Era: 1910–1917*. New York: Harper & Row, 1954.

Livingston, James. *Origins of the Federal Reserve System: Money, Class, and Corporate Capitalism 1890–1913*. Ithaca, NY: Cornell University Press, 1986.

Lohr, Steve. "Like J. P. Morgan, Warren E. Buffet Braves a Crisis." *New York Times*, October 5, 2008, www.nytimes.com/2008/10/06/business/06buffett.html?scp=1&sq =Like%20J.P.%20Morgan,%20Warren%20E.%20Buffet%20Braves%20a%20Crisis &st=Search.

Lopez, Brian. "Critical Infrastructure Protection in the United States since 1993." In *Seeds of Disaster, Roots of Response: How Private Action Can Reduce Public Vulnerability*, edited by Philip E. Auerswald, Lewis M. Branscomb, Todd M. La Porte, and Erwann O. Michel-Kerjan, 37–50. New York: Cambridge University Press, 2006.

———. "Evolution of Vulnerability Assessment Methods." In Philip Auerswald et al., eds., *Seeds of Disaster*, 51–70.

Lovecek, Tomas, Jozef Ristvej, and Ladislav Simak. "Critical Infrastructure Protection Systems Effectiveness Evaluation." *Journal of Homeland Security and Emergency Management*, vol. 7, no. 1, art. 34 (2009): 1–34.

Marshall, Edward. "Edison's Plan for Preparedness: The Inventor Tells How We Could Be Made Invincible in War without Overburdening Ourselves with Taxation." *New York Times*, May 30, 1915, SM6, http://query.nytimes.com/gst/abstract.html?res =F60F12F9385C13738DDDA90B94DD405B858DF1D3.

McAdams, Jennifer. "Bridging the Gap: What Makes Public/Private Security Alliances Succeed? It's Not Just about the Money—Except When It Is." *Federal Computer Week: Special Report; Homeland Security* (February 26, 2007): 30–34.

McEntire, David A. *Disaster Response and Recovery*. Hoboken, NJ: John Wiley and Sons, 2007.

McKay, Jim. "Former DHS Assistant Secretary Bob Liscouski Discusses Critical Infrastructure," *Emergency Management*, August 18, 2009, www.emergencymgmt.com/safety/Robert-Liscouski-Critical-Infrastructure.html.

McNeill, Jena Baker. "More than Lip Service: Why Private Sector Engagement Is Essential." *Homeland Security 2020: The Future of Defending the Homeland*, Heritage Foundation, no. 3 (August 25, 2010): 1–2.

Meltzer, Allan H. *A History of the Federal Reserve*. Volume 1, *1913–1951*. Chicago: University of Chicago Press, 2003.

Mileti, Dennis M. *Disasters by Design: A Reassessment of Natural Hazards in the United States*. Washington, DC: Joseph Henry Press, 2004.

Miskel, James F. *Disaster Response and Homeland Security: What Works, What Doesn't.* Stanford, CA: Stanford University Press, 2008.

Monroe, Linda. "Uncommon Valor: Winner: Verizon Building at 140 West Street, New York City." *Buildings Magazine*, May 2005, www.buildings.com/Article Details/tabid/3321/ArticleID/2530/Default.aspx.

Moore, Carl H. *The Federal Reserve System: A History of the First 75 Years.* Jefferson, McFarland & Company, 1990.

Moss, Mitchell, Charles Schellhamer, and David A. Berman. "The Stafford Act and Priorities for Reform." *Journal of Homeland Security and Emergency Management*, vol. 6, no. 1, art. 13 (2009): 1–21.

Nagorski, Thomas. "Editors Notebook: Afghan War Now Country's Longest, Afghan War Now Marks Another Grim Milestone," *ABC News*, June 7, 2010, http://abcnews .go.com/Politics/afghan-war-now-longest-war-us-history/story?id=10849303.

Nash, William A. "Emergency and Asset Currency." *New York Times*, February 14, 1910.

National Commission on Terrorist Attacks upon the United States (9/11 Commission). *The 9/11 Commission Report: Final Report of the National Commission on Terrorist Attacks upon the United States.* New York: W. W. Norton, 2004.

———. *Staff Statement No. 14: Crisis Management,* May 19, 2004.

Norris, Floyd, and Jonathan Fuerbringer, "A Day of Terror: The Markets; Stocks Tumble Abroad; Exchanges in New York Never Opened for the Day," *New York Times*, September 12, 2001, www.nytimes.com/2001/09/12/business/day-terror-markets -stocks-tumble-abroad-exchanges-new-york-never-opened-for-day.html.

Ohl, John K. "The Navy, the War Industries Board, and the Industrial Mobilization for War, 1917–1918." *Society for Military History* 40, no. 1 (February 1976): 17–22.

Paxson, Fredric L. "The American War Government, 1917–1918." *American Historical Association* 26, no. 1 (October 1920): 54–76.

Platt, Rutherford H. *Disasters and Democracy.* Washington, DC: Island Press, 1999.

Powers, John R. "An Alternative Approach to Disaster Relief." *Journal of Homeland Security and Emergency Management* 6, no. 1, art. 60 (2009): 1–5.

President's Commission on Critical Infrastructure Protection (PCCIP). *Critical Foundations: Protecting America's Infrastructures; The Report of the President's Commission on Critical Infrastructure Protection,* Washington DC, October 1997.

Priest, Dana, and William M. Arkin, "Top Secret America, A Washington Post Investigation; A Hidden World, Growing beyond Control," *Washington Post*, July 19, 2010, http://projects.washingtonpost.com/top-secret-america/articles/a-hidden-world -growing-beyond-control/.

Prieto, Daniel B., III. "Information Sharing with the Private Sector: History, Challenges, Innovations, and Prospects." In *Seeds of Disaster, Roots of Response: How Private Action Can Reduce Public Vulnerability*, edited by Philip E. Auerswald, Lewis M. Branscomb, Todd M. La Porte, and Erwann O. Michel-Kerjan, 404–28. New York: Cambridge University Press, 2006.

Pringle, Henry F. *The Life and Times of William Howard Taft*, Vol. 2. New York: Farrar and Rinehart, 1939.

Quarantelli, E. L. "Catastrophes Are Different from Disasters: Some Implications for Crisis Planning and Managing Drawn from Katrina." *Social Science Research Council*, June 11, 2006. http://understandingkatrina.ssrc.org/Quarantelli/.

Ridge, Tom. *The Test of Our Times: America Under Siege . . . And How We Can Be Safe Again*. With Larry Bloom. New York: Thomas Dunne Books, 2009.

Ripley, Amanda. *The Unthinkable: Who Survives When Disaster Strikes and Why*. New York, Three Rivers Press, 2008.

Robinson, Lisa A., James K. Hammit, Joseph E. Aldy, Alan Krupnick, and Jennifer Baxter. "Valuing the Risk of Death from Terrorist Attacks." *Journal of Homeland Security and Emergency Management* 7, no. 1, art. 14 (2010): 1–25.

Romero, Simon. "Houston Finds Business Boon after Katrina," *New York Times*, September 6, 2005, www.nytimes.com/2005/09/06/business/06goldrush.html.

———. "Using a Cellphone Signal to Hunt for a Victim in Desperate Need," *New York Times*, September 20, 2001, www.nytimes.com/2001/09/20/technology/circuits/20CELL.html.

Rose, Adam Z. "A Framework for Analyzing the Total Economic Impacts of Terrorist Attacks and Natural Disasters." In *Journal of Homeland Security* 6, no. 1, art. 9, 2009, 1–27.

Rosegrant, Susan. "Wal-Mart's Response to Hurricane Katrina: Striving for a Public–Private Partnership." Case Program, John F. Kennedy School of Government, Harvard University, C16-07-1876.0, August 28, 2007.

Rosenau, J. *Along the Domestic-Foreign Frontier*. Cambridge: Cambridge University Press, 1997.

Rothbard, Murray N. *A History of Money and Banking in the United States: The Colonial Era to World War II*. Auburn: Ludwig von Mises Institute, 2005.

Rothkopf, David. *Superclass: The Global Power Elite and the World They Are Making*. New York: Farrar, Straus and Giroux, 2008.

Rowe, J. Z. *The Public–Private Character of United States Central Banking*. New Brunswick, NJ: Rutgers University Press, 1965.

Russell, Joy D. "Verizon Deals with Loss of Employees and Outages: Nearly 500 Verizon Employees Were in the North Tower at the Time of Attack." *VARBusiness*, September 12, 2001. www.crn.com/news/channel-programs/18836626/verizon-deals-with-loss-of-employees-and-outages.htm.

Salkowe, Richard S., and Jayajit Charkraborty. "Federal Disaster Relief in the US: The Role of Political Partisanship and Preference in Presidential Disaster Declarations and Turndowns." *Journal of Homeland Security and Emergency Management* 6, no. 1, art. 28 (2009): 1–21.

Schaeffer, Peter V., and Scott Loveridge. "Toward an Understanding of Public–Private Cooperation." *Public Performance and Management Review* 26, no. 2 (December 2002): 169–89.

Schwab, Anna K., Katherine Eschelbach, and David J. Browner. *Hazard Mitigation and Preparedness*. Hoboken, NJ: John Wiley and Sons, 2007.

Scott, Lloyd N. *Naval Consulting Board of the United States*. Washington, DC: Government Printing Office, 1920.

Shughart, William F., II. "Katrinanomics: The Politics and Economics of Disaster Relief." *Public Choice* 127, no. 1/2 (April 2006): 31–53.

Shull, Bernard. *The Fourth Branch: The Federal Reserve's Unlikely Rise to Power and Influence.* Westport, CT: Greenwood, 2005.

Steinhauer, Jennifer, and Eric Lipton, "FEMA, Slow to the Rescue, Now Stumbles in Aid Effort," *New York Times*, September 17, 2005, www.nytimes.com/2005/09/17/national/nationalspecial/17fema.html.

Strange, Susan. *The Retreat of the State: The Diffusion of Power in the World Economy.* Cambridge: Cambridge University Press, 1996.

———. "States, Firms and Diplomacy." *International Affairs* 68, no. 1 (January 1992): 1–15.

Straw, Joseph. "Food Sector Abandons Its ISAC." *Security Management*, September 2008, accessed January 6, 2010, www.securitymanagement.com/article/food-sector-abandons-its-isac-004590.

Sunstein, Cass R. *Worst Case Scenarios.* Cambridge, MA: Harvard University Press, 2007.

Teeple, Gary. *Globalization and the Decline of Social Reform.* Ontario: Garamond Press, 2000.

Terriff, Terry. "Of Romans and Dragons: Preparing the US Marine Corps for Future Warfare." *Contemporary Security Policy* 28, no. 1 (April 2007): 143–62.

Thomas, Evan. "How Bush Blew It: Bureaucratic Timidity. Bad Phone Lines. And a Failure of Imagination. Why the Government Was So Slow to Respond to Catastrophe." *Newsweek*, September 28, 2005, http://homepage.mac.com/davidbellel/%20HowBushBlewIt.pdf.

United Nations International Strategy for Disaster Reduction (UNISDR). *2009 UNISDR Terminology on Disaster Risk Reduction.* New York: United Nations, May 2009.

US Chamber of Commerce. *From Relief to Recovery: The 2005 US Business Response to the Southeast Asia Tsunami and the Gulf Coast Hurricanes.* Washington, DC: US Chamber of Commerce, Business Civic Leadership Center, March 2006.

Warburg, Paul M. *The Federal Reserve System: Its Origin and Growth.* Vol. 2, *Addresses and Essays 1907–1924.* New York: MacMillan, 1930.

Wein, Lawrence M. "Got Toxic Milk?" *New York Times*, May 30, 2005, www.nytimes.com/2005/05/30/opinion/30wein.html?_r=1&n=Top/Opinion/Editorial.

Wells, Donald R. *The Federal Reserve System: A History.* Jefferson, NC: McFarland and Company, 2004.

Wiebe, Robert H. *The Search for Order 1877–1920.* New York: Hill and Wang, 1967.

Willis, Henry Parker. *The Federal Reserve System: Legislation, Organization and Operation.* New York: Ronald Press Company, 1923.

Wise, Charles R. "Organizing for Homeland Security after Katrina: Is Adaptive Management What's Missing?" *Public Administration Review* 66, no. 3 (May–June 2006): 302–18.

Yoshpe, Harry B. "Bernard M. Baruch: Civilian Godfather of the Military M-Day Plan." *Military Affairs* 29, no. 1 (Spring 1965): 1–15.

PUBLIC LAWS

Federal Reserve Act of 1913. Pub. L. 63-43, 38 Stat. 251 (1913).

Homeland Security Act of 2002. Pub. L. 107-296, 116 Stat. 2135 (2002).

Implementing Recommendations of the 9/11 Commission Act of 2007. Pub. L. 110-53,121 Stat. 266 (2007).

Intelligence Reform and Terrorism Prevention Act of 2004. Pub. L. 108-458, 118 Stat. 3638 (2004).

Post–Katrina Emergency Management Reform Act of 2006. Pub. L. 109-295, Title VI-National Emergency Management, 120 Stat. 1355 (2006).

Reducing Over-Classification Act. Pub. L. 111-258, 124 Stat. 2648 (2010).

The Robert T. Stafford Disaster Relief and Emergency Assistance Act, as amended, 42 U.S.C. 5121–5207, and Related Authorities. Pub. L. 93-288, June 2007.

USA Patriot Act of 2001. Pub. L. 107-56, 115 Stat. 272 (2001).

Year 2000 Information and Readiness Disclosure Act, Pub. L. 105-271, 112 Stat. 2386 (1998).

GOVERNMENT DOCUMENTS AND REPORTS

Department of Homeland Security. *Critical Infrastructure Partnership Advisory Council Annual,* Washington, DC, 2009.

———. *Interim National Infrastructure Protection Plan (NIPP).* Washington, DC, February 2005.

———. *National Infrastructure Protection Plan (NIPP).* Washington, DC, January 2009.

———. *National Mitigation Framework: Working Draft, Pre-Decisional.* Washington, DC, May 1, 2012.

———. *National Preparedness Goal.* Washington, DC, September 2011.

———. *National Preparedness Guidelines.* Washington DC, September 2007.

———. *National Prevention Framework: Working Draft, Pre-Decisional.* Washington, DC, May 1, 2012.

———. *National Protection Framework: Working Draft, Pre-Decisional.* Washington, DC, May 1, 2012.

———. *National Response Framework.* Washington, DC, January 2008.

———. *National Response Framework: Working Draft, Pre-Decisional.* Washington, DC, May 1, 2012.

———. *National Response Plan.* Washington, DC, December 2004.

———. *Written Testimony of Federal Emergency Management Agency Federal Insurance and Mitigation Administration Associate Administrator David Miller for a House Committee on Transportation and Infrastructure, Subcommittee on Economic Development, Public Buildings, and Emergency Management Hearing titled* "Current Programs and Initiatives," Washington, DC, July 24, 2012. http://www.dhs.gov/ynews/ testimony/20120724-fema-building-codes-and-mitigation-htic.shtm.

Department of Homeland Security, Federal Emergency Management Agency. *The Federal Emergency Management Agency*, Washington, DC, November 2010.

―――. *National Disaster Recovery Framework* (Draft), Washington, DC, February 5, 2010.

―――. *Project Impact: Building a Disaster-Resistant Community*, Washington, DC, November 22, 1999. www.fema.gov/news/newsrelease.fema?id=8895.

Department of Homeland Security, History Office. *Brief Documentary History of the Department of Homeland Security 2001–2008*, Washington, DC, 2008.

Department of Homeland Security, National Infrastructure Advisory Council (DHS, NIAC). *Critical Infrastructure and Resilience: Final Report and Recommendations*, Washington DC, September 8, 2009.

―――. *Public–Private Sector Intelligence Coordination: Final Report and Recommendations by the Council*, Washington DC, July 11, 2006.

Department of Homeland Security, Office of the Inspector General (DHS, OIG). *Relationships between Fusion Centers and Emergency Operations Centers*. OIG-12-15, Washington, DC, December 2011.

Government Accountability Office (GAO). *Catastrophic Disasters: Enhanced Leadership, Capabilities, and Accountability Controls Will Improve the Effectiveness of the Nation's Preparedness, Response, and Recovery System*. GAO-06-618, September 2006.

―――. *Critical Infrastructure Protection: Improving Information Sharing with Infrastructure Sectors*. GAO-04-780, July 2004.

―――. *Department of Homeland Security: A Comprehensive and Sustained Approach Needed to Achieve Management Integration, Report to Congress*. GAO-05-139, March 2005.

―――. *Homeland Security: Federal Efforts Are Helping to Alleviate Some Challenges Encountered by State and Local Information Fusion Centers, Report to Congressional Committees*. GAO-08-35, October 2007

―――. *Information Sharing: DHS Could Better Define How It Plans to Meet Its State and Local Mission and Improve Performance Accountability, Report to the Chairman: Committee on Homeland Security, House of Representatives*. GAO-11-223, December 2010.

―――. *Information Sharing: Federal Agencies Are Helping Fusion Centers Build and Sustain Capabilities and Protect Privacy, but Could Better Measure Results, Report to Congressional Requesters*. GAO-10-972, September 2010.

―――. *Information Sharing: Progress Made and Challenges Remaining in Sharing Terrorism-Related Information*. Statement for the Record to the Committee on Homeland Security and Governmental Affairs, US Senate. GAO-12-144T, October 12, 2011.

―――. *National Preparedness: FEMA Has Made Progress but Needs to Complete and Integrate Planning, Exercise and Assessment Efforts, Report to Congress*. GAO-09-369, April 2009.

———. *Terrorist Financing: US Agencies Should Systematically Assess Terrorists' Use of Alternative Financing Mechanisms.* November 2003.

General Accounting Office (GAO). *Year 2000 Computing Challenge: Lessons Learned Can Be Applied to Other Management Challenges.* Report to the Chairman, Subcommittee on Government Management, Information and Technology, Committee on Government Reform, House of Representatives. GAO/AIMD-00-290, September 2000.

House of Representatives, Democratic Staff of the US House Committee on Homeland Security. *Leaving the Nation at Risk: 33 Unfulfilled Promises from the Department of Homeland Security; Investigative Report.* Washington, DC, December 27, 2005.

Senate. *Digest of the Proceedings of the Council of National Defense during the World War.* Franklin H. Martin, 73rd Cong., 2nd Session, Doc. No. 193, Washington DC, 1934.

White House. *Executive Order 12968: Access to Classified Information.* Washington, DC, August 2, 1995.

———. *Executive Order 13073: Year 2000 Conversion.* Washington, DC, February 4, 1998.

———. *Executive Order 13010: Critical Infrastructure Protection.* Washington, DC, July 15, 1996.

———. *Executive Order 13288: Establishing the Office of Homeland Security and the Homeland Security Council. Federal Register*: Washington, DC, vol. 66, no. 196, October 10, 2001.

———. *Federal Response to Hurricane Katrina: Lessons Learned.* Washington, DC, February 2006.

———. *Homeland Security Presidential Directive 5 (HSPD 5): Management of Domestic Incidents.* Washington, DC, February 28, 2003.

———. *Homeland Security Presidential Directive 7 (HSPD-7): Homeland Security Advisory System.* Washington, DC, March 11, 2002.

———. *Homeland Security Presidential Directive 8 (HSPD-8): National Preparedness.* Washington, DC, December 17, 2003.

———. *National Security Directive 63: Single Scope Background Investigations.* Washington, DC, October 21, 1991.

———. *National Strategy for Homeland Security,* Homeland Security Council, October 2007.

———. *National Strategy for Homeland Security,* Office of Homeland Security, July 2002.

———. *National Strategy to Secure Cyberspace.* Washington, DC, February 2003.

———. *Our Presidents: No. 27 William Howard Taft 1909–1913.* Washington, DC, www.whitehouse.gov/about/presidents/WilliamhowardTaft/.

———. *Presidential Decision Directive 39 (PDD 39).* Washington, DC, June 21, 1995.

———. *Presidential Decision Directive 63 (PDD 63).* Washington, DC, May 22, 1998.

ARCHIVAL MATERIAL

Parsonage, E. E. "Correspondence to C. S. Brantingham." In *Records of the War Industries Board*, November 16, 1918, US National Archives and Records Administration, College Park, Maryland, RG 61, File 21A-A4.

Records of the US House of Representatives, 60th Congress. "Committee on Banking & Currency, Currency & Banking Reform," US National Archives and Records Administration, Washington, DC, RG 233, HR60A-H4, boxes 667–71.

Records of the US House of Representatives, 62nd Congress. "Committee on Banking & Currency, Currency & Banking Reform," US National Archives and Records Administration, Washington, DC, RG 233, HR62A-F2.1–F2.3.

Records of the War Industries Board. "Memorandum for Consideration of Priority Committee." Undated, US National Archives and Records Administration, College Park, Maryland, RG 61, File 21A-A4, Box 1163.

Senate, Special Committee to Investigate the Munitions Industry. *Munitions Industry: Final Report of the Chairman of the United States War Industries Board to the President of the United States, February 1919.* 74th Cong., 1st sess, 1935, Senate Committee print no. 3, US National Archives and Records Administration, RG 287, Box No. Y 5932.

INDEX

Note: Tables are represented by page numbers in italics.